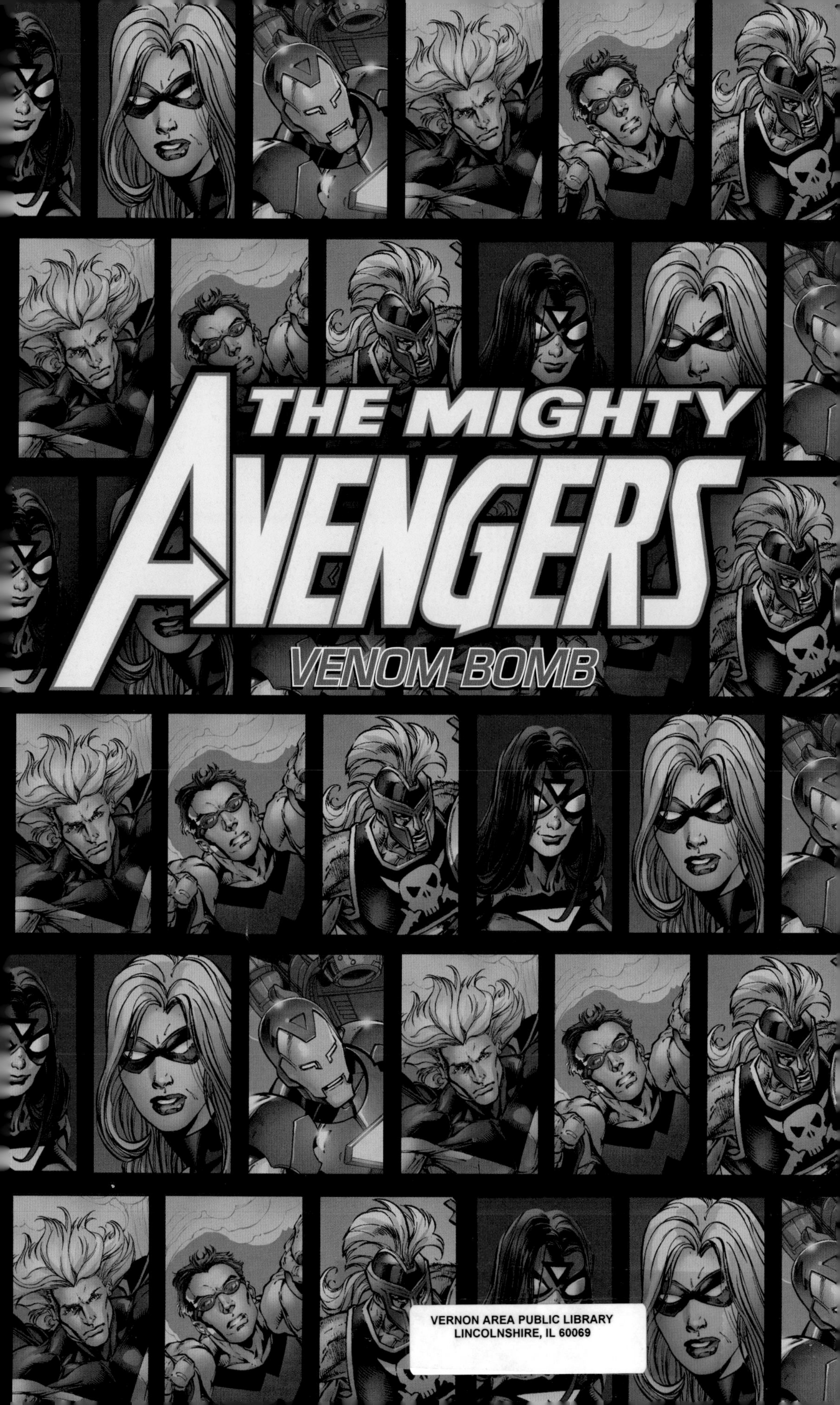
THE MIGHTY
AVENGERS
VENOM BOMB

THE MIGHTY AVENGERS
VENOM BOMB

WRITER: **Brian Michael Bendis**

PENCILS: **Mark Bagley**

INKERS: **Danny Miki & Crime Lab Studios'**
Allen Martinez & Victor Olazaba

ADDITONAL ART (ISSUES #9 & #11): **Marko Djurdjevic**

COLORS: **Justin Ponsor & Stephane Peru**

LETTERER: **Artmonkeys' Dave Lanphear**

COVER ART: **Mark Bagley with Frank Cho (Issue #7)**

ASSISTANT EDITOR: **Molly Lazer**

EDITOR: **Tom Brevoort**

COLLECTION EDITOR: **Jennifer Grünwald**

ASSISTANT EDITORS: **Cory Levine & John Denning**

EDITOR, SPECIAL PROJECTS: **Mark D. Beazley**

SENIOR EDITOR, SPECIAL PROJECTS: **Jeff Youngquist**

SENIOR VICE PRESIDENT OF SALES: **David Gabriel**

PRODUCTION: **Nelson Ribeiro**

BOOK DESIGNER: **Carrie Beadle**

EDITOR IN CHIEF: **Joe Quesada**

PUBLISHER: **Dan Buckley**

ERS VOL. 2: VENOM BOMB. Contains material originally published in magazine form as MIGHTY AVENGERS #7-11. First printing 2008. Hardcover ISBN# 978-0-7851-2641-6. Softcover ISBN#
9-9. Published by MARVEL PUBLISHING, INC., a subsidiary of MARVEL ENTERTAINMENT, INC. OFFICE OF PUBLICATION: 417 5th Avenue, New York, NY 10016. Copyright © 2007 and 2008 Marvel
ll rights reserved. Hardcover: $19.99 per copy in the U.S. and $21.00 in Canada (GST #127032852). Softcover: $14.99 per copy in the U.S. and $15.75 in Canada (GST #127032852). Canadian
68537. All characters featured in this issue and the distinctive names and likenesses thereof, and all related indicia are trademarks of Marvel Characters, Inc. No similarity between any of
acters, persons, and/or institutions in this magazine with those of any living or dead person or institution is intended, and any such similarity which may exist is purely coincidental. **Printed**
AN FINE, CEO Marvel Toys & Publishing Divisions and CMO Marvel Entertainment, Inc.; DAVID GABRIEL, SVP of Publishing Sales & Circulation; DAVID BOGART, SVP of Business Affairs & Talent
CHAEL PASCIULLO, VP of Merchandising & Communications; JIM O'KEEFE, VP of Operations & Logistics; DAN CARR, Executive Director of Publishing Technology; JUSTIN F. GABRIE, Director of
ns; SUSAN CRESPI, Editorial Operations Manager; OMAR OTIEKU, Production Manager; STAN LEE, Chairman Emeritus. For information regarding advertising in Marvel Comics or on Marvel.com,

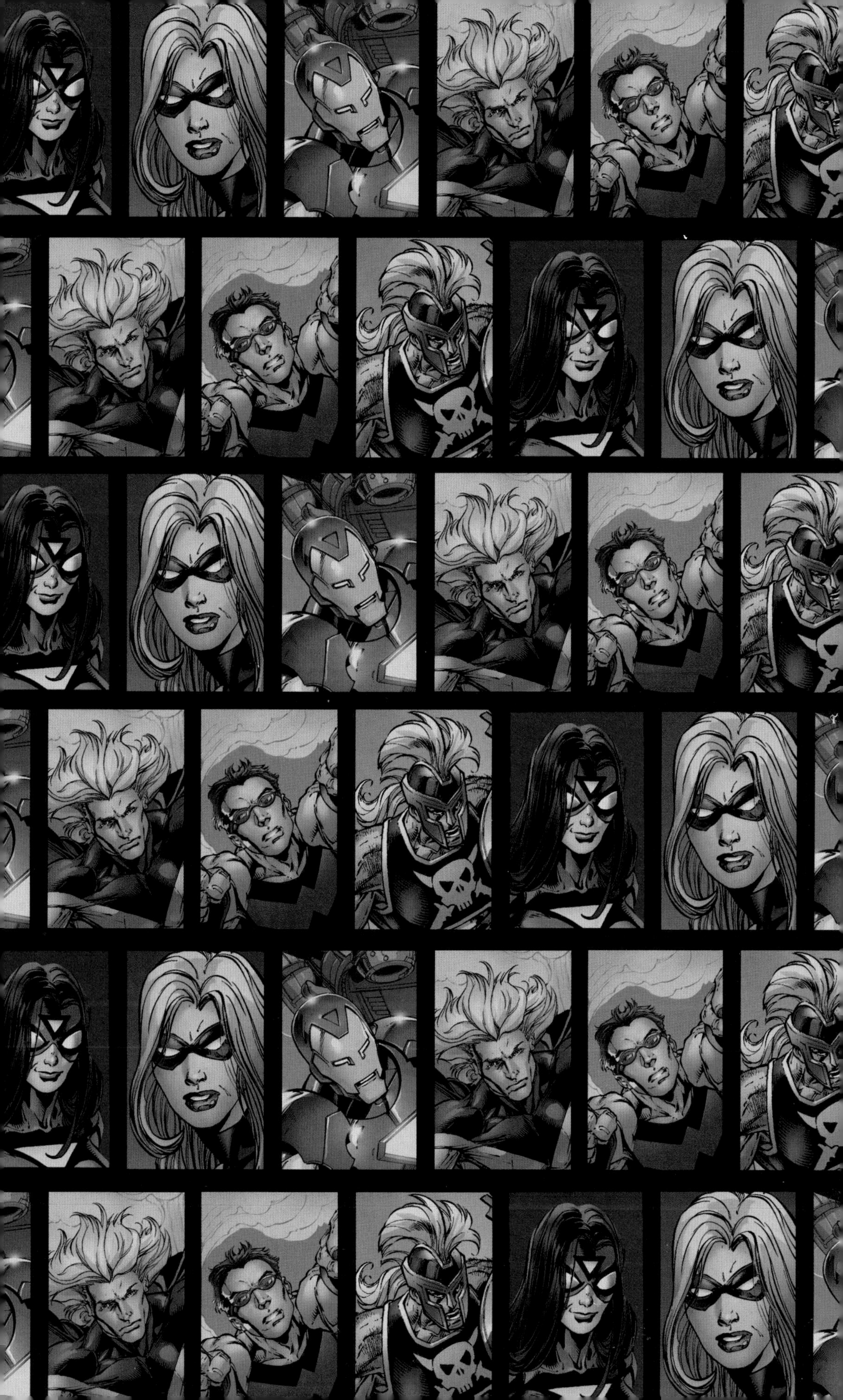

And there came a day, a day unlike any other, when Earth's Mightiest Heroes found themselves united against a common threat! On that day, the Avengers were born, to fight the foes no single super hero could withstand!

THE MIGHTY AVENGERS

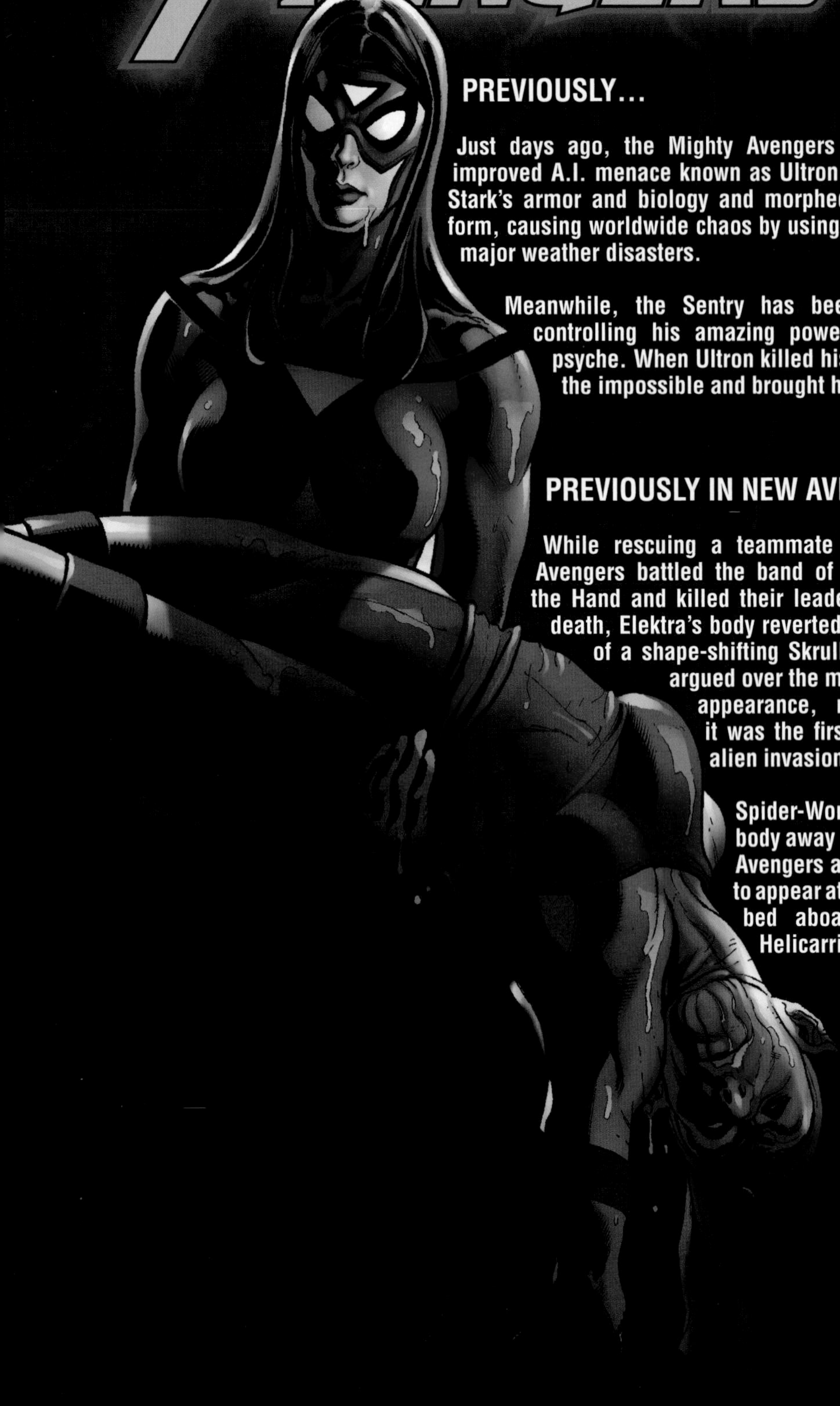

PREVIOUSLY...

Just days ago, the Mighty Avengers faced the new and improved A.I. menace known as Ultron, who took over Tony Stark's armor and biology and morphed into a new female form, causing worldwide chaos by using Starktech to unleash major weather disasters.

Meanwhile, the Sentry has been having problems controlling his amazing powers and his troubled psyche. When Ultron killed his wife, the Sentry did the impossible and brought her back to life.

PREVIOUSLY IN NEW AVENGERS...

While rescuing a teammate in Japan, the New Avengers battled the band of assassins known as the Hand and killed their leader, Elektra. Upon her death, Elektra's body reverted to its true form, that of a shape-shifting Skrull. The New Avengers argued over the meaning of the Skrull's appearance, most believing that it was the first hint of a full-scale alien invasion.

Spider-Woman took the Skrull body away from the underground Avengers and disappeared, only to appear at Tony Stark's recovery bed aboard the S.H.I.E.L.D. Helicarrier.

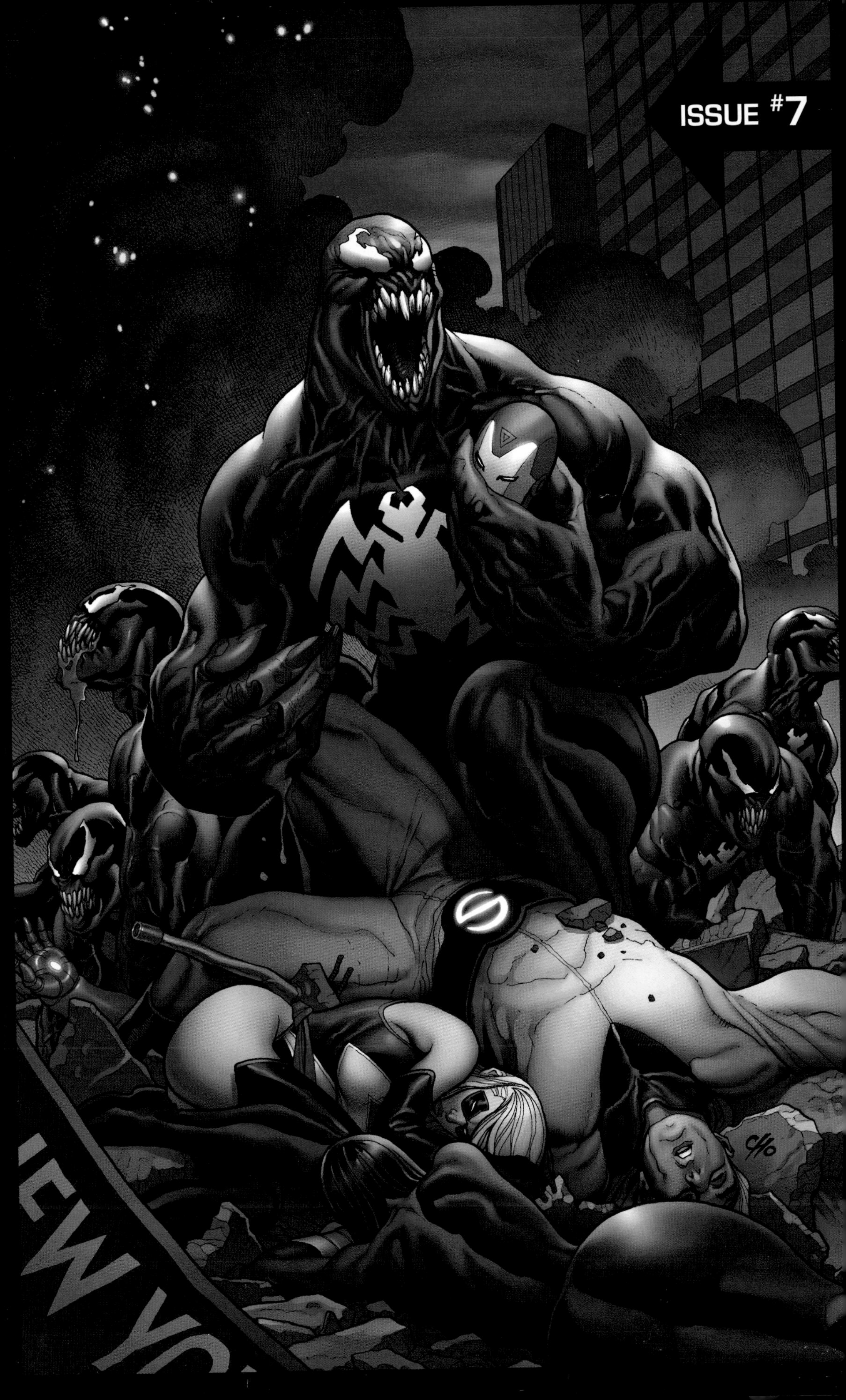
ISSUE #7

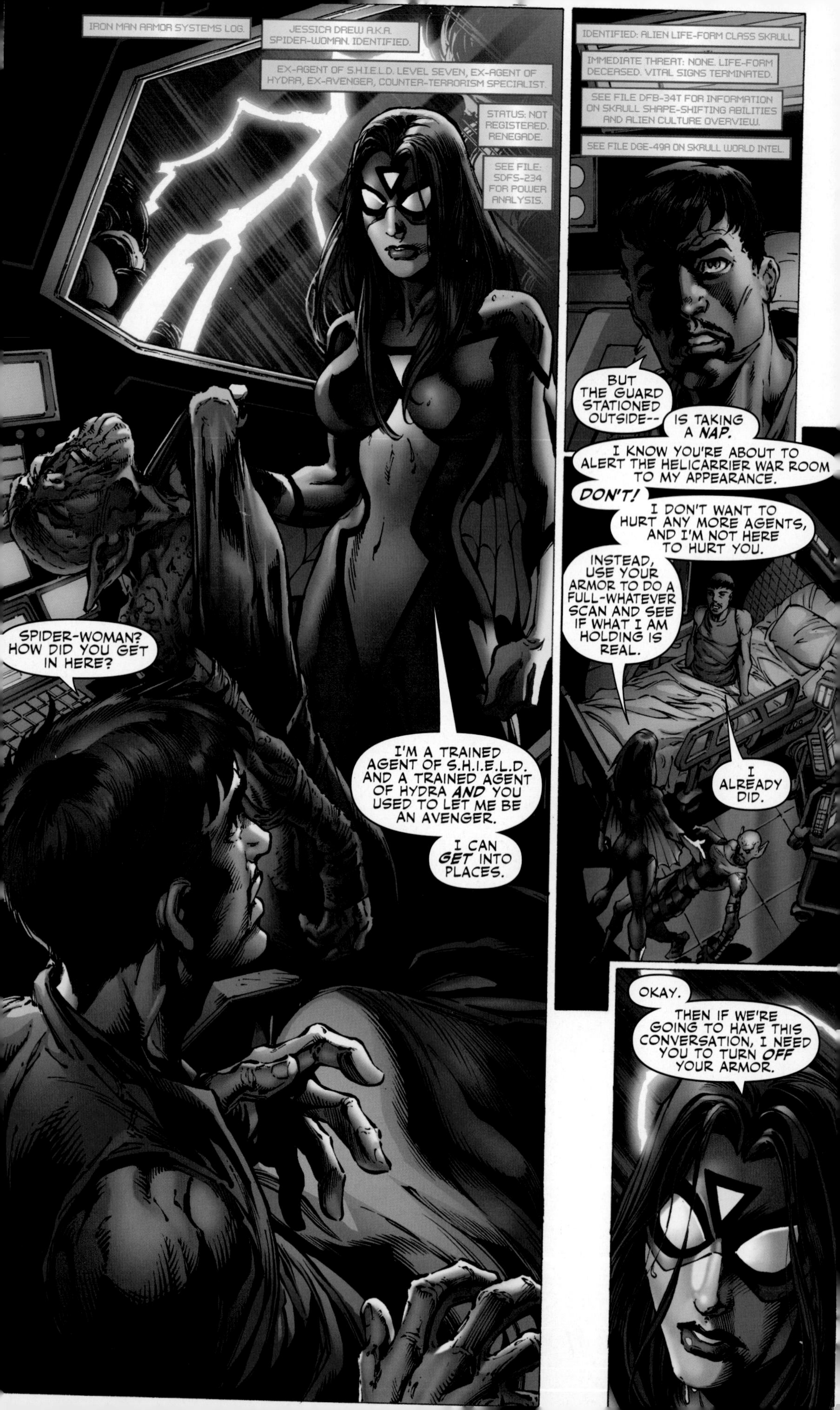

IRON MAN ARMOR SYSTEMS LOG.
JESSICA DREW A.K.A. SPIDER-WOMAN. IDENTIFIED.
EX-AGENT OF S.H.I.E.L.D. LEVEL SEVEN, EX-AGENT OF HYDRA, EX-AVENGER, COUNTER-TERRORISM SPECIALIST.
STATUS: NOT REGISTERED. RENEGADE.
SEE FILE: SDFS-234 FOR POWER ANALYSIS.
SPIDER-WOMAN? HOW DID YOU GET IN HERE?
I'M A TRAINED AGENT OF S.H.I.E.L.D. AND A TRAINED AGENT OF HYDRA *AND* YOU USED TO LET ME BE AN AVENGER.
I CAN *GET* INTO PLACES.
IDENTIFIED: ALIEN LIFE-FORM CLASS SKRULL.
IMMEDIATE THREAT: NONE. LIFE-FORM DECEASED. VITAL SIGNS TERMINATED.
SEE FILE DFB-34T FOR INFORMATION ON SKRULL SHAPE-SHIFTING ABILITIES AND ALIEN CULTURE OVERVIEW.
SEE FILE DGE-49A ON SKRULL WORLD INTEL.
BUT THE GUARD STATIONED OUTSIDE--
IS TAKING A *NAP.*
I KNOW YOU'RE ABOUT TO ALERT THE HELICARRIER WAR ROOM TO MY APPEARANCE.
DON'T!
I DON'T WANT TO HURT ANY MORE AGENTS, AND I'M NOT HERE TO HURT YOU.
INSTEAD, USE YOUR ARMOR TO DO A FULL-WHATEVER SCAN AND SEE IF WHAT I AM HOLDING IS REAL.
I ALREADY DID.
OKAY.
THEN IF WE'RE GOING TO HAVE THIS CONVERSATION, I NEED YOU TO TURN *OFF* YOUR ARMOR.

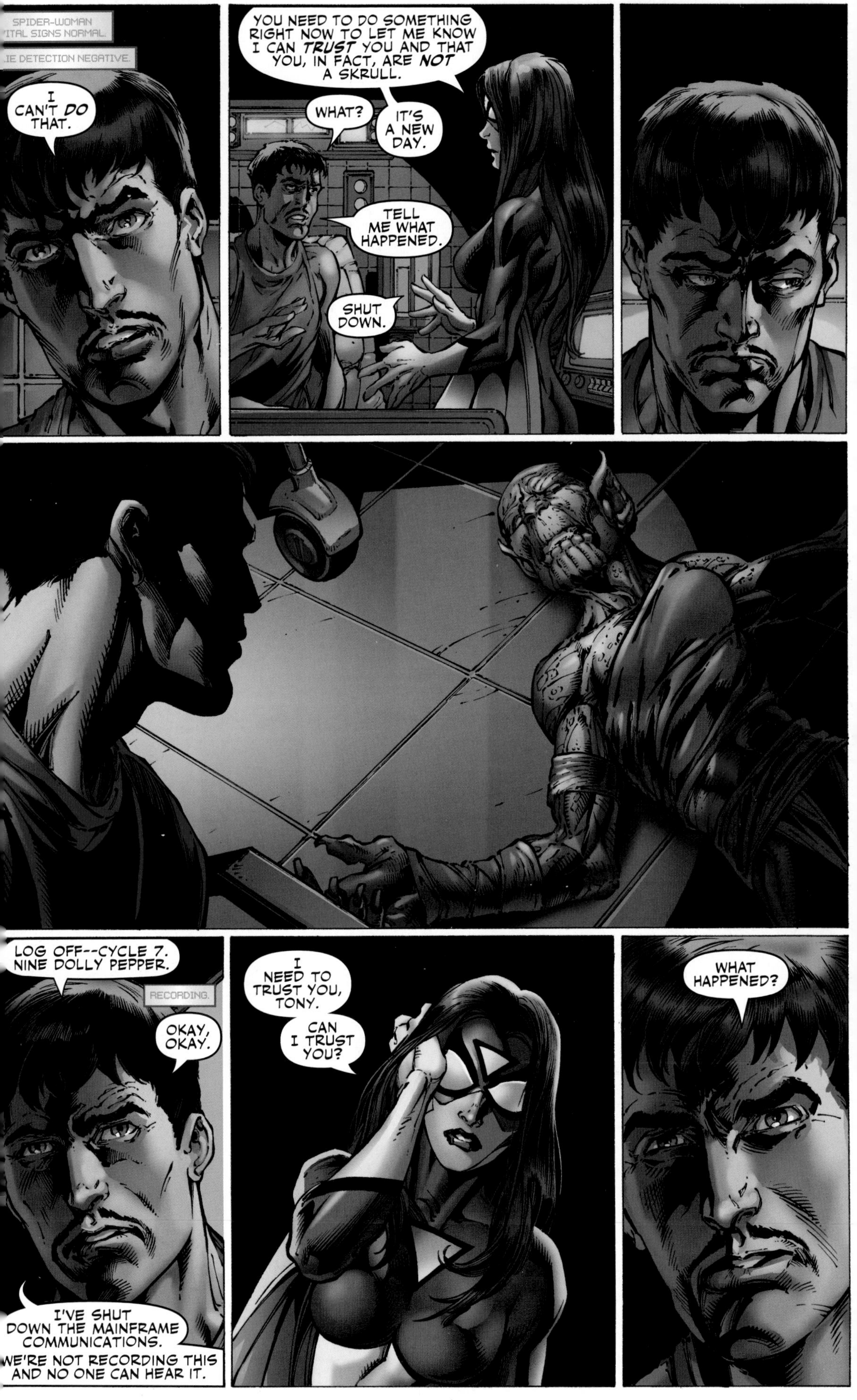
SPIDER-WOMAN
VITAL SIGNS NORMAL.
LIE DETECTION NEGATIVE.
I CAN'T *DO* THAT.
YOU NEED TO DO SOMETHING RIGHT NOW TO LET ME KNOW I CAN *TRUST* YOU AND THAT YOU, IN FACT, ARE *NOT* A SKRULL.
WHAT?
IT'S A NEW DAY.
TELL ME WHAT HAPPENED.
SHUT DOWN.
LOG OFF--CYCLE 7. NINE DOLLY PEPPER.
RECORDING.
OKAY, OKAY.
I'VE SHUT DOWN THE MAINFRAME COMMUNICATIONS.
WE'RE NOT RECORDING THIS AND NO ONE CAN HEAR IT.
I NEED TO TRUST YOU, TONY.
CAN I TRUST YOU?
WHAT HAPPENED?

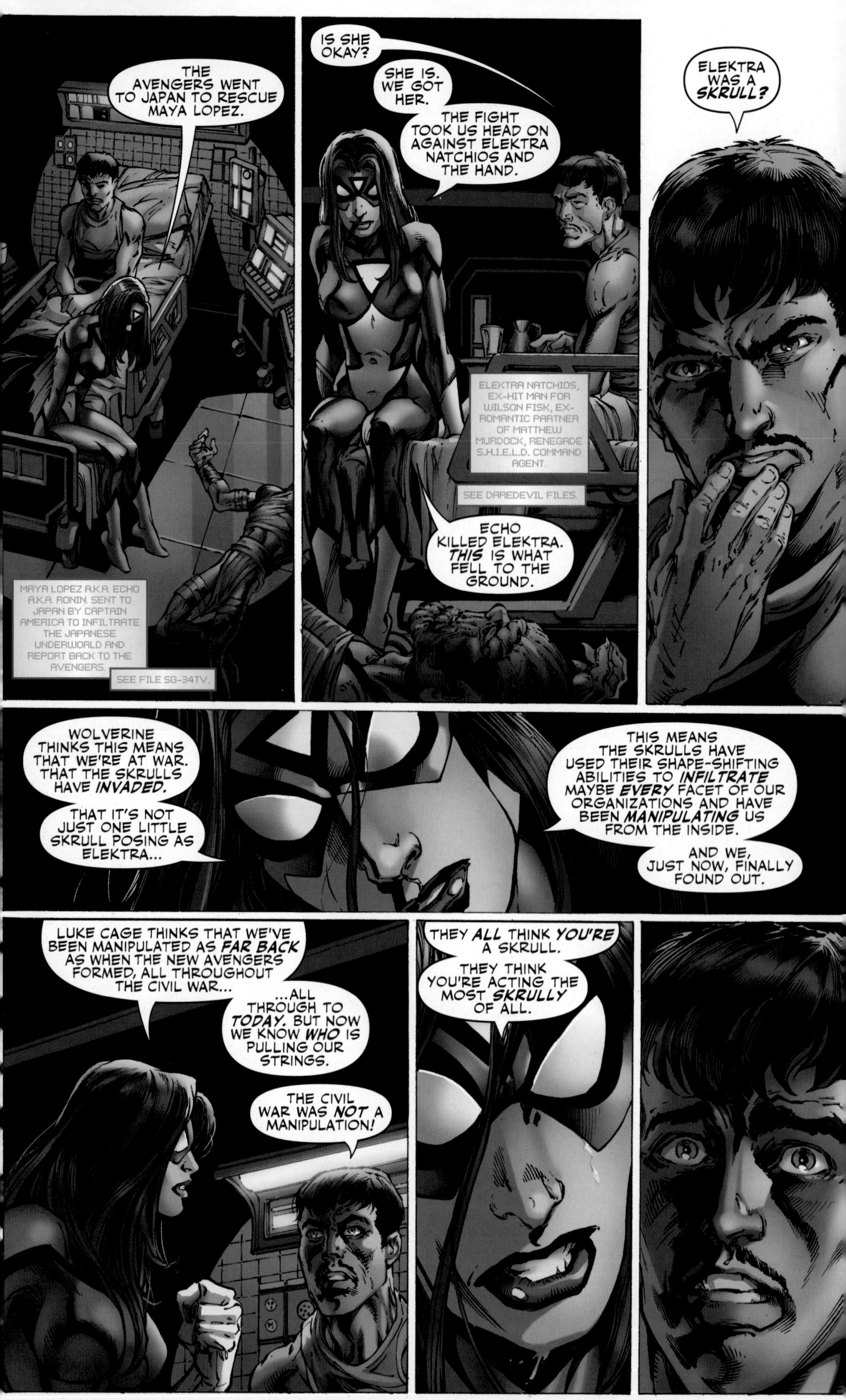
THE AVENGERS WENT TO JAPAN TO RESCUE MAYA LOPEZ.
MAYA LOPEZ A.K.A. ECHO A.K.A. RONIN. SENT TO JAPAN BY CAPTAIN AMERICA TO INFILTRATE THE JAPANESE UNDERWORLD AND REPORT BACK TO THE AVENGERS.
SEE FILE SG-34TV.
IS SHE OKAY?
SHE IS. WE GOT HER.
THE FIGHT TOOK US HEAD ON AGAINST ELEKTRA NATCHIOS AND THE HAND.
ELEKTRA NATCHIOS, EX-HIT MAN FOR WILSON FISK, EX-ROMANTIC PARTNER OF MATTHEW MURDOCK, RENEGADE S.H.I.E.L.D. COMMAND AGENT.
SEE DAREDEVIL FILES.
ECHO KILLED ELEKTRA. THIS IS WHAT FELL TO THE GROUND.
ELEKTRA WAS A SKRULL?
WOLVERINE THINKS THIS MEANS THAT WE'RE AT WAR. THAT THE SKRULLS HAVE INVADED.
THAT IT'S NOT JUST ONE LITTLE SKRULL POSING AS ELEKTRA...
THIS MEANS THE SKRULLS HAVE USED THEIR SHAPE-SHIFTING ABILITIES TO INFILTRATE MAYBE EVERY FACET OF OUR ORGANIZATIONS AND HAVE BEEN MANIPULATING US FROM THE INSIDE.
AND WE, JUST NOW, FINALLY FOUND OUT.
LUKE CAGE THINKS THAT WE'VE BEEN MANIPULATED AS FAR BACK AS WHEN THE NEW AVENGERS FORMED, ALL THROUGHOUT THE CIVIL WAR...
...ALL THROUGH TO TODAY. BUT NOW WE KNOW WHO IS PULLING OUR STRINGS.
THE CIVIL WAR WAS NOT A MANIPULATION!
THEY ALL THINK YOU'RE A SKRULL.
THEY THINK YOU'RE ACTING THE MOST SKRULLY OF ALL.

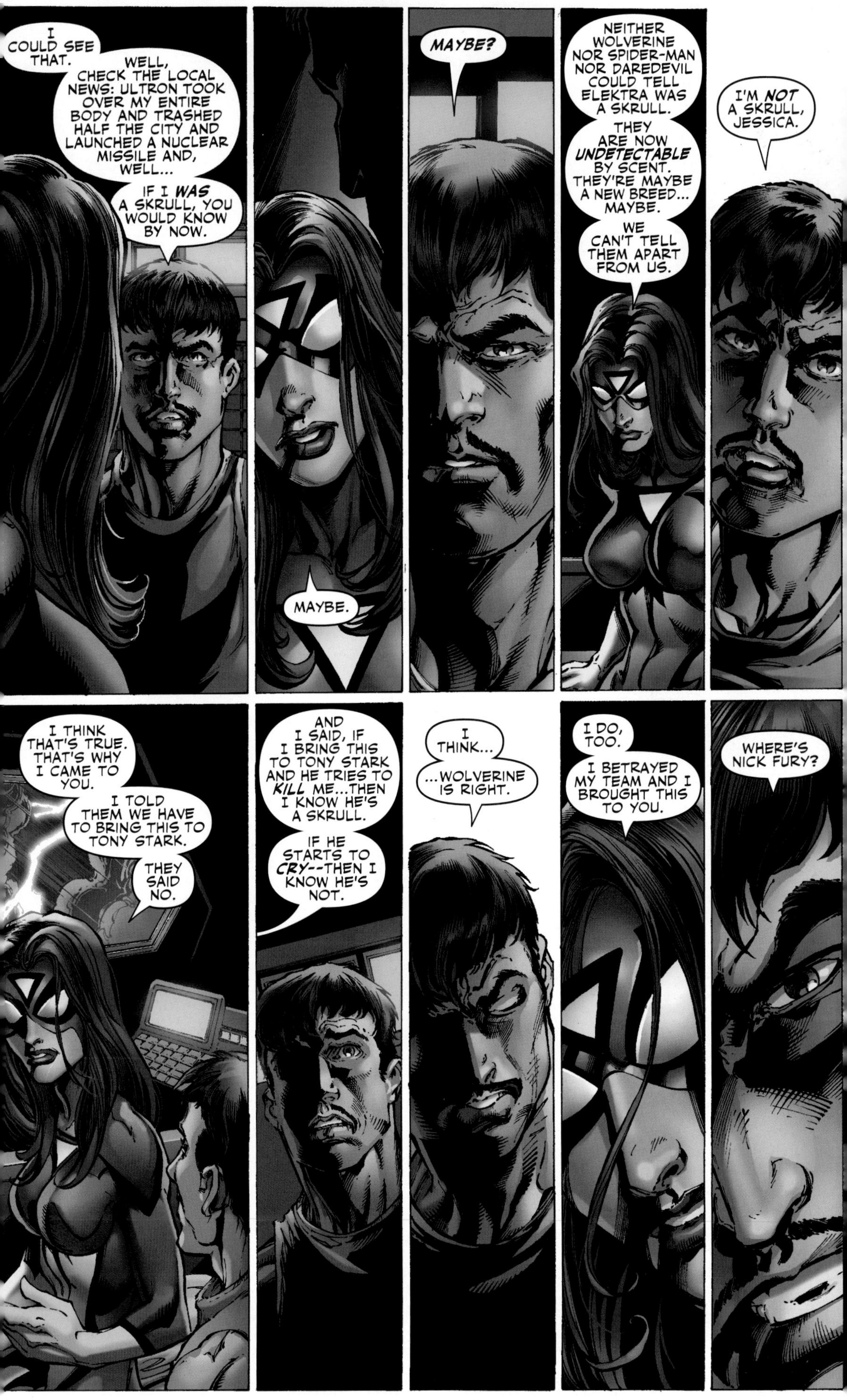
I COULD SEE THAT.
WELL, CHECK THE LOCAL NEWS: ULTRON TOOK OVER MY ENTIRE BODY AND TRASHED HALF THE CITY AND LAUNCHED A NUCLEAR MISSILE AND, WELL...
IF I WAS A SKRULL, YOU WOULD KNOW BY NOW.
MAYBE.
MAYBE?
NEITHER WOLVERINE NOR SPIDER-MAN NOR DAREDEVIL COULD TELL ELEKTRA WAS A SKRULL.
THEY ARE NOW UNDETECTABLE BY SCENT. THEY'RE MAYBE A NEW BREED... MAYBE.
WE CAN'T TELL THEM APART FROM US.
I'M NOT A SKRULL, JESSICA.
I THINK THAT'S TRUE. THAT'S WHY I CAME TO YOU.
I TOLD THEM WE HAVE TO BRING THIS TO TONY STARK.
THEY SAID NO.
AND I SAID, IF I BRING THIS TO TONY STARK AND HE TRIES TO KILL ME...THEN I KNOW HE'S A SKRULL.
IF HE STARTS TO CRY--THEN I KNOW HE'S NOT.
I THINK...
...WOLVERINE IS RIGHT.
I DO, TOO.
I BETRAYED MY TEAM AND I BROUGHT THIS TO YOU.
WHERE'S NICK FURY?

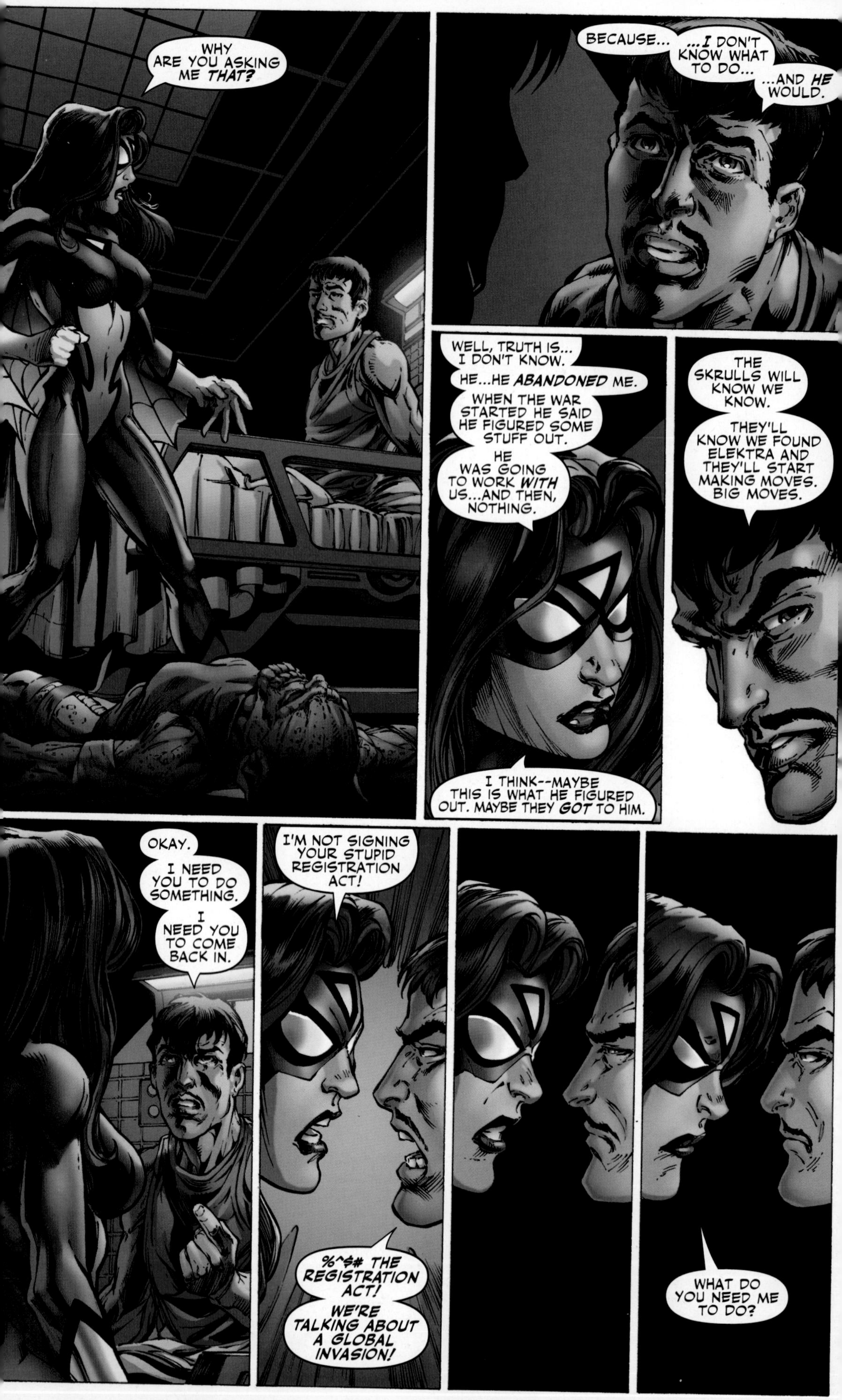
WHY ARE YOU ASKING ME THAT?
BECAUSE...
...I DON'T KNOW WHAT TO DO...
...AND HE WOULD.
WELL, TRUTH IS... I DON'T KNOW.
HE...HE ABANDONED ME.
WHEN THE WAR STARTED HE SAID HE FIGURED SOME STUFF OUT.
HE WAS GOING TO WORK WITH US...AND THEN, NOTHING.
I THINK--MAYBE THIS IS WHAT HE FIGURED OUT. MAYBE THEY GOT TO HIM.
THE SKRULLS WILL KNOW WE KNOW.
THEY'LL KNOW WE FOUND ELEKTRA AND THEY'LL START MAKING MOVES. BIG MOVES.
OKAY.
I NEED YOU TO DO SOMETHING.
I NEED YOU TO COME BACK IN.
I'M NOT SIGNING YOUR STUPID REGISTRATION ACT!
%^$# THE REGISTRATION ACT!
WE'RE TALKING ABOUT A GLOBAL INVASION!
WHAT DO YOU NEED ME TO DO?

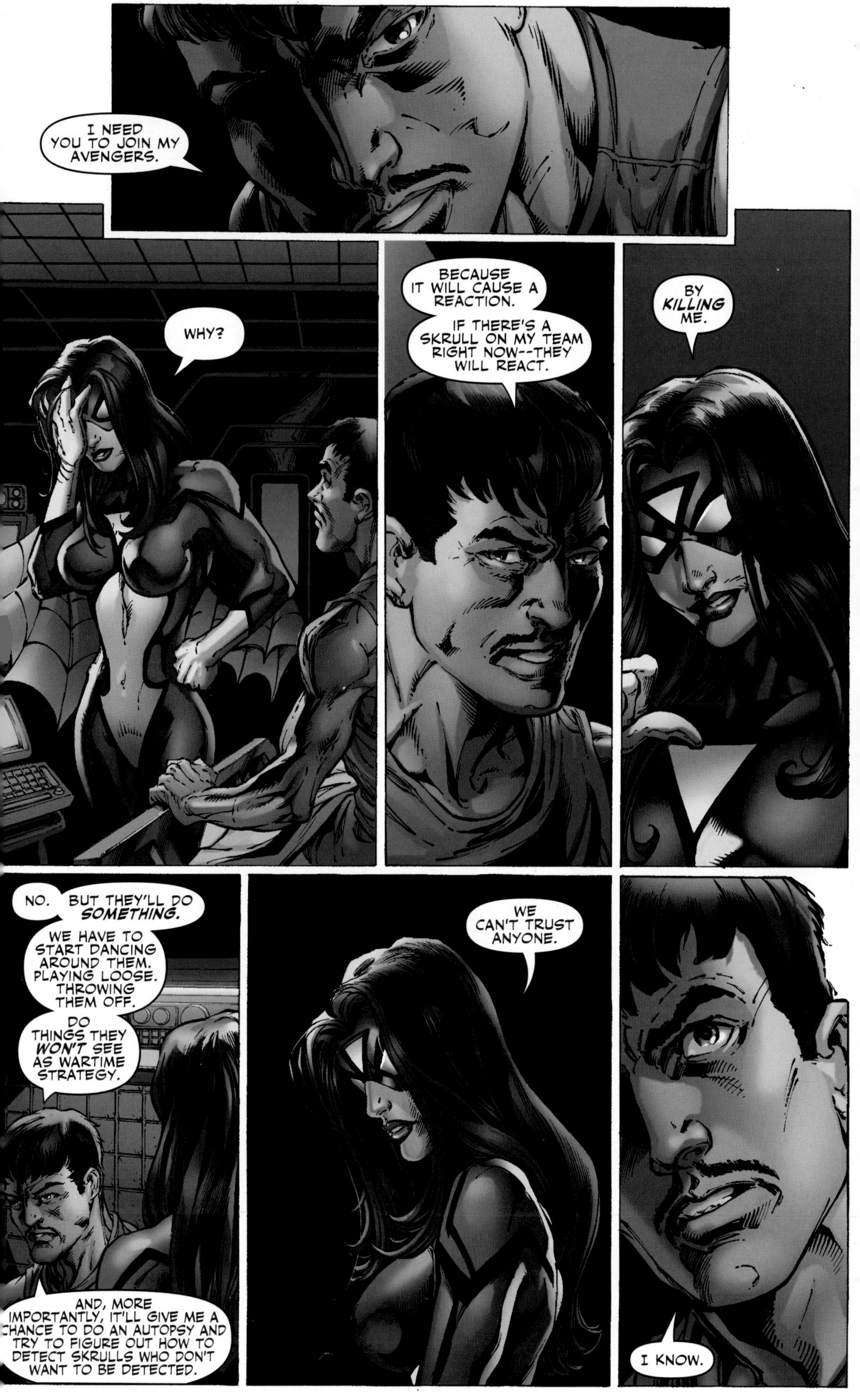

I NEED YOU TO JOIN MY AVENGERS.
WHY?
BECAUSE IT WILL CAUSE A REACTION.
IF THERE'S A SKRULL ON MY TEAM RIGHT NOW--THEY WILL REACT.
BY *KILLING* ME.
NO.
BUT THEY'LL DO *SOMETHING.*
WE HAVE TO START DANCING AROUND THEM. PLAYING LOOSE. THROWING THEM OFF.
DO THINGS THEY *WON'T* SEE AS WARTIME STRATEGY.
AND, MORE IMPORTANTLY, IT'LL GIVE ME A CHANCE TO DO AN AUTOPSY AND TRY TO FIGURE OUT HOW TO DETECT SKRULLS WHO DON'T WANT TO BE DETECTED.
WE CAN'T TRUST ANYONE.
I KNOW.

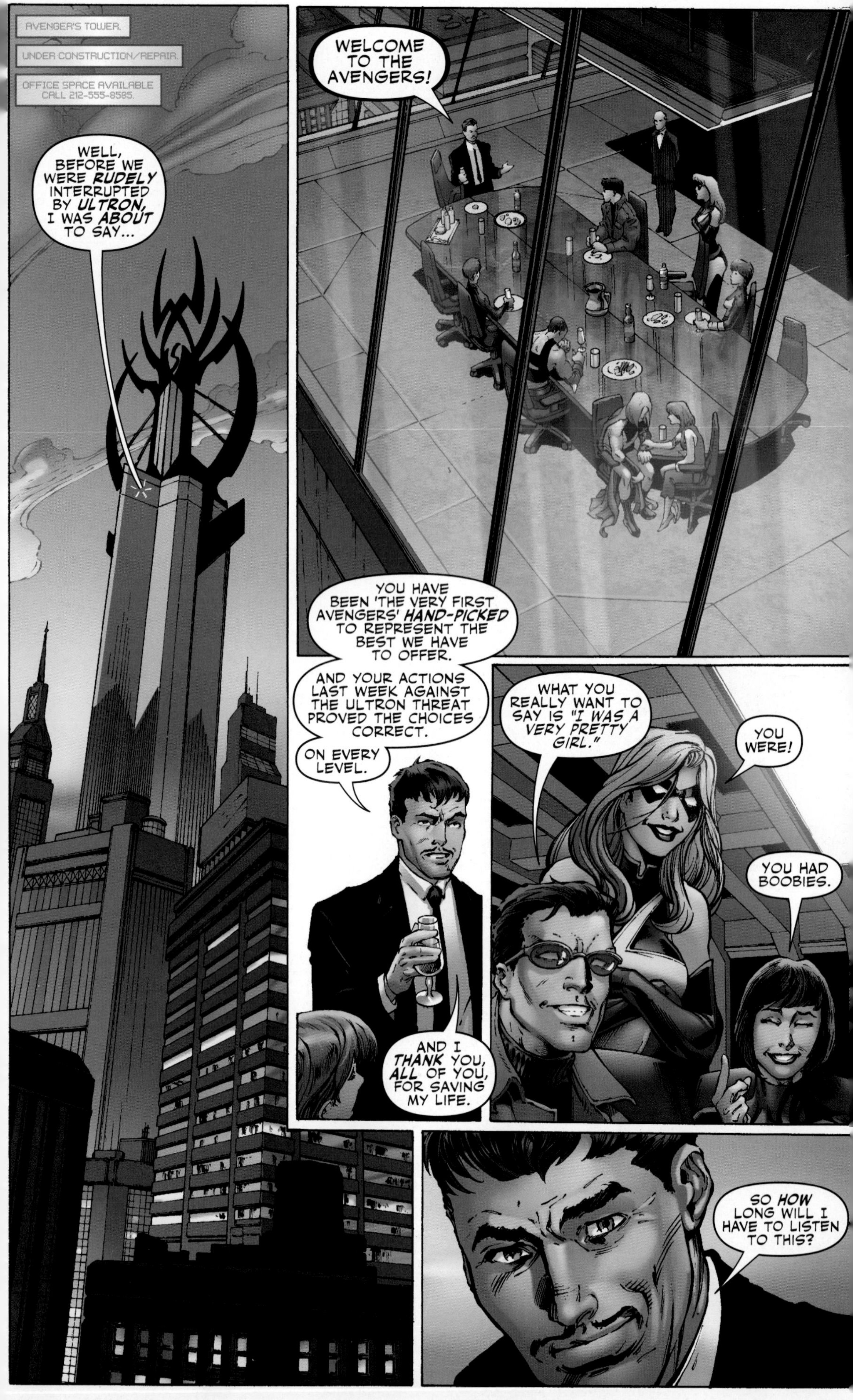

AVENGER'S TOWER.
UNDER CONSTRUCTION/REPAIR.
OFFICE SPACE AVAILABLE CALL 212-555-8585.
WELL, BEFORE WE WERE RUDELY INTERRUPTED BY ULTRON, I WAS ABOUT TO SAY...
WELCOME TO THE AVENGERS!
YOU HAVE BEEN 'THE VERY FIRST AVENGERS' HAND-PICKED TO REPRESENT THE BEST WE HAVE TO OFFER.
AND YOUR ACTIONS LAST WEEK AGAINST THE ULTRON THREAT PROVED THE CHOICES CORRECT.
ON EVERY LEVEL.
AND I THANK YOU, ALL OF YOU, FOR SAVING MY LIFE.
WHAT YOU REALLY WANT TO SAY IS "I WAS A VERY PRETTY GIRL."
YOU WERE!
YOU HAD BOOBIES.
SO HOW LONG WILL I HAVE TO LISTEN TO THIS?

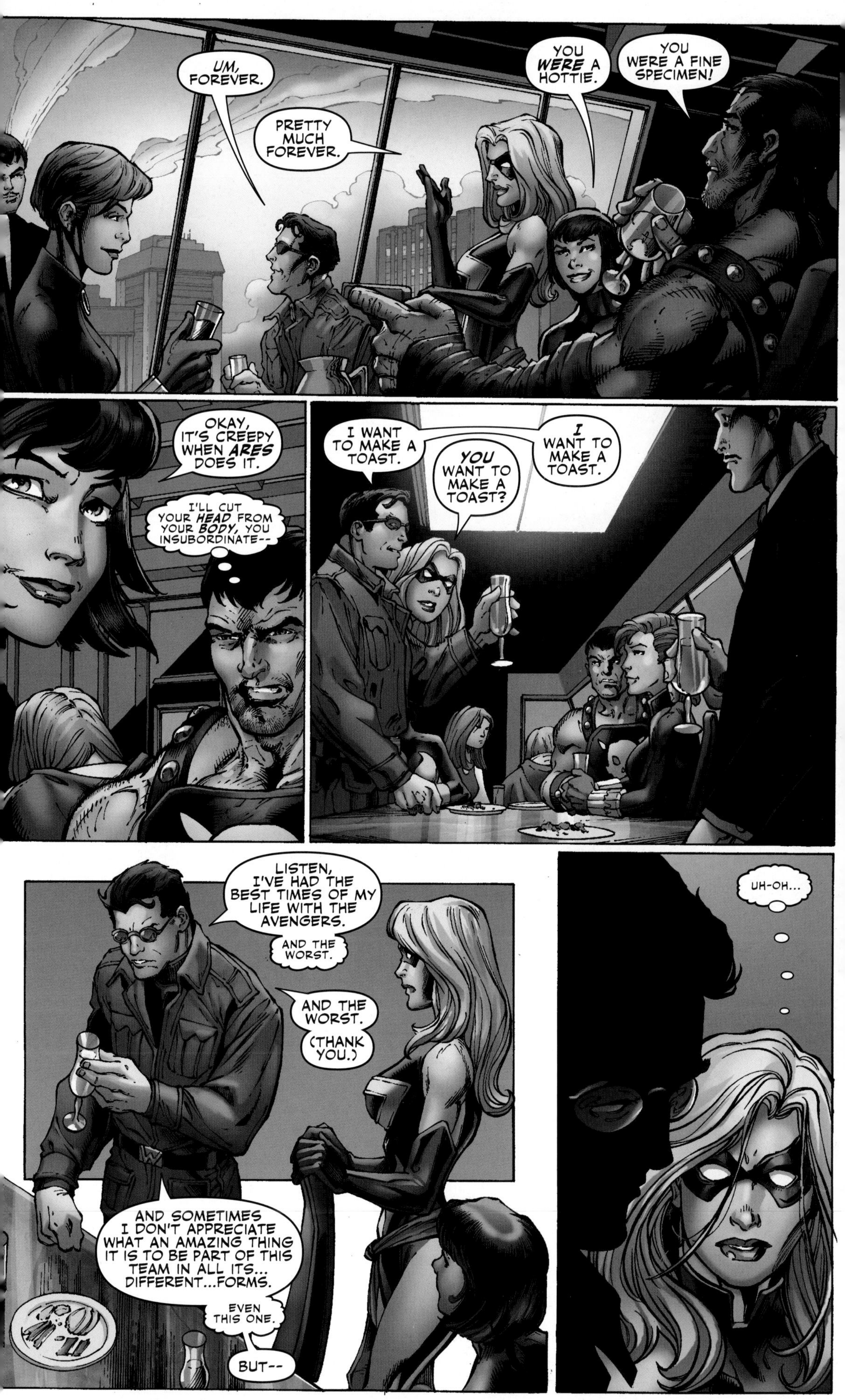
UM, FOREVER.
PRETTY MUCH FOREVER.
YOU *WERE* A HOTTIE.
YOU WERE A FINE SPECIMEN!
OKAY, IT'S CREEPY WHEN *ARES* DOES IT.
I'LL CUT YOUR *HEAD* FROM YOUR *BODY*, YOU INSUBORDINATE--
I WANT TO MAKE A TOAST.
YOU WANT TO MAKE A TOAST?
I WANT TO MAKE A TOAST.
LISTEN, I'VE HAD THE BEST TIMES OF MY LIFE WITH THE AVENGERS.
AND THE WORST.
AND THE WORST. (THANK YOU.)
AND SOMETIMES I DON'T APPRECIATE WHAT AN AMAZING THING IT IS TO BE PART OF THIS TEAM IN ALL ITS... DIFFERENT...FORMS.
EVEN THIS ONE.
BUT--
UH-OH...

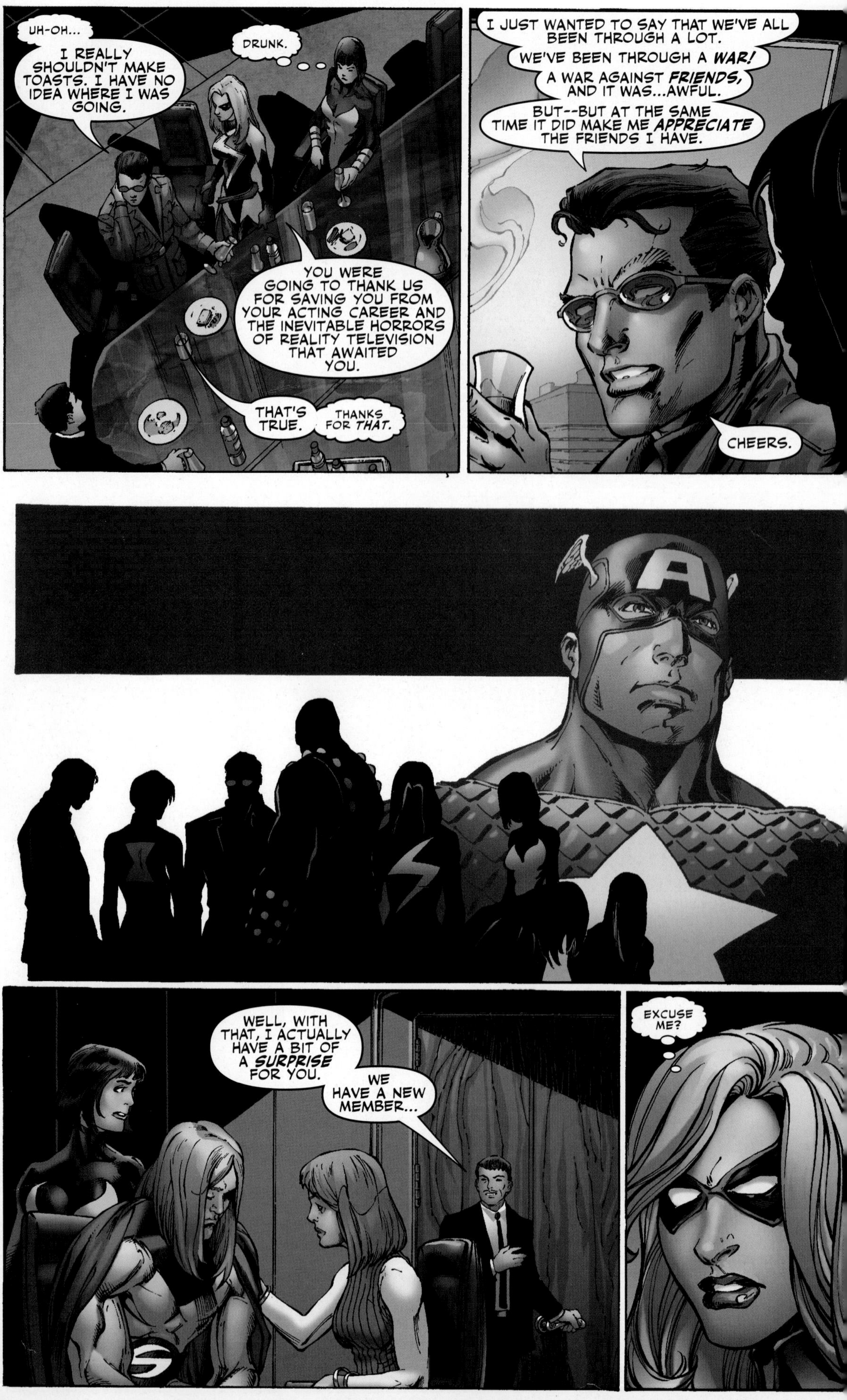
UH-OH...
I REALLY SHOULDN'T MAKE TOASTS. I HAVE NO IDEA WHERE I WAS GOING.
DRUNK.
YOU WERE GOING TO THANK US FOR SAVING YOU FROM YOUR ACTING CAREER AND THE INEVITABLE HORRORS OF REALITY TELEVISION THAT AWAITED YOU.
THAT'S TRUE.
THANKS FOR *THAT*.
I JUST WANTED TO SAY THAT WE'VE ALL BEEN THROUGH A LOT.
WE'VE BEEN THROUGH A *WAR!*
A WAR AGAINST *FRIENDS,* AND IT WAS...AWFUL.
BUT--BUT AT THE SAME TIME IT DID MAKE ME *APPRECIATE* THE FRIENDS I HAVE.
CHEERS.
WELL, WITH THAT, I ACTUALLY HAVE A BIT OF A *SURPRISE* FOR YOU.
WE HAVE A NEW MEMBER...
EXCUSE ME?

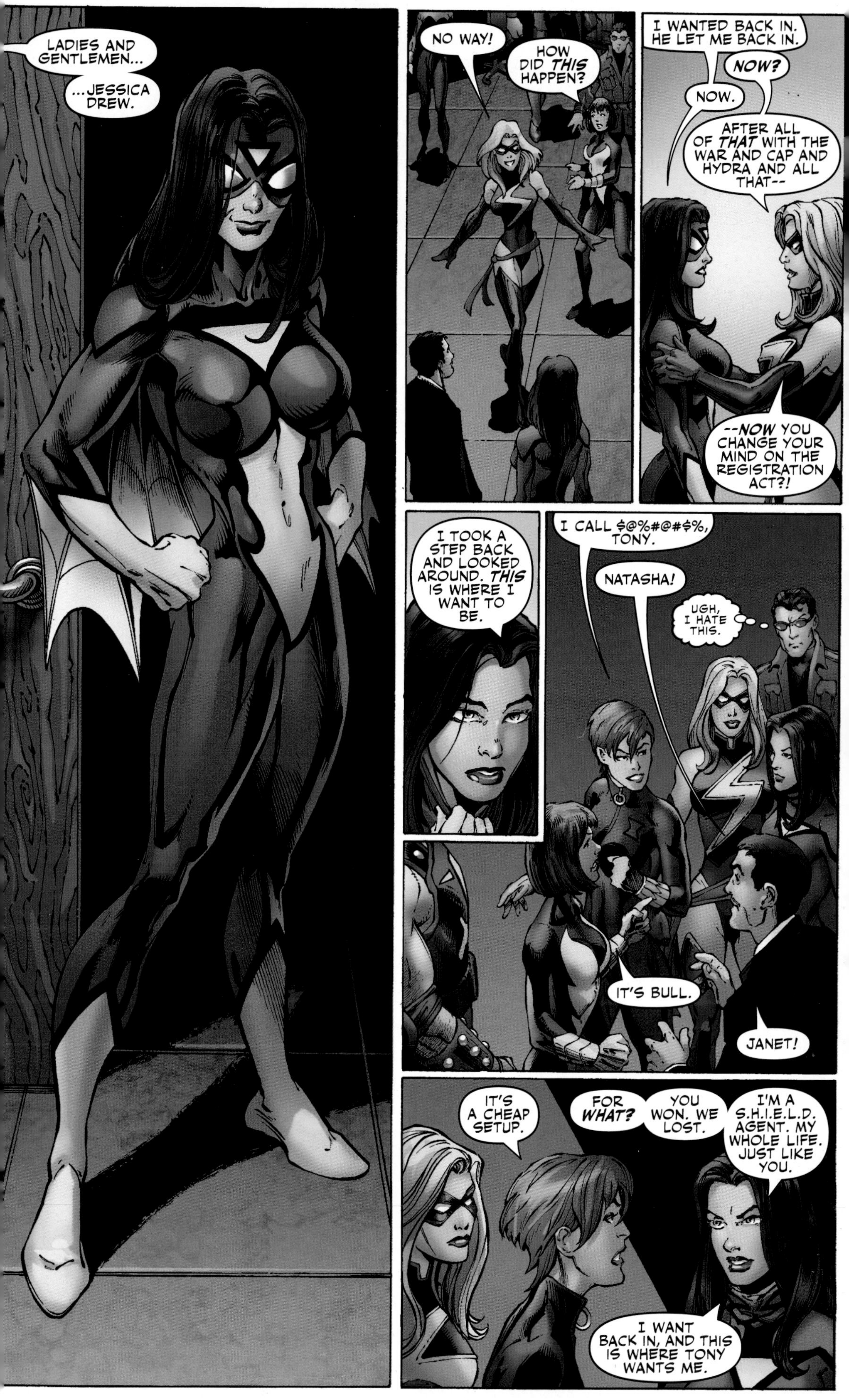
LADIES AND GENTLEMEN...
...JESSICA DREW.
NO WAY!
HOW DID THIS HAPPEN?
I WANTED BACK IN. HE LET ME BACK IN.
NOW?
NOW.
AFTER ALL OF THAT WITH THE WAR AND CAP AND HYDRA AND ALL THAT--
--NOW YOU CHANGE YOUR MIND ON THE REGISTRATION ACT?!
I TOOK A STEP BACK AND LOOKED AROUND. THIS IS WHERE I WANT TO BE.
I CALL $@%#@#$%, TONY.
NATASHA!
UGH, I HATE THIS.
IT'S BULL.
JANET!
IT'S A CHEAP SETUP.
FOR WHAT?
YOU WON. WE LOST.
I'M A S.H.I.E.L.D. AGENT. MY WHOLE LIFE. JUST LIKE YOU.
I WANT BACK IN, AND THIS IS WHERE TONY WANTS ME.

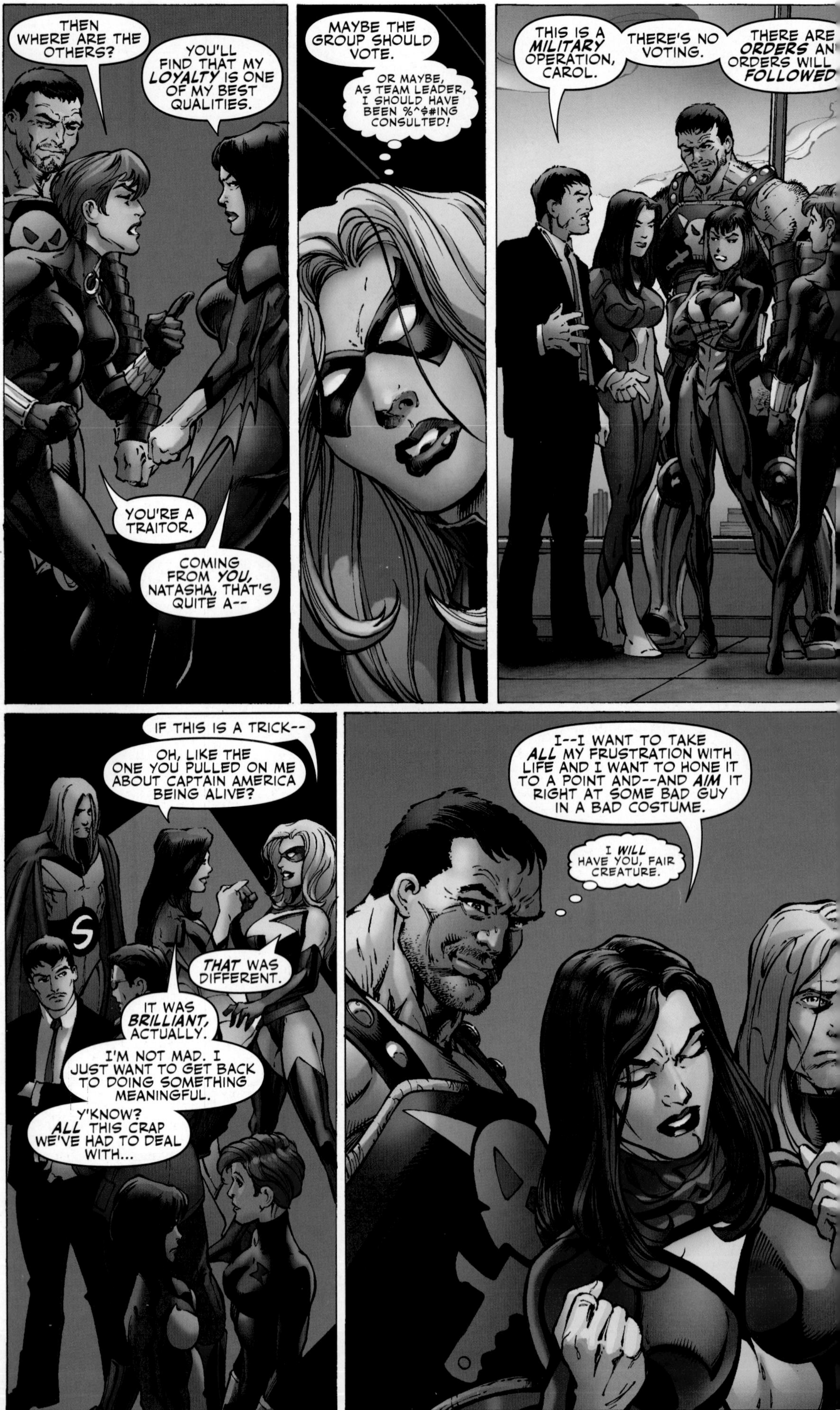
THEN WHERE ARE THE OTHERS?
YOU'LL FIND THAT MY LOYALTY IS ONE OF MY BEST QUALITIES.
YOU'RE A TRAITOR.
COMING FROM YOU, NATASHA, THAT'S QUITE A--
MAYBE THE GROUP SHOULD VOTE.
OR MAYBE, AS TEAM LEADER, I SHOULD HAVE BEEN %^$#ING CONSULTED!
THIS IS A MILITARY OPERATION, CAROL.
THERE'S NO VOTING.
THERE ARE ORDERS AN ORDERS WILL FOLLOWED
IF THIS IS A TRICK--
OH, LIKE THE ONE YOU PULLED ON ME ABOUT CAPTAIN AMERICA BEING ALIVE?
THAT WAS DIFFERENT.
IT WAS BRILLIANT, ACTUALLY.
I'M NOT MAD. I JUST WANT TO GET BACK TO DOING SOMETHING MEANINGFUL.
Y'KNOW? ALL THIS CRAP WE'VE HAD TO DEAL WITH...
I--I WANT TO TAKE ALL MY FRUSTRATION WITH LIFE AND I WANT TO HONE IT TO A POINT AND--AND AIM IT RIGHT AT SOME BAD GUY IN A BAD COSTUME.
I WILL HAVE YOU, FAIR CREATURE.

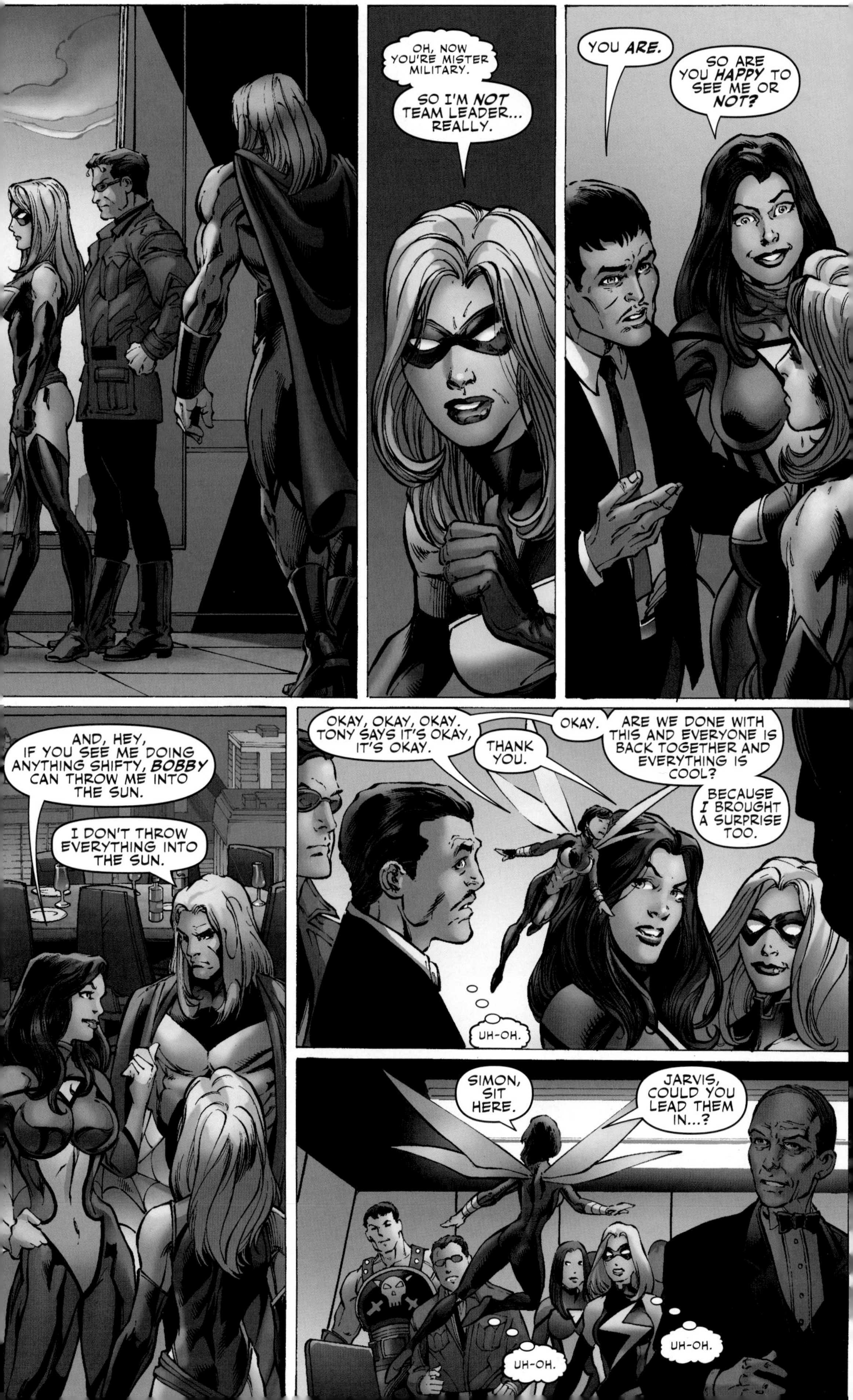

OH, NOW YOU'RE MISTER MILITARY.
SO I'M NOT TEAM LEADER... REALLY.
YOU ARE.
SO ARE YOU HAPPY TO SEE ME OR NOT?
AND, HEY, IF YOU SEE ME DOING ANYTHING SHIFTY, BOBBY CAN THROW ME INTO THE SUN.
I DON'T THROW EVERYTHING INTO THE SUN.
OKAY, OKAY, OKAY. TONY SAYS IT'S OKAY, IT'S OKAY.
THANK YOU.
OKAY.
ARE WE DONE WITH THIS AND EVERYONE IS BACK TOGETHER AND EVERYTHING IS COOL?
BECAUSE I BROUGHT A SURPRISE TOO.
UH-OH.
SIMON, SIT HERE.
JARVIS, COULD YOU LEAD THEM IN...?
UH-OH.
UH-OH.

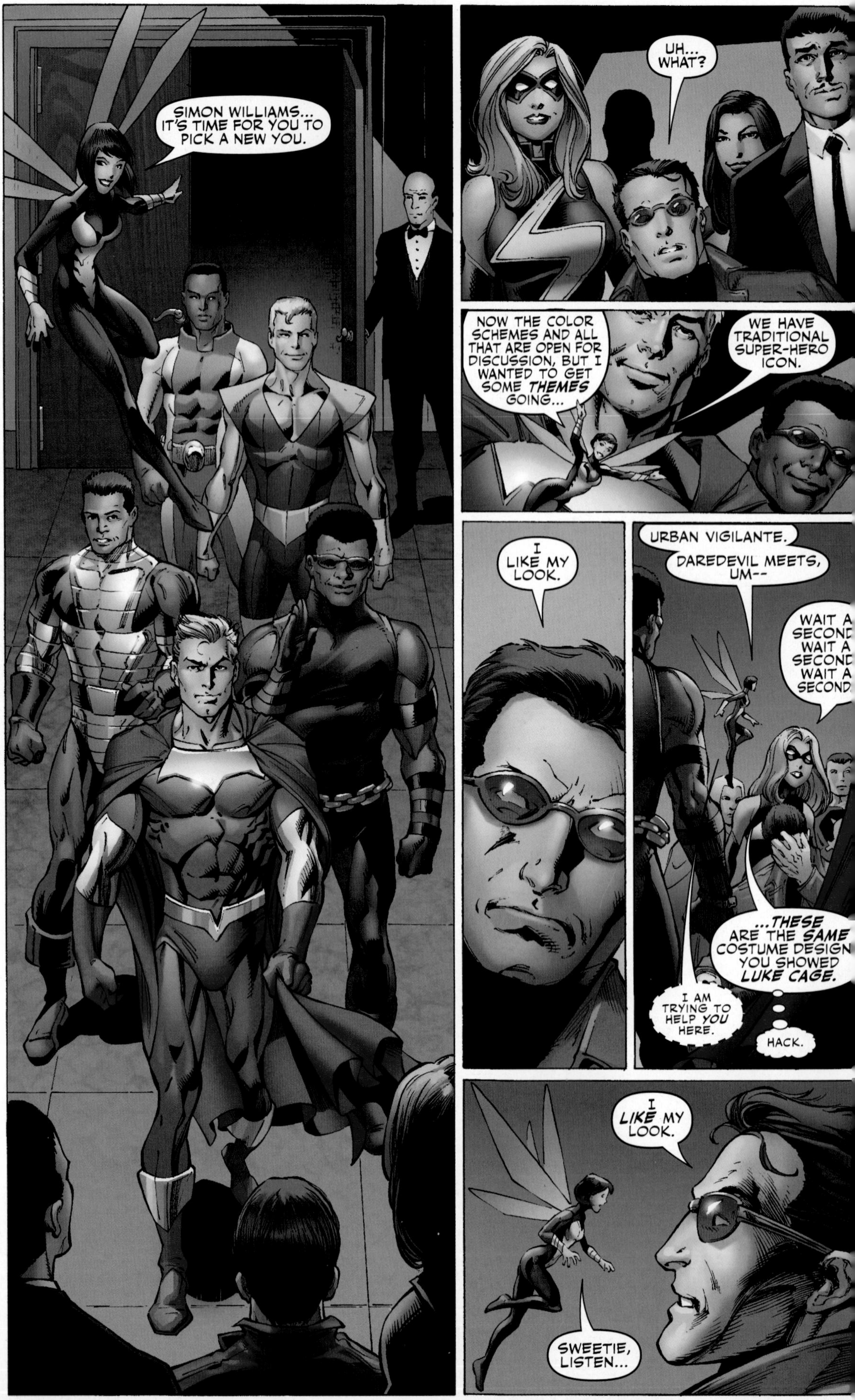
SIMON WILLIAMS... IT'S TIME FOR YOU TO PICK A NEW YOU.
UH... WHAT?
NOW THE COLOR SCHEMES AND ALL THAT ARE OPEN FOR DISCUSSION, BUT I WANTED TO GET SOME THEMES GOING...
WE HAVE TRADITIONAL SUPER-HERO ICON.
URBAN VIGILANTE.
DAREDEVIL MEETS, UM--
I LIKE MY LOOK.
WAIT A SECOND WAIT A SECOND WAIT A SECOND
...THESE ARE THE SAME COSTUME DESIGN YOU SHOWED LUKE CAGE.
I AM TRYING TO HELP YOU HERE.
HACK.
I LIKE MY LOOK.
SWEETIE, LISTEN...

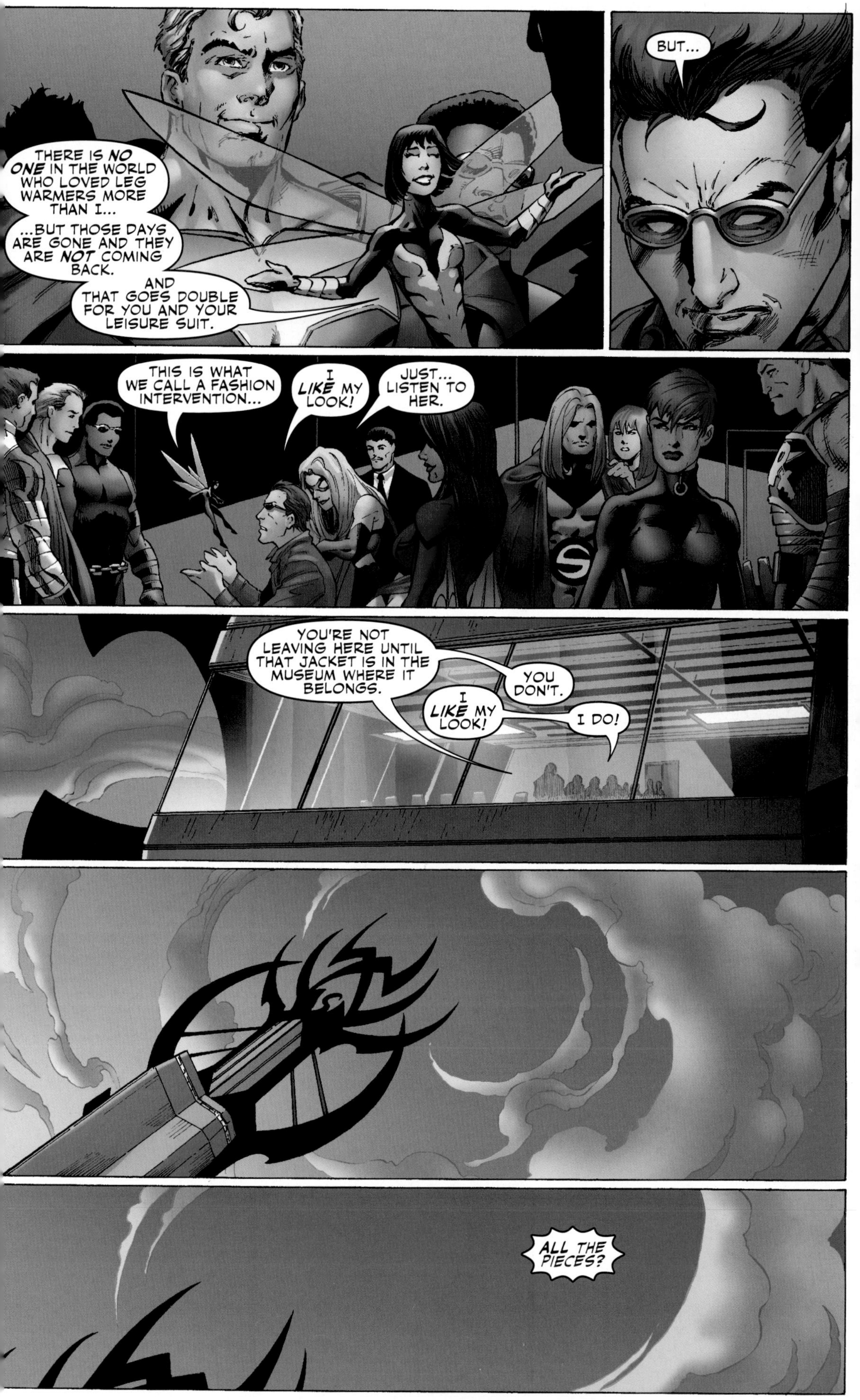
THERE IS NO ONE IN THE WORLD WHO LOVED LEG WARMERS MORE THAN I...
...BUT THOSE DAYS ARE GONE AND THEY ARE NOT COMING BACK.
AND THAT GOES DOUBLE FOR YOU AND YOUR LEISURE SUIT.
BUT...
THIS IS WHAT WE CALL A FASHION INTERVENTION...
I LIKE MY LOOK!
JUST... LISTEN TO HER.
YOU'RE NOT LEAVING HERE UNTIL THAT JACKET IS IN THE MUSEUM WHERE IT BELONGS.
YOU DON'T.
I LIKE MY LOOK!
I DO!
ALL THE PIECES?

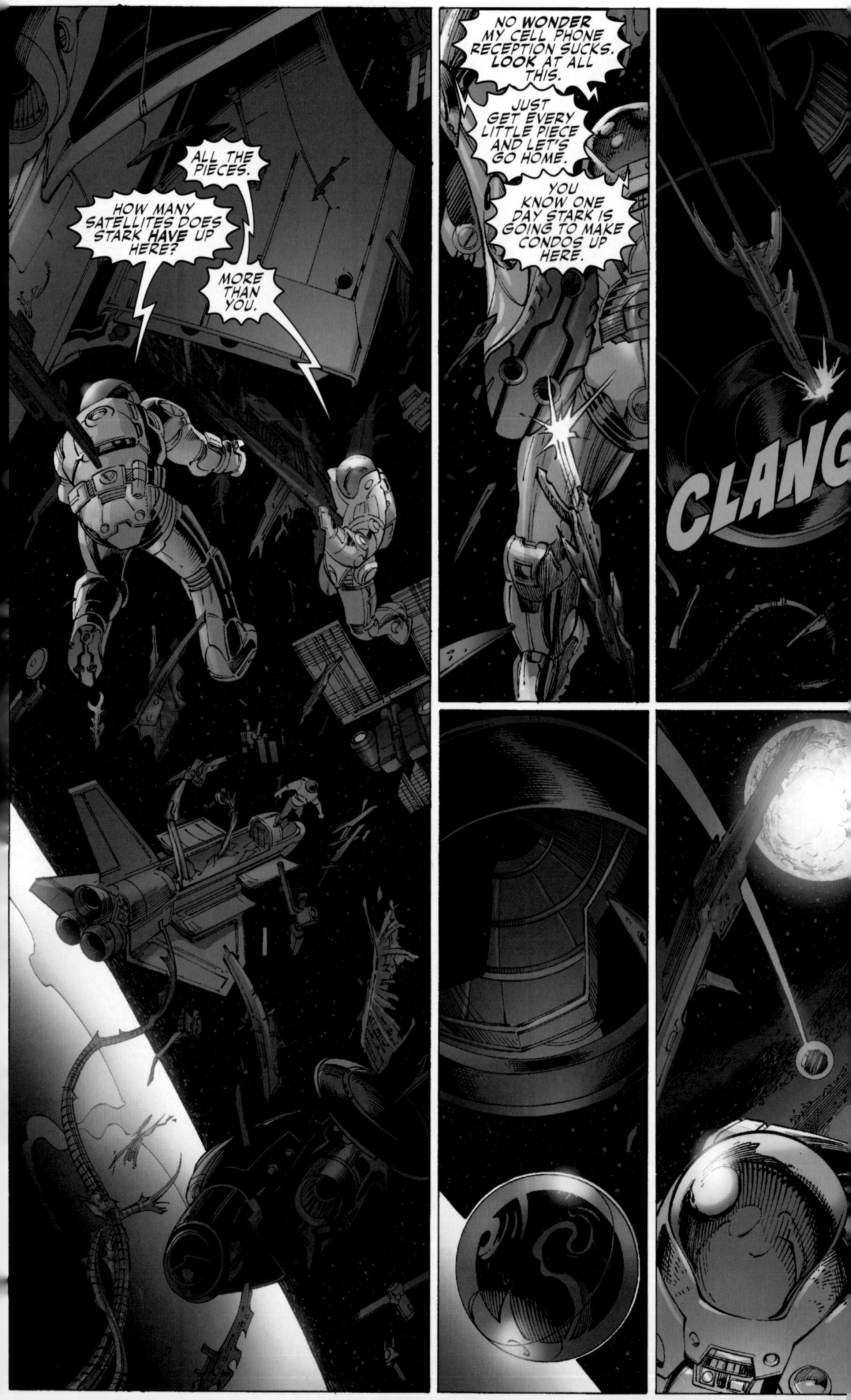

ALL THE PIECES.
HOW MANY SATELLITES DOES STARK HAVE UP HERE?
MORE THAN YOU.
NO WONDER MY CELL PHONE RECEPTION SUCKS. LOOK AT ALL THIS.
JUST GET EVERY LITTLE PIECE AND LET'S GO HOME.
YOU KNOW ONE DAY STARK IS GOING TO MAKE CONDOS UP HERE.
CLANG

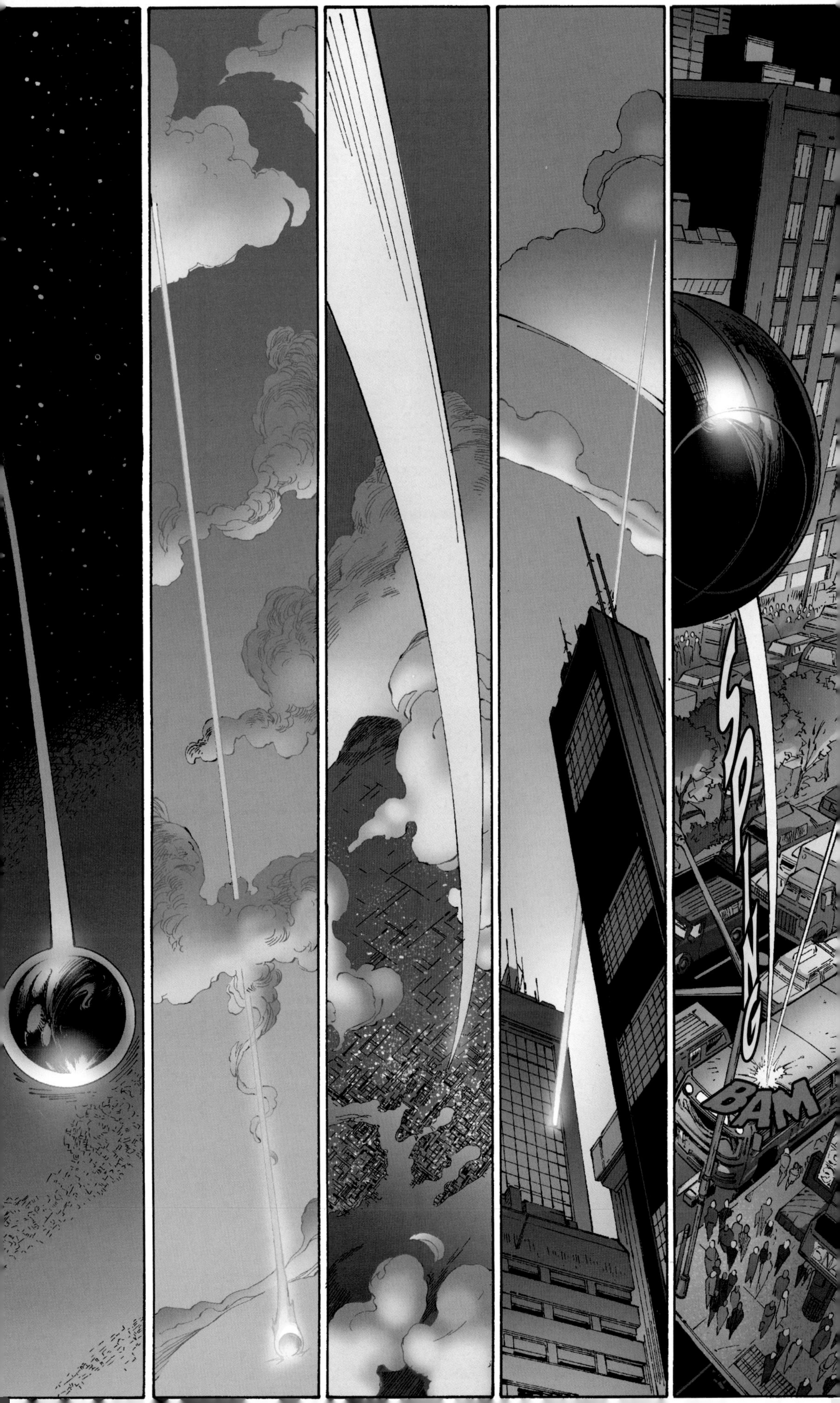
SPING
BAM

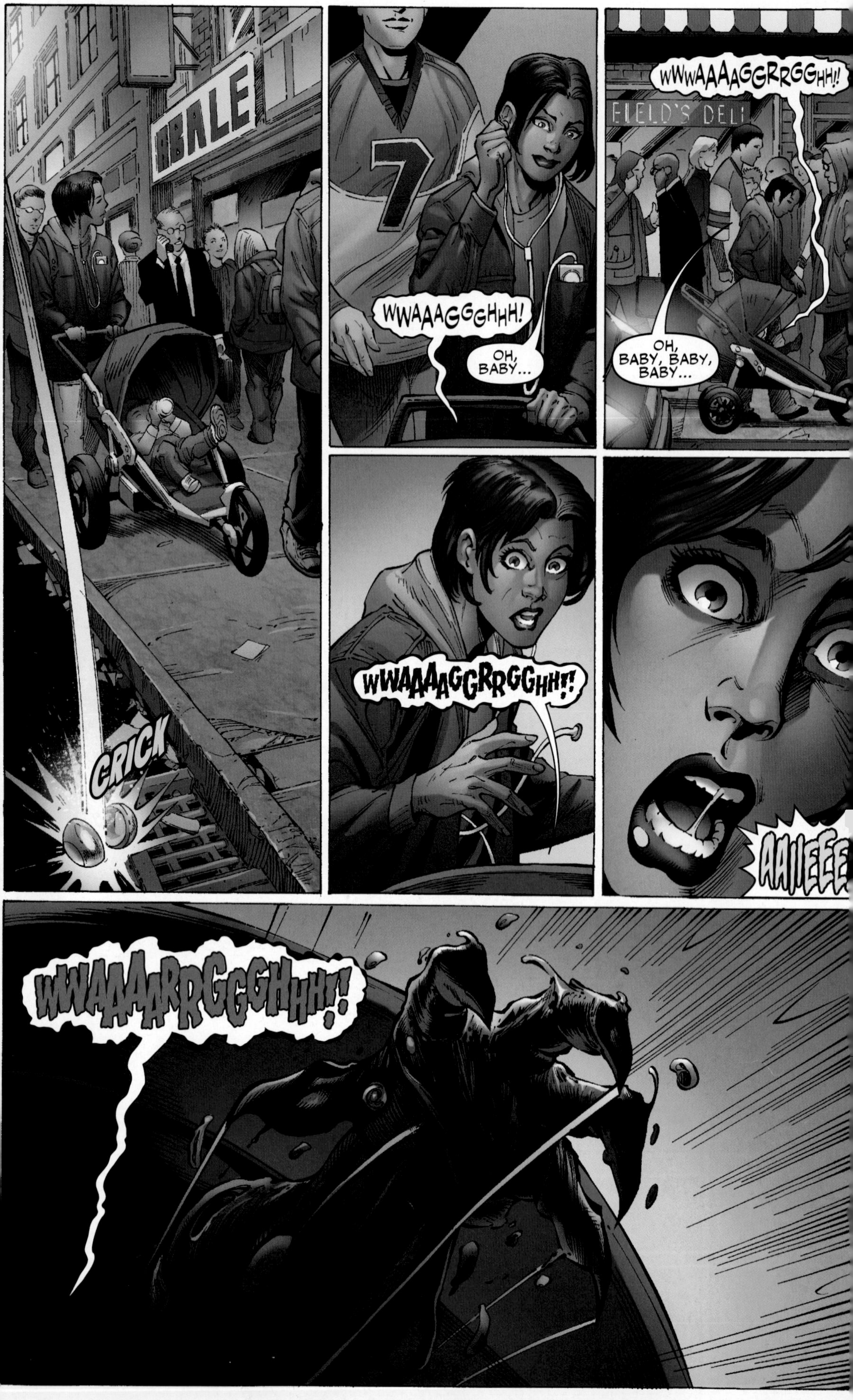

ABALE
CRICK
WWAAAGGGHHH!
OH, BABY...
WWWAAAAGGRRGGHH!!
FIELD'S DELI
OH, BABY, BABY, BABY...
WWAAAAGGRRGGHH!!
AAIIEEE
WWAAAARRGGGHHH!!

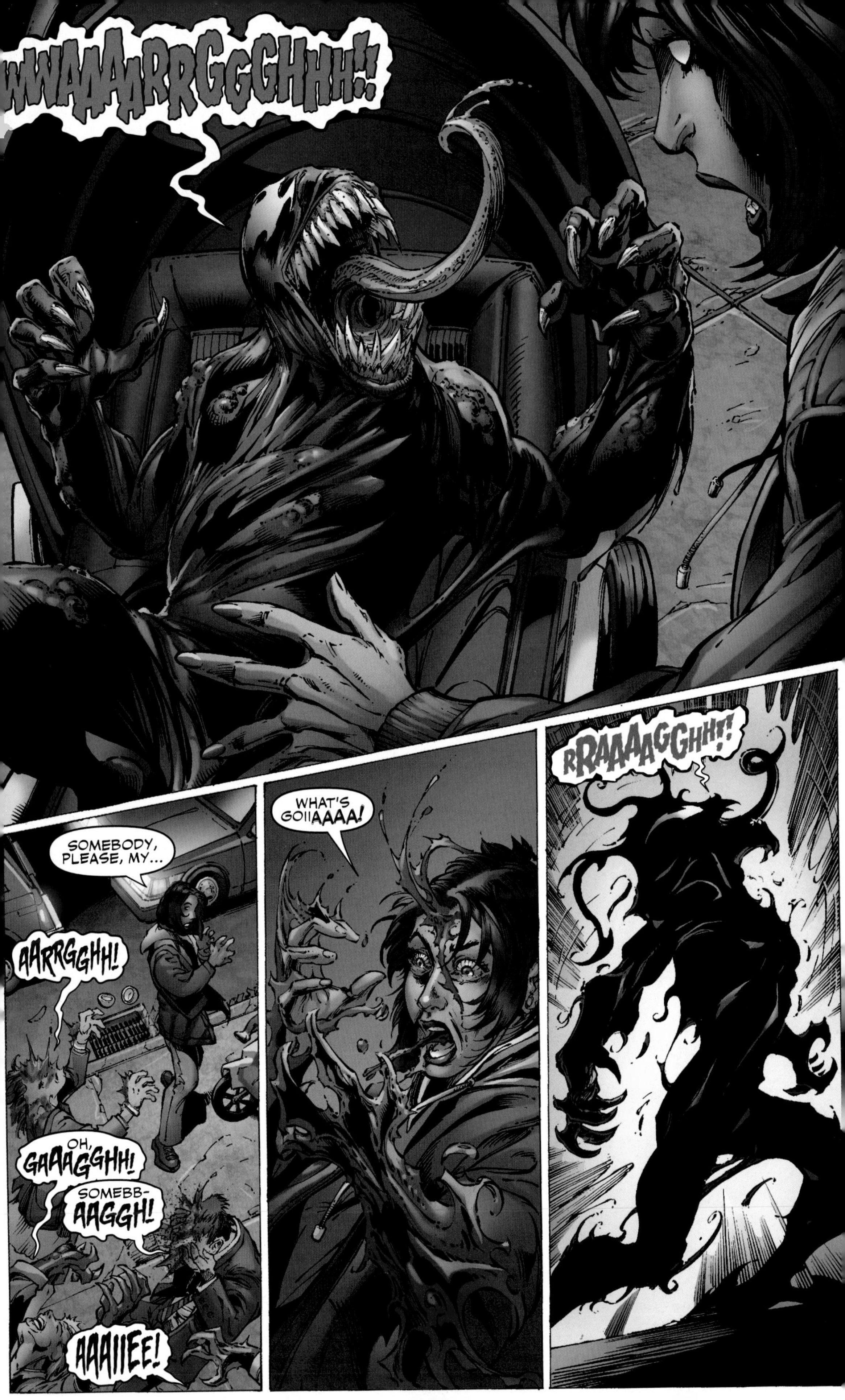
WWAAAARRGGGHHH!!
SOMEBODY, PLEASE, MY...
AARRGGHH!
OH, GAAAGGHH!
SOMEBB-AAGGH!
AAAIIEE!
WHAT'S GOIIAAAA!
RRAAAAGGHH!!

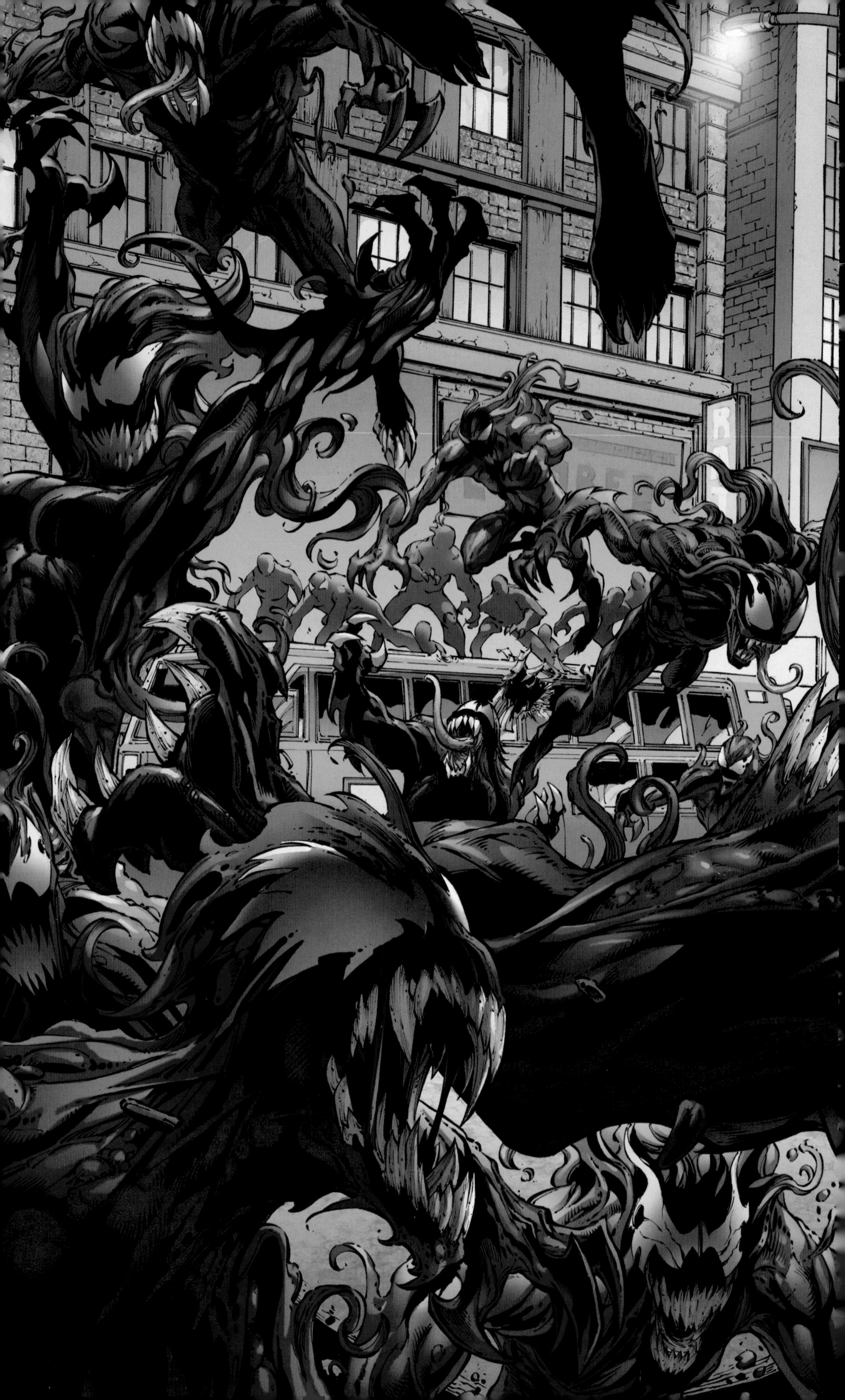

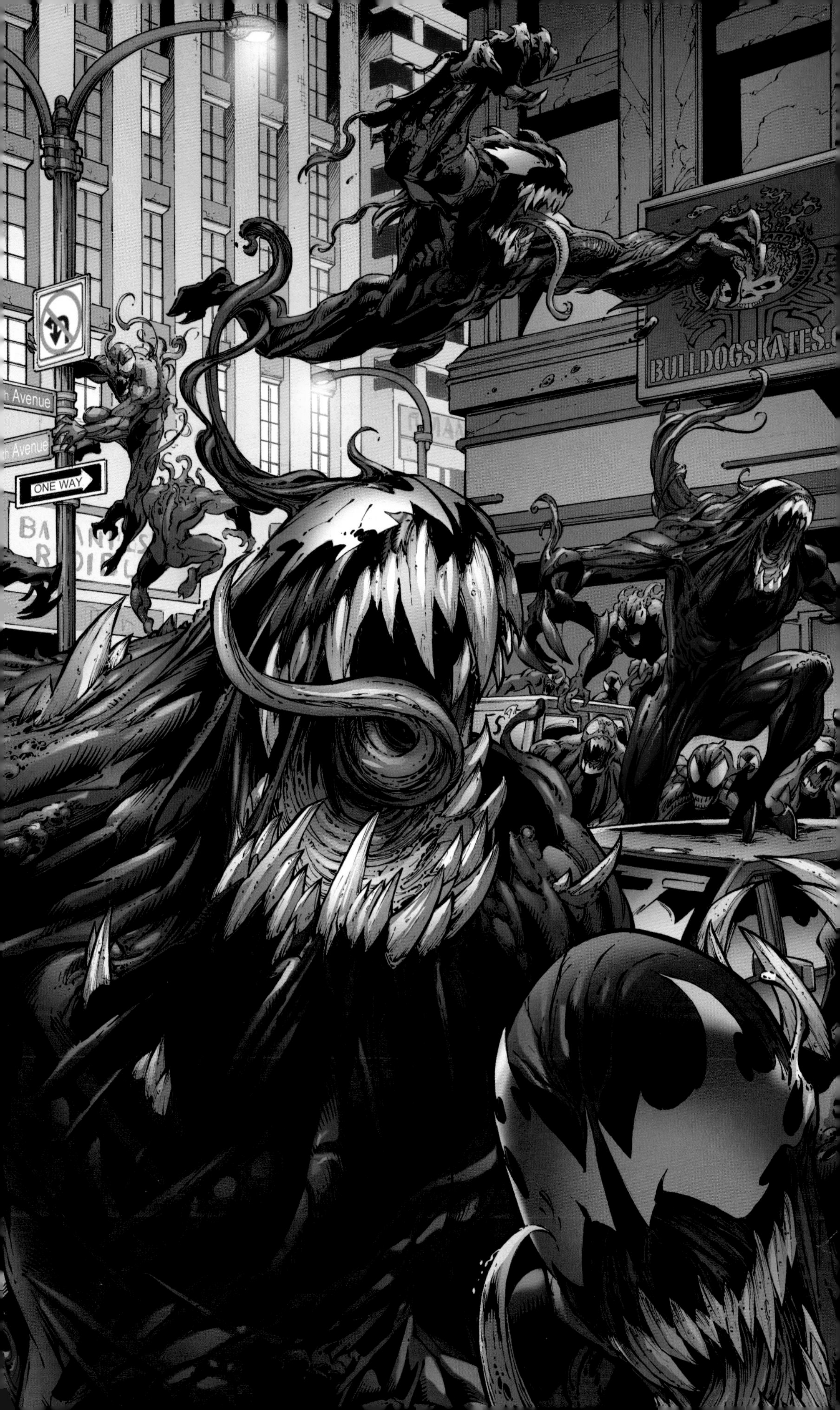
BULLDOGSKATES.C
h Avenue
th Avenue
ONE WAY

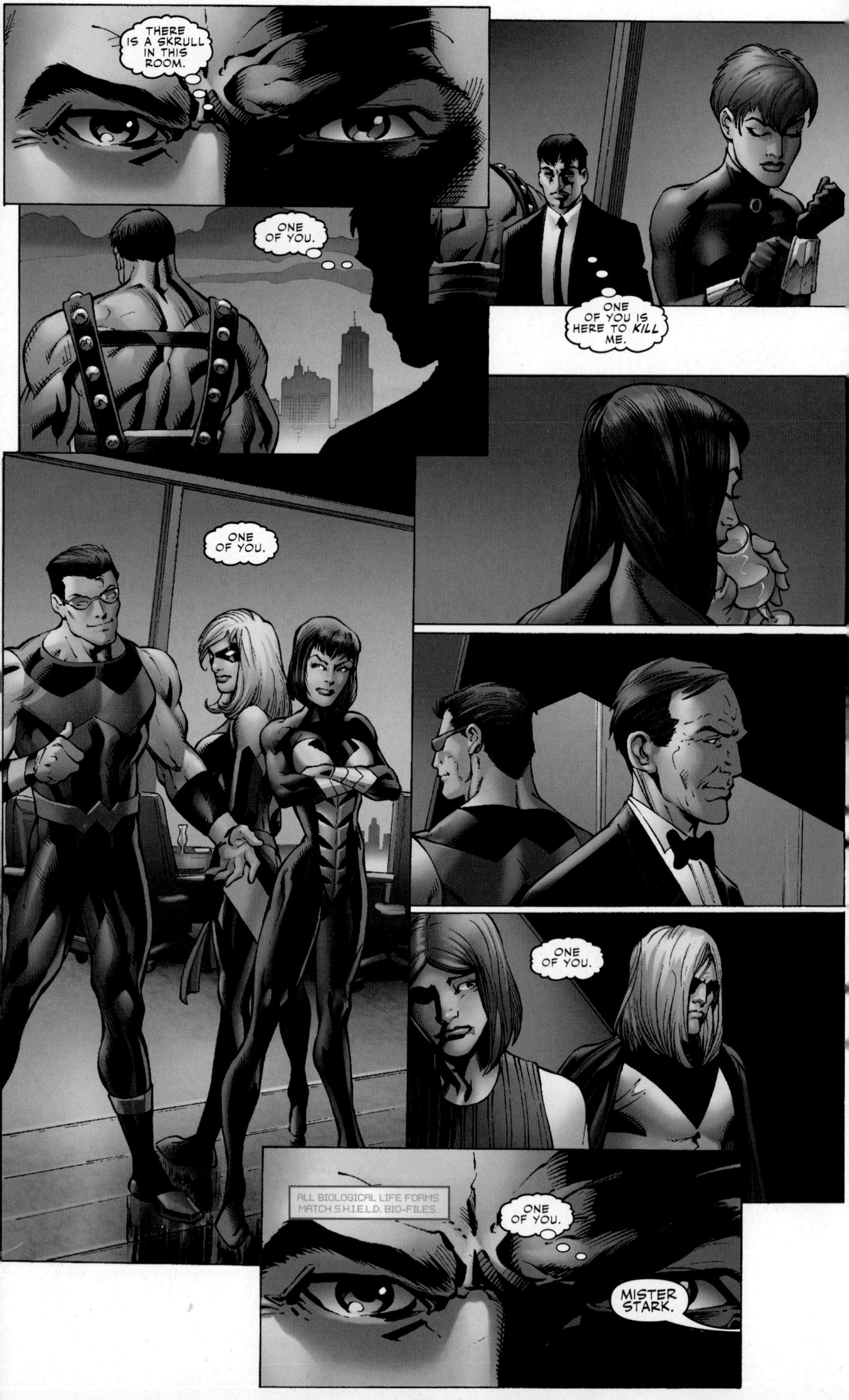
THERE IS A SKRULL IN THIS ROOM.
ONE OF YOU.
ONE OF YOU IS HERE TO KILL ME.
ONE OF YOU.
ONE OF YOU.
ALL BIOLOGICAL LIFE FORMS MATCH S.H.I.E.L.D. BIO-FILES.
ONE OF YOU.
MISTER STARK.

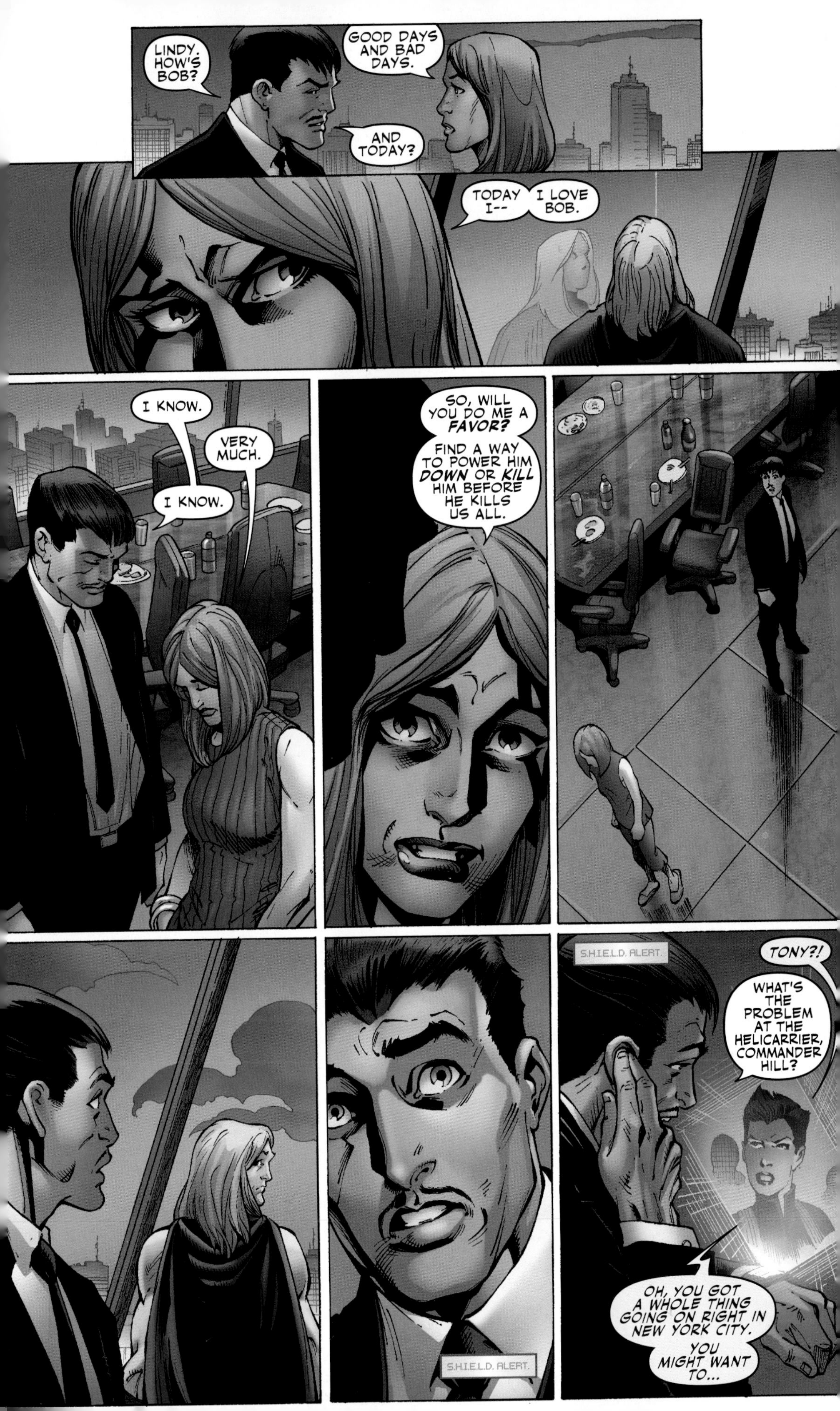
LINDY. HOW'S BOB?
GOOD DAYS AND BAD DAYS.
AND TODAY?
TODAY I--
I LOVE BOB.
I KNOW.
VERY MUCH.
I KNOW.
SO, WILL YOU DO ME A FAVOR?
FIND A WAY TO POWER HIM DOWN OR KILL HIM BEFORE HE KILLS US ALL.
S.H.I.E.L.D. ALERT.
S.H.I.E.L.D. ALERT.
TONY?!
WHAT'S THE PROBLEM AT THE HELICARRIER, COMMANDER HILL?
OH, YOU GOT A WHOLE THING GOING ON RIGHT IN NEW YORK CITY.
YOU MIGHT WANT TO...

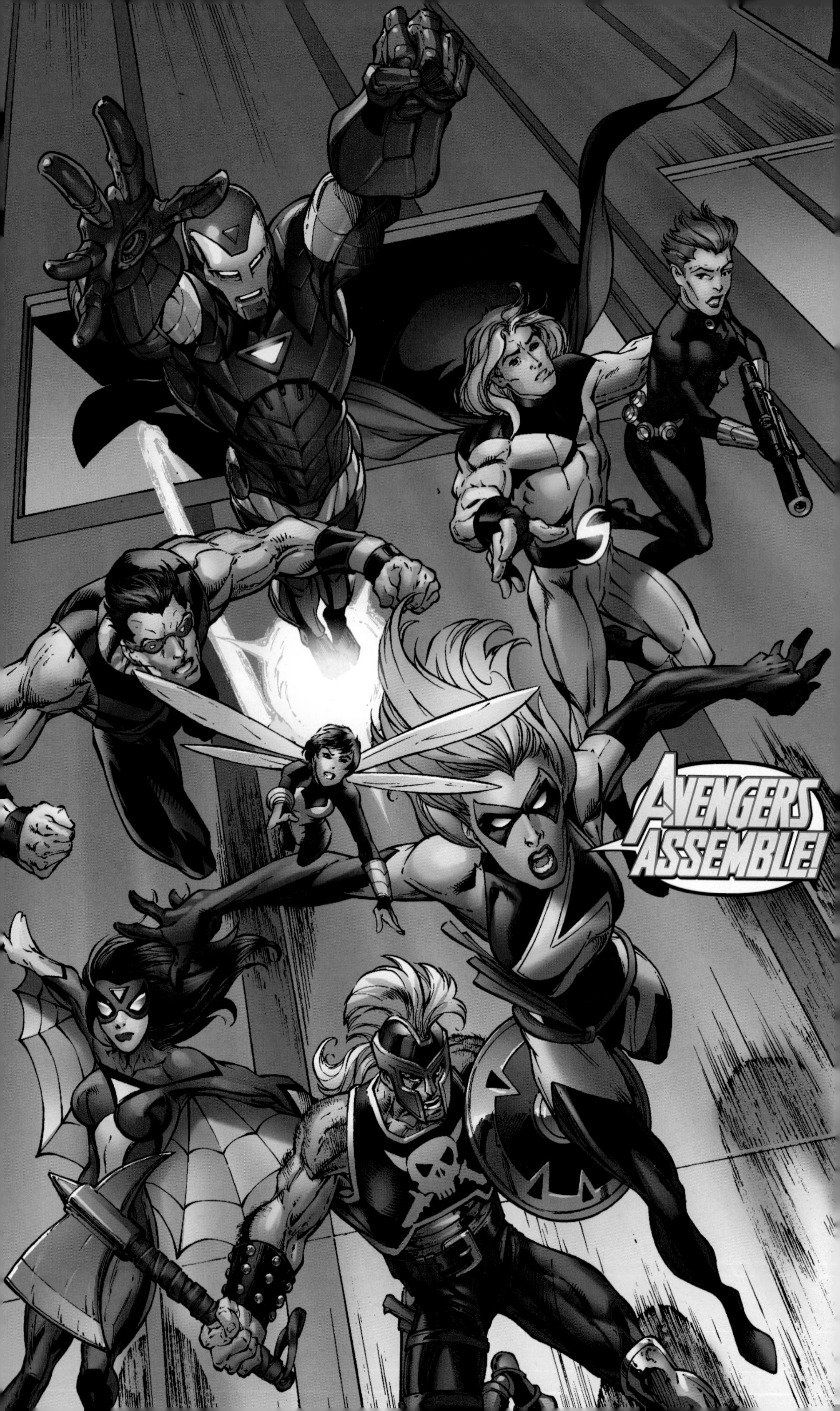
AVENGERS ASSEMBLE!

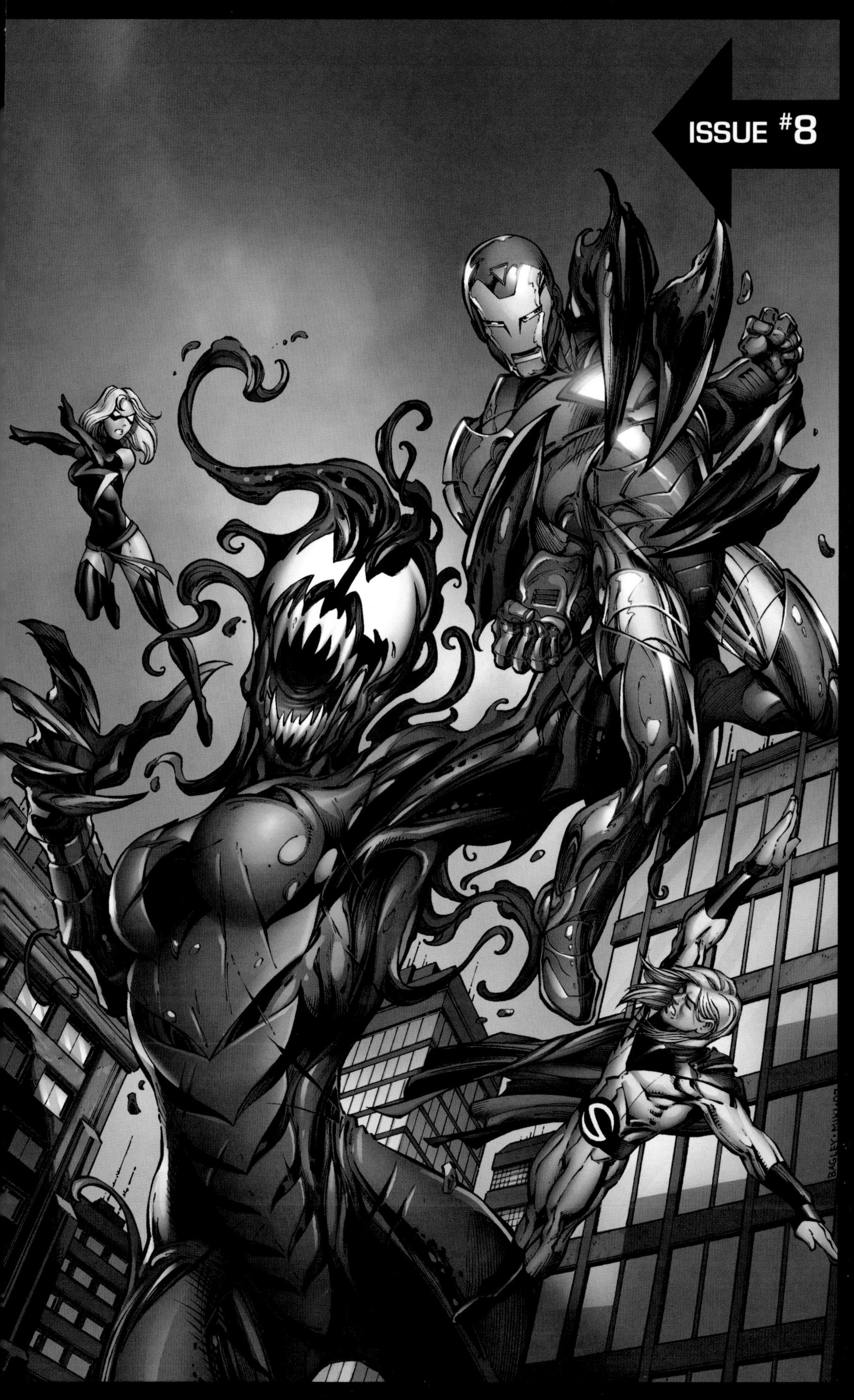
ISSUE #8

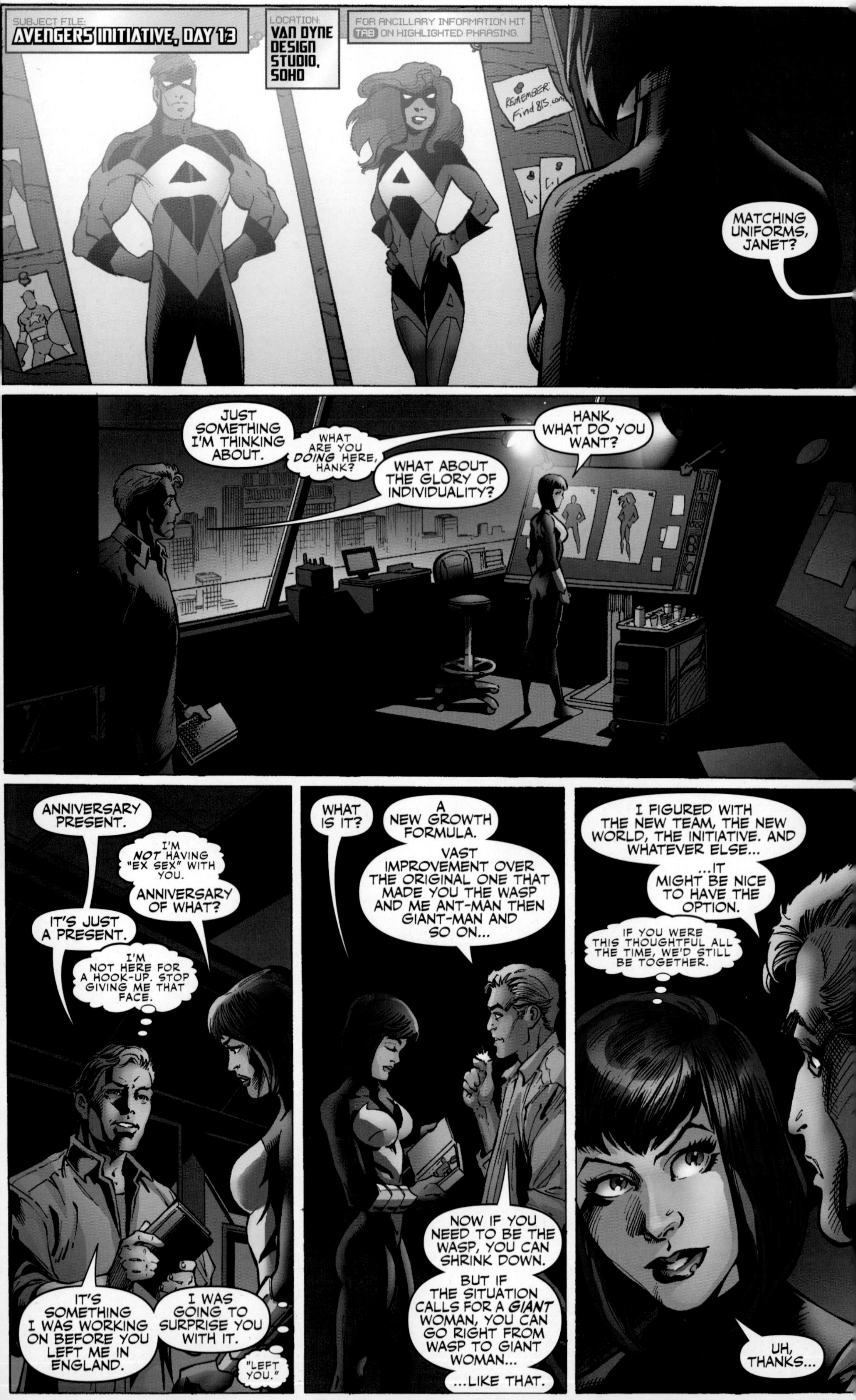

SUBJECT FILE:
AVENGERS INITIATIVE, DAY 13
LOCATION:
VAN DYNE DESIGN STUDIO, SOHO
FOR ANCILLARY INFORMATION HIT TAB ON HIGHLIGHTED PHRASING.
REMEMBER: Find815.com
MATCHING UNIFORMS, JANET?
JUST SOMETHING I'M THINKING ABOUT.
WHAT ARE YOU DOING HERE, HANK?
WHAT ABOUT THE GLORY OF INDIVIDUALITY?
HANK, WHAT DO YOU WANT?
ANNIVERSARY PRESENT.
I'M NOT HAVING "EX SEX" WITH YOU.
ANNIVERSARY OF WHAT?
IT'S JUST A PRESENT.
I'M NOT HERE FOR A HOOK-UP. STOP GIVING ME THAT FACE.
IT'S SOMETHING I WAS WORKING ON BEFORE YOU LEFT ME IN ENGLAND.
I WAS GOING TO SURPRISE YOU WITH IT.
"LEFT YOU."
WHAT IS IT?
A NEW GROWTH FORMULA.
VAST IMPROVEMENT OVER THE ORIGINAL ONE THAT MADE YOU THE WASP AND ME ANT-MAN THEN GIANT-MAN AND SO ON...
NOW IF YOU NEED TO BE THE WASP, YOU CAN SHRINK DOWN.
BUT IF THE SITUATION CALLS FOR A GIANT WOMAN, YOU CAN GO RIGHT FROM WASP TO GIANT WOMAN...
...LIKE THAT.
I FIGURED WITH THE NEW TEAM, THE NEW WORLD, THE INITIATIVE. AND WHATEVER ELSE...
...IT MIGHT BE NICE TO HAVE THE OPTION.
IF YOU WERE THIS THOUGHTFUL ALL THE TIME, WE'D STILL BE TOGETHER.
UH, THANKS...

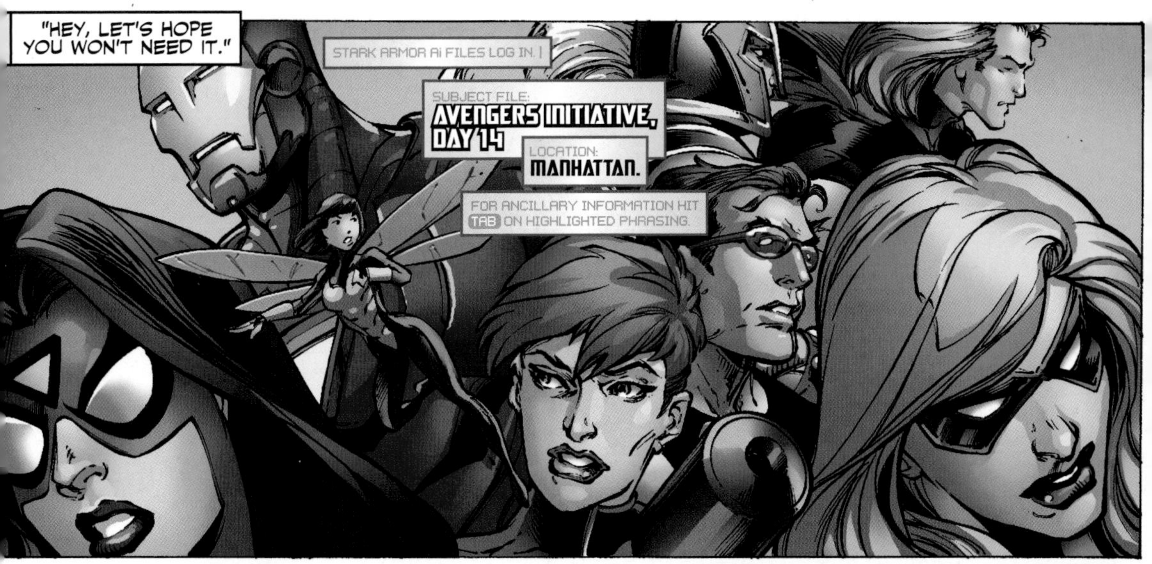
"HEY, LET'S HOPE YOU WON'T NEED IT."
STARK ARMOR Ai FILES LOG IN.
SUBJECT FILE: AVENGERS INITIATIVE, DAY 14
LOCATION: MANHATTAN.
FOR ANCILLARY INFORMATION HIT TAB ON HIGHLIGHTED PHRASING.

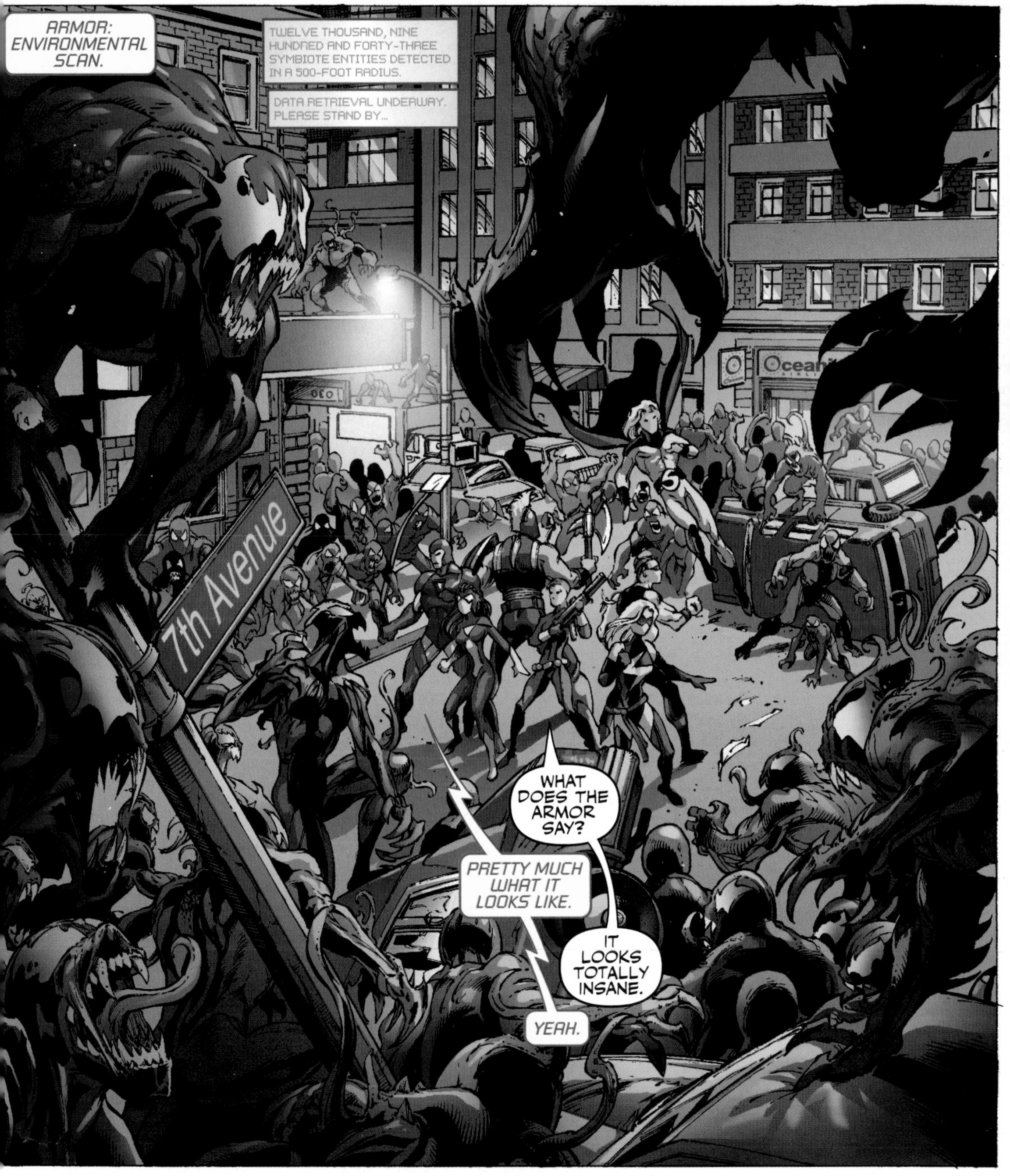
ARMOR: ENVIRONMENTAL SCAN.
TWELVE THOUSAND, NINE HUNDRED AND FORTY-THREE SYMBIOTE ENTITIES DETECTED IN A 500-FOOT RADIUS.
DATA RETRIEVAL UNDERWAY. PLEASE STAND BY...
7th Avenue
WHAT DOES THE ARMOR SAY?
PRETTY MUCH WHAT IT LOOKS LIKE.
IT LOOKS TOTALLY INSANE.
YEAH.

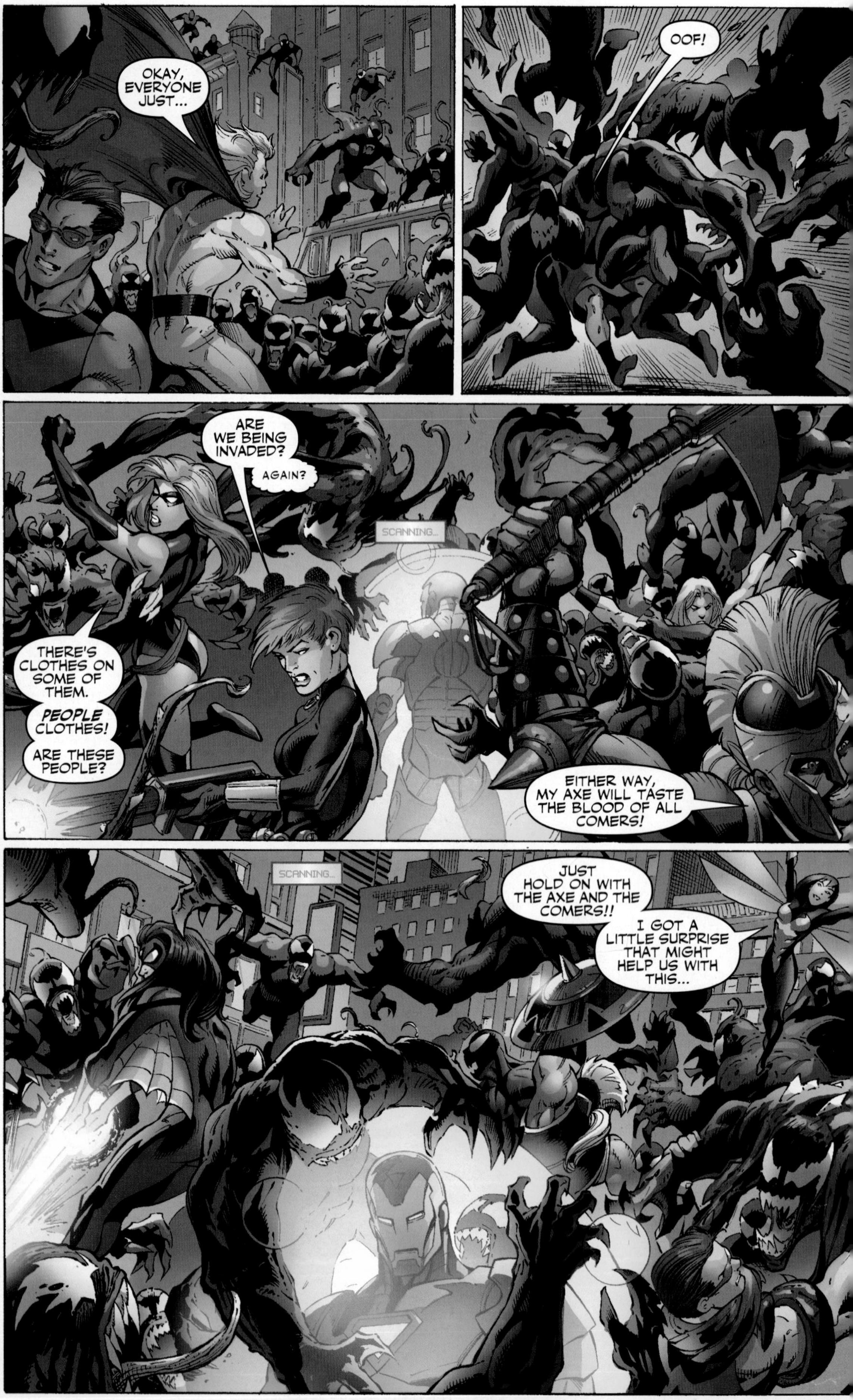
OKAY, EVERYONE JUST...
OOF!
ARE WE BEING INVADED?
AGAIN?
SCANNING...
THERE'S CLOTHES ON SOME OF THEM.
PEOPLE CLOTHES!
ARE THESE PEOPLE?
EITHER WAY, MY AXE WILL TASTE THE BLOOD OF ALL COMERS!
SCANNING...
JUST HOLD ON WITH THE AXE AND THE COMERS!!
I GOT A LITTLE SURPRISE THAT MIGHT HELP US WITH THIS...

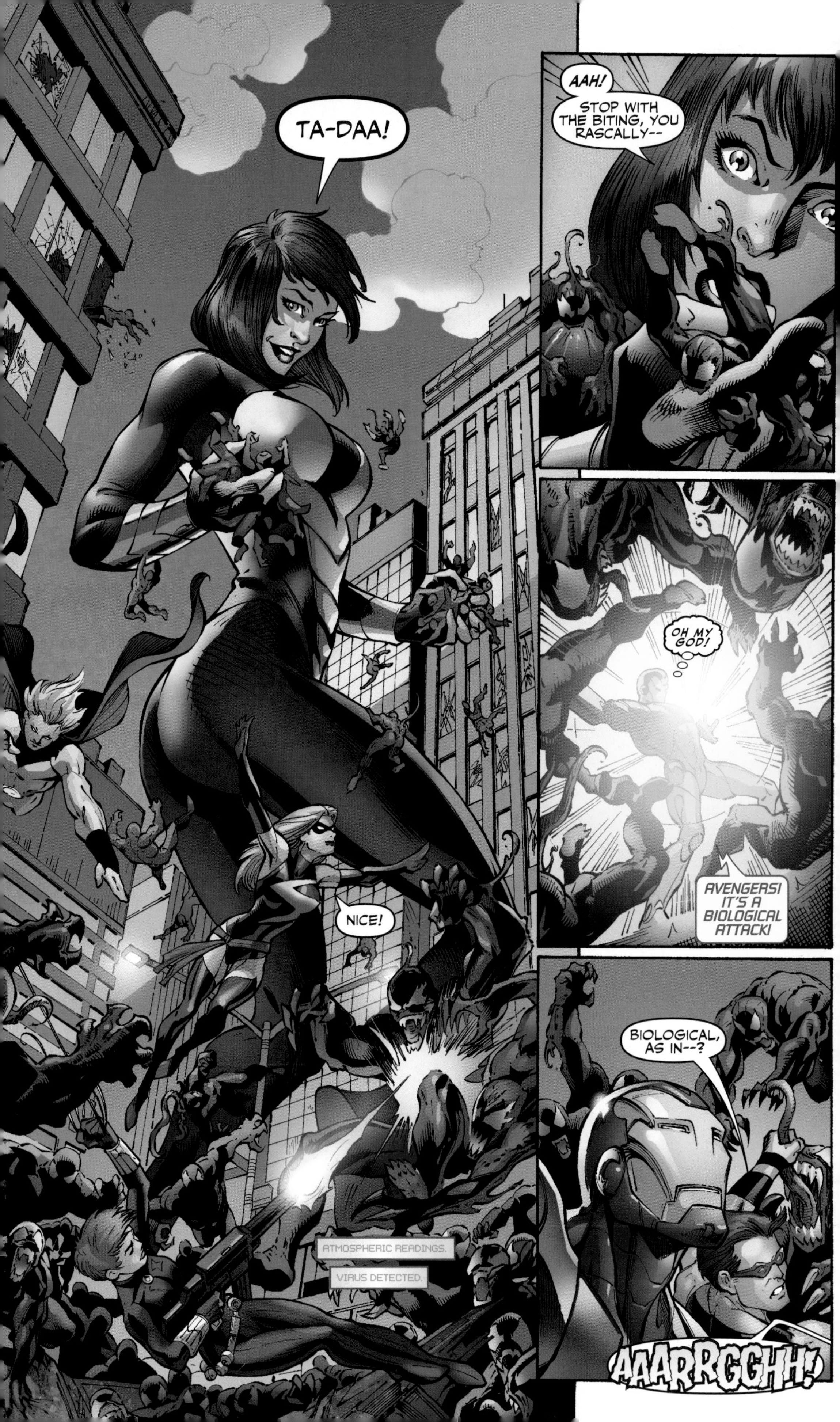
TA-DAA!
NICE!
ATMOSPHERIC READINGS.
VIRUS DETECTED.
AAH!
STOP WITH THE BITING, YOU RASCALLY--
OH MY GOD!
AVENGERS! IT'S A BIOLOGICAL ATTACK!
BIOLOGICAL, AS IN--?
AAARRGGHH!

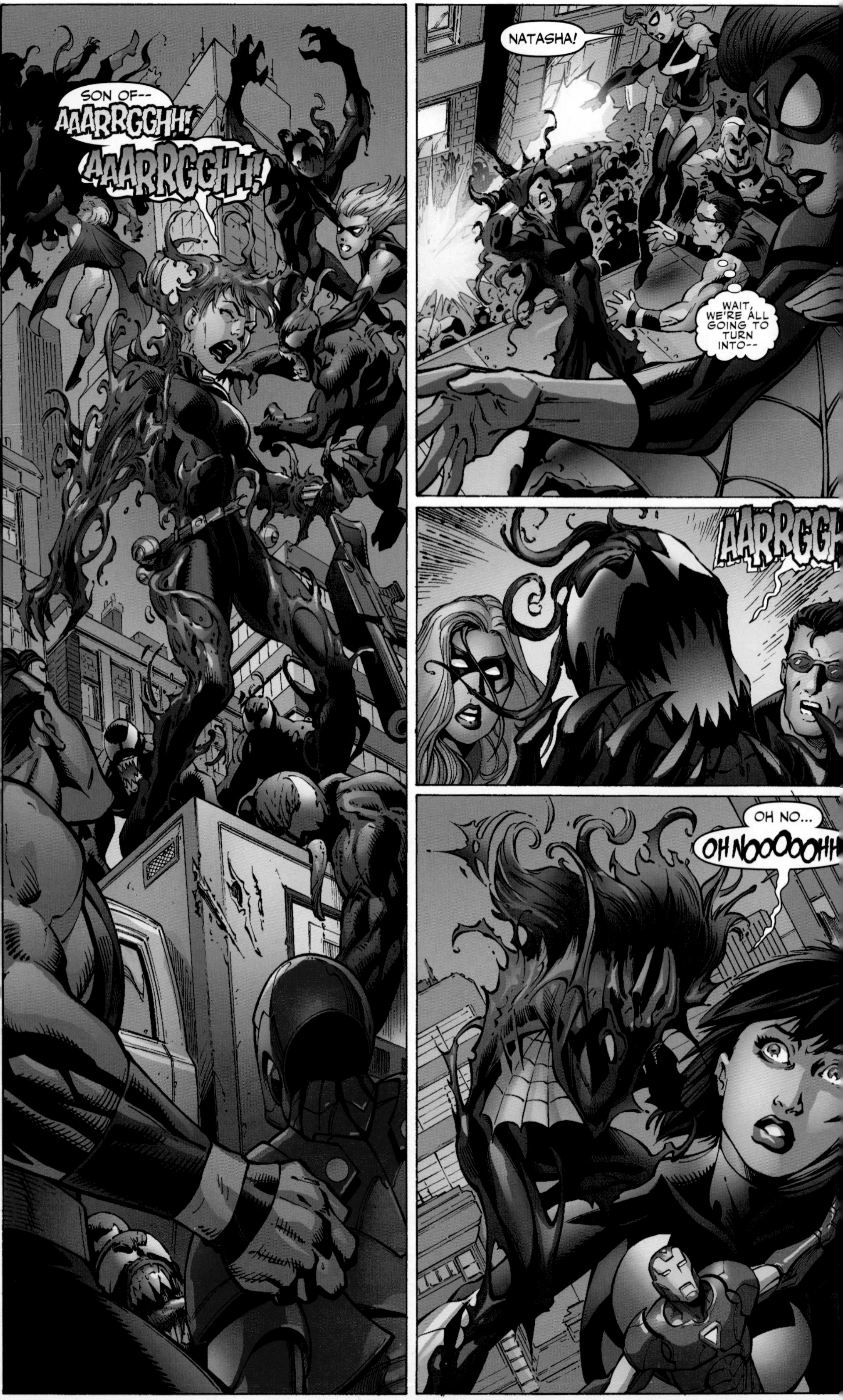
SON OF--
AAARRGGHH!
AAARRGGHH!
NATASHA!
WAIT, WE'RE ALL GOING TO TURN INTO--
AARRGGH
OH NO...
OH NOOOOOHH

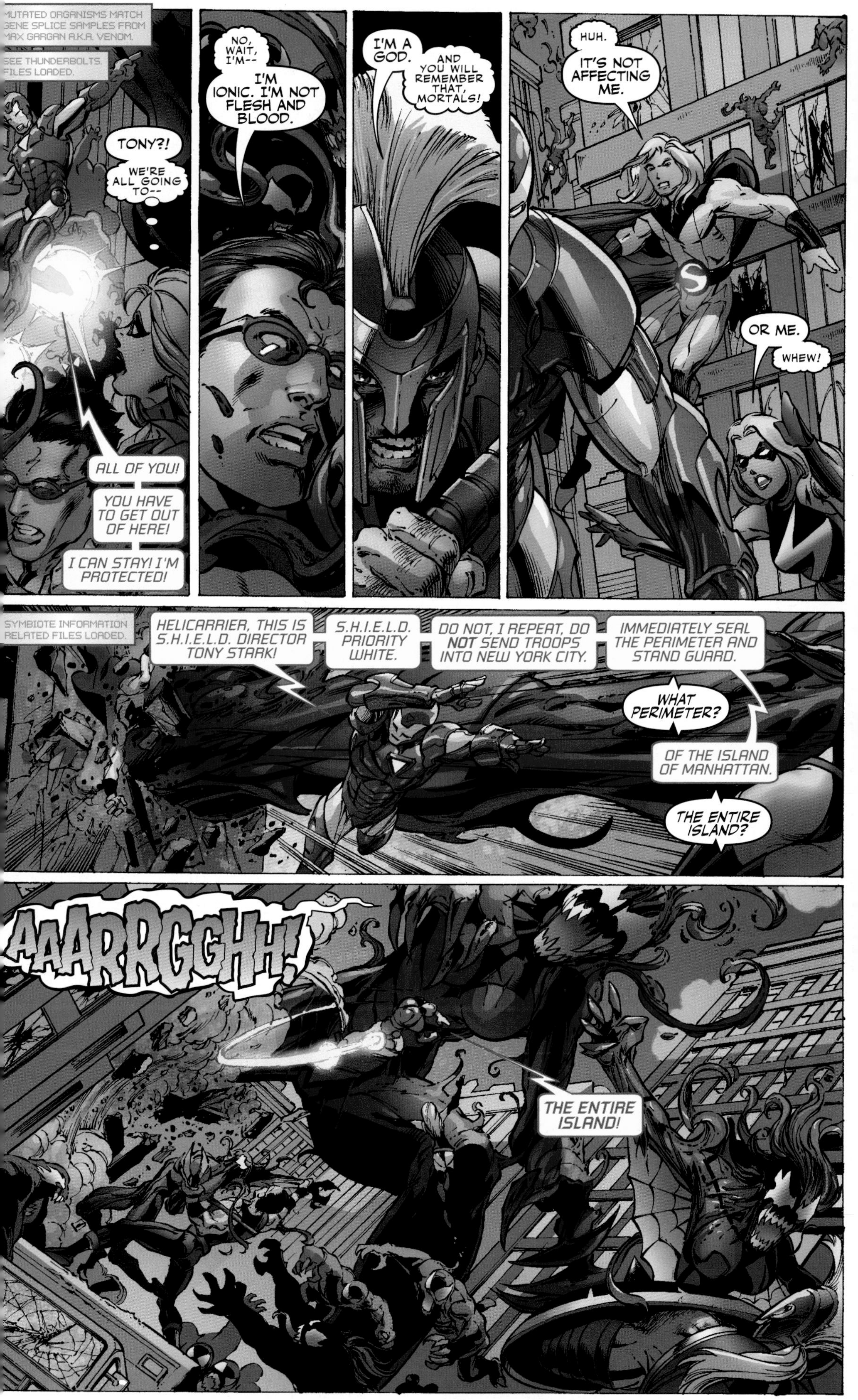
MUTATED ORGANISMS MATCH GENE SPLICE SAMPLES FROM MAX GARGAN A.K.A. VENOM.
SEE THUNDERBOLTS. FILES LOADED.
TONY?!
WE'RE ALL GOING TO--
ALL OF YOU!
YOU HAVE TO GET OUT OF HERE!
I CAN STAY! I'M PROTECTED!
NO, WAIT, I'M--
I'M IONIC. I'M NOT FLESH AND BLOOD.
I'M A GOD.
AND YOU WILL REMEMBER THAT, MORTALS!
HUH.
IT'S NOT AFFECTING ME.
OR ME.
WHEW!
SYMBIOTE INFORMATION RELATED FILES LOADED.
HELICARRIER, THIS IS S.H.I.E.L.D. DIRECTOR TONY STARK!
S.H.I.E.L.D. PRIORITY WHITE.
DO NOT, I REPEAT, DO NOT SEND TROOPS INTO NEW YORK CITY.
IMMEDIATELY SEAL THE PERIMETER AND STAND GUARD.
WHAT PERIMETER?
OF THE ISLAND OF MANHATTAN.
THE ENTIRE ISLAND?
AAARRGGHH!
THE ENTIRE ISLAND!

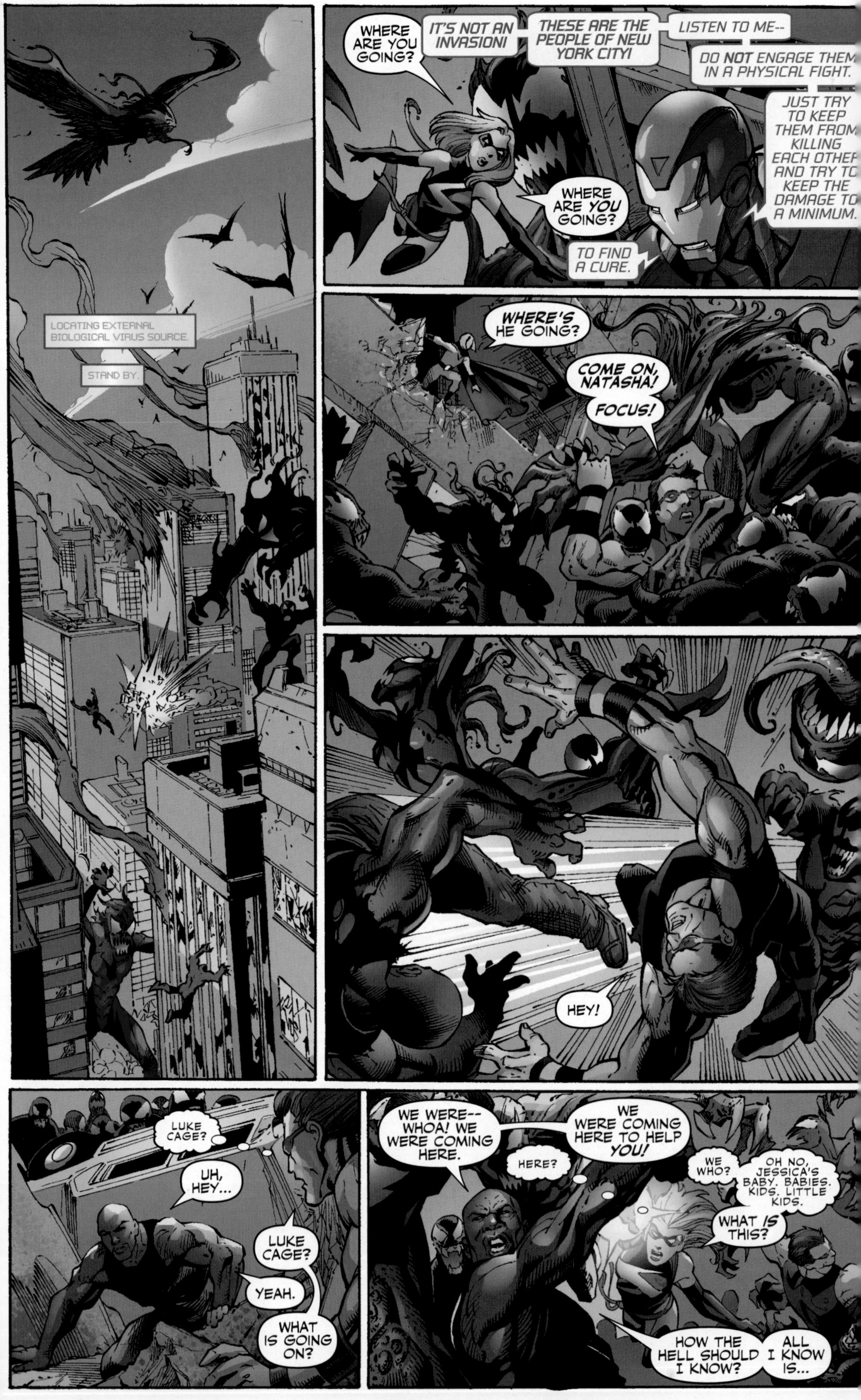

LOCATING EXTERNAL BIOLOGICAL VIRUS SOURCE.
STAND BY.
WHERE ARE YOU GOING?
IT'S NOT AN INVASION!
THESE ARE THE PEOPLE OF NEW YORK CITY!
LISTEN TO ME--
DO NOT ENGAGE THEM IN A PHYSICAL FIGHT.
JUST TRY TO KEEP THEM FROM KILLING EACH OTHER AND TRY TO KEEP THE DAMAGE TO A MINIMUM.
WHERE ARE YOU GOING?
TO FIND A CURE.
WHERE'S HE GOING?
COME ON, NATASHA!
FOCUS!
HEY!
LUKE CAGE?
UH, HEY...
LUKE CAGE?
YEAH.
WHAT IS GOING ON?
WE WERE-- WHOA! WE WERE COMING HERE.
WE WERE COMING HERE TO HELP YOU!
HERE?
WE WHO?
OH NO, JESSICA'S BABY. BABIES. KIDS. LITTLE KIDS.
WHAT IS THIS?
HOW THE HELL SHOULD I KNOW?
ALL I KNOW IS...

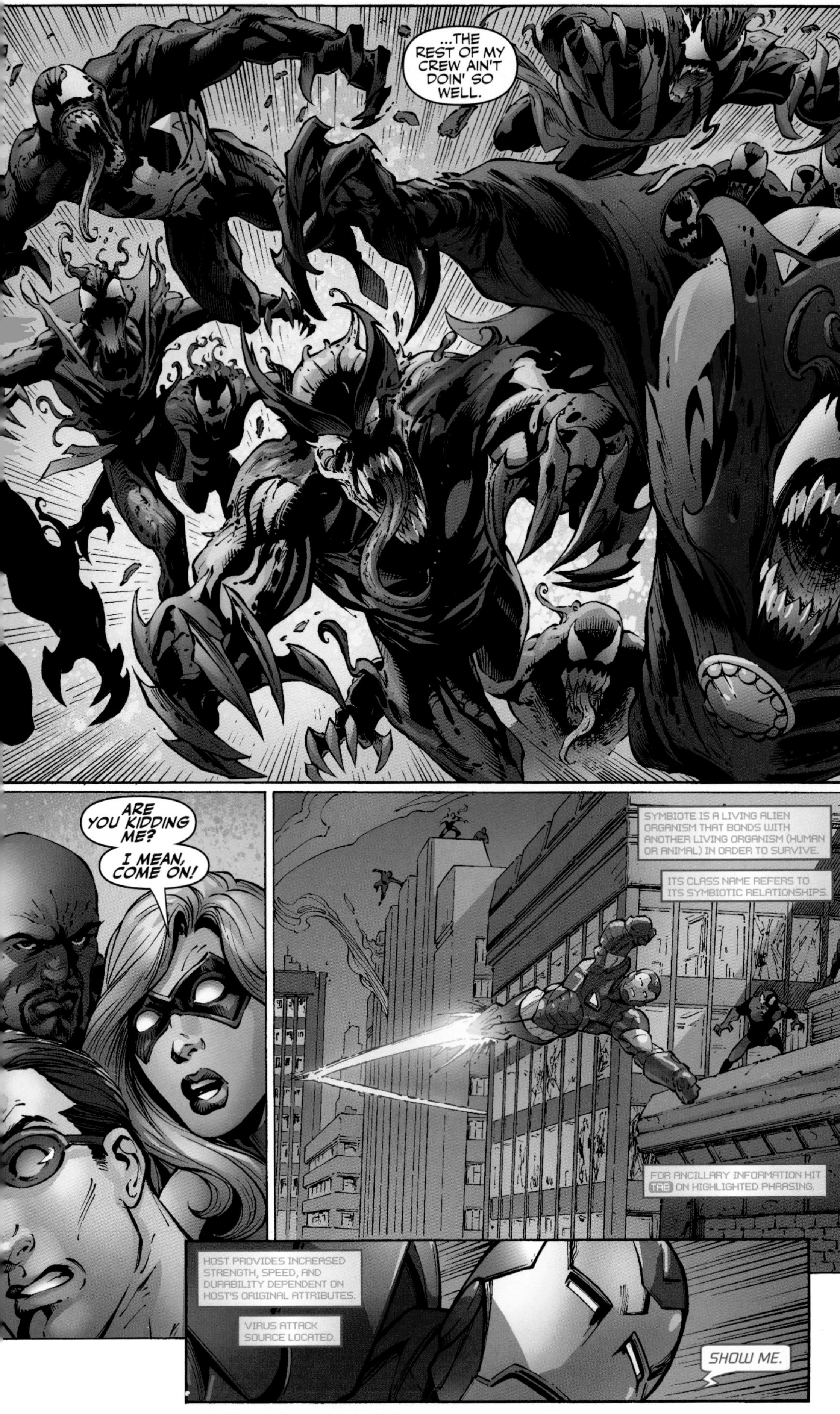
...THE REST OF MY CREW AIN'T DOIN' SO WELL.
ARE YOU KIDDING ME?
I MEAN, COME ON!
SYMBIOTE IS A LIVING ALIEN ORGANISM THAT BONDS WITH ANOTHER LIVING ORGANISM (HUMAN OR ANIMAL) IN ORDER TO SURVIVE.
ITS CLASS NAME REFERS TO ITS SYMBIOTIC RELATIONSHIPS.
FOR ANCILLARY INFORMATION HIT TAB ON HIGHLIGHTED PHRASING.
HOST PROVIDES INCREASED STRENGTH, SPEED, AND DURABILITY DEPENDENT ON HOST'S ORIGINAL ATTRIBUTES.
VIRUS ATTACK SOURCE LOCATED.
SHOW ME.

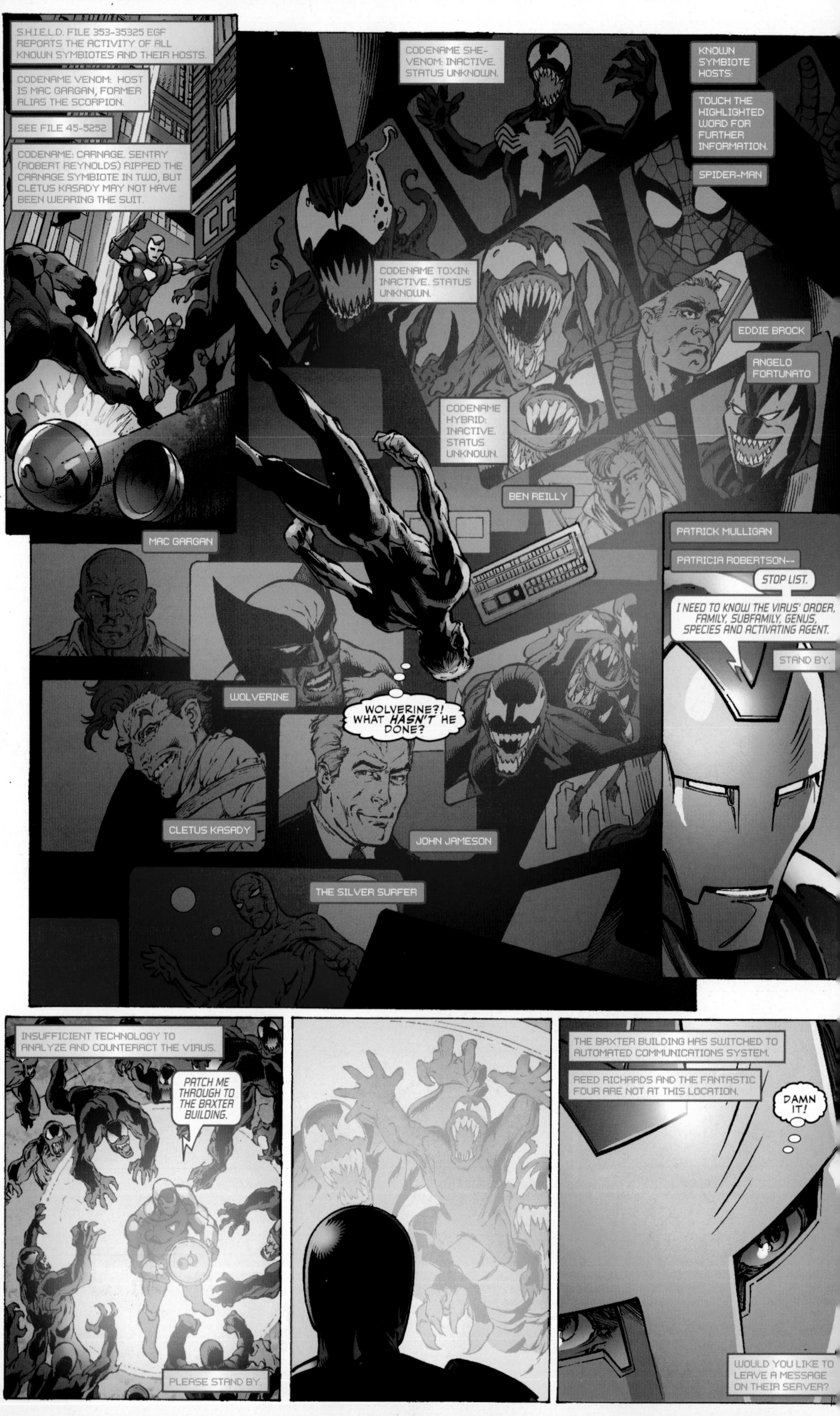

S.H.I.E.L.D. FILE 353-35325 EGF REPORTS THE ACTIVITY OF ALL KNOWN SYMBIOTES AND THEIR HOSTS.
CODENAME VENOM: HOST IS MAC GARGAN, FORMER ALIAS THE SCORPION.
SEE FILE 45-5252
CODENAME: CARNAGE. SENTRY (ROBERT REYNOLDS) RIPPED THE CARNAGE SYMBIOTE IN TWO, BUT CLETUS KASADY MAY NOT HAVE BEEN WEARING THE SUIT.
CODENAME SHE-VENOM: INACTIVE. STATUS UNKNOWN.
KNOWN SYMBIOTE HOSTS:
TOUCH THE HIGHLIGHTED WORD FOR FURTHER INFORMATION.
SPIDER-MAN
CODENAME TOXIN: INACTIVE. STATUS UNKNOWN.
EDDIE BROCK
ANGELO FORTUNATO
CODENAME HYBRID: INACTIVE. STATUS UNKNOWN.
BEN REILLY
MAC GARGAN
PATRICK MULLIGAN
PATRICIA ROBERTSON--
STOP LIST.
I NEED TO KNOW THE VIRUS' ORDER, FAMILY, SUBFAMILY, GENUS, SPECIES AND ACTIVATING AGENT.
STAND BY.
WOLVERINE
WOLVERINE?! WHAT HASN'T HE DONE?
CLETUS KASADY
JOHN JAMESON
THE SILVER SURFER
INSUFFICIENT TECHNOLOGY TO ANALYZE AND COUNTERACT THE VIRUS.
PATCH ME THROUGH TO THE BAXTER BUILDING.
PLEASE STAND BY.
THE BAXTER BUILDING HAS SWITCHED TO AUTOMATED COMMUNICATIONS SYSTEM.
REED RICHARDS AND THE FANTASTIC FOUR ARE NOT AT THIS LOCATION.
DAMN IT!
WOULD YOU LIKE TO LEAVE A MESSAGE ON THEIR SERVER?

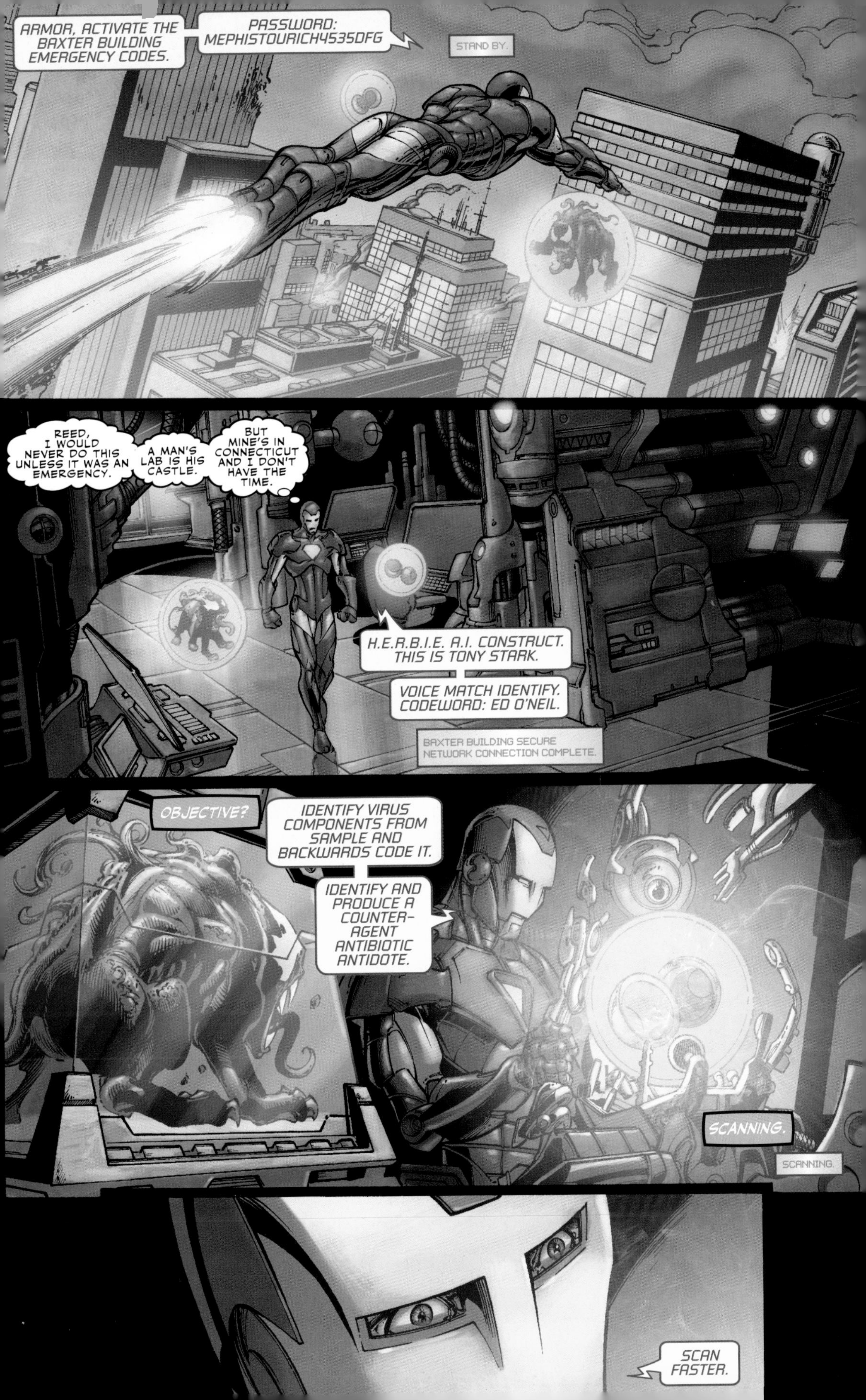

ARMOR, ACTIVATE THE BAXTER BUILDING EMERGENCY CODES.
PASSWORD: MEPHISTOURICH4535DFG
STAND BY.
REED, I WOULD NEVER DO THIS UNLESS IT WAS AN EMERGENCY.
A MAN'S LAB IS HIS CASTLE.
BUT MINE'S IN CONNECTICUT AND I DON'T HAVE THE TIME.
H.E.R.B.I.E. A.I. CONSTRUCT. THIS IS TONY STARK.
VOICE MATCH IDENTIFY. CODEWORD: ED O'NEIL.
BAXTER BUILDING SECURE NETWORK CONNECTION COMPLETE.
OBJECTIVE?
IDENTIFY VIRUS COMPONENTS FROM SAMPLE AND BACKWARDS CODE IT.
IDENTIFY AND PRODUCE A COUNTER-AGENT ANTIBIOTIC ANTIDOTE.
SCANNING.
SCANNING.
SCAN FASTER.

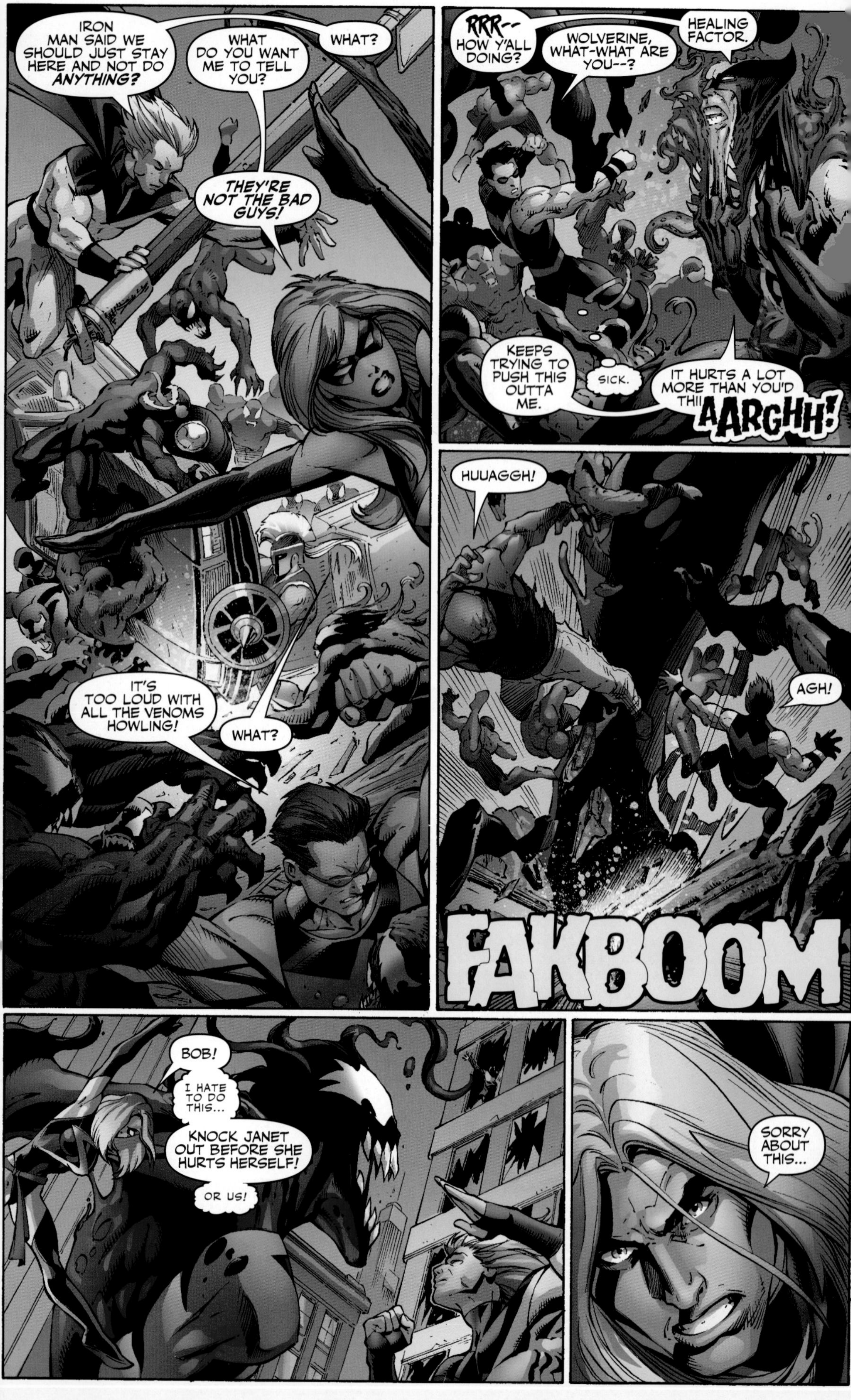
IRON MAN SAID WE SHOULD JUST STAY HERE AND NOT DO *ANYTHING?*
WHAT DO YOU WANT ME TO TELL YOU?
WHAT?
THEY'RE NOT THE BAD GUYS!
IT'S TOO LOUD WITH ALL THE VENOMS HOWLING!
WHAT?
RRR-- HOW Y'ALL DOING?
WOLVERINE, WHAT-WHAT ARE YOU--?
HEALING FACTOR.
KEEPS TRYING TO PUSH THIS OUTTA ME.
SICK.
IT HURTS A LOT MORE THAN YOU'D THI!
AARGHH!
HUUAGGH!
AGH!
FAKBOOM
BOB!
I HATE TO DO THIS...
KNOCK JANET OUT BEFORE SHE HURTS HERSELF!
OR US!
SORRY ABOUT THIS...

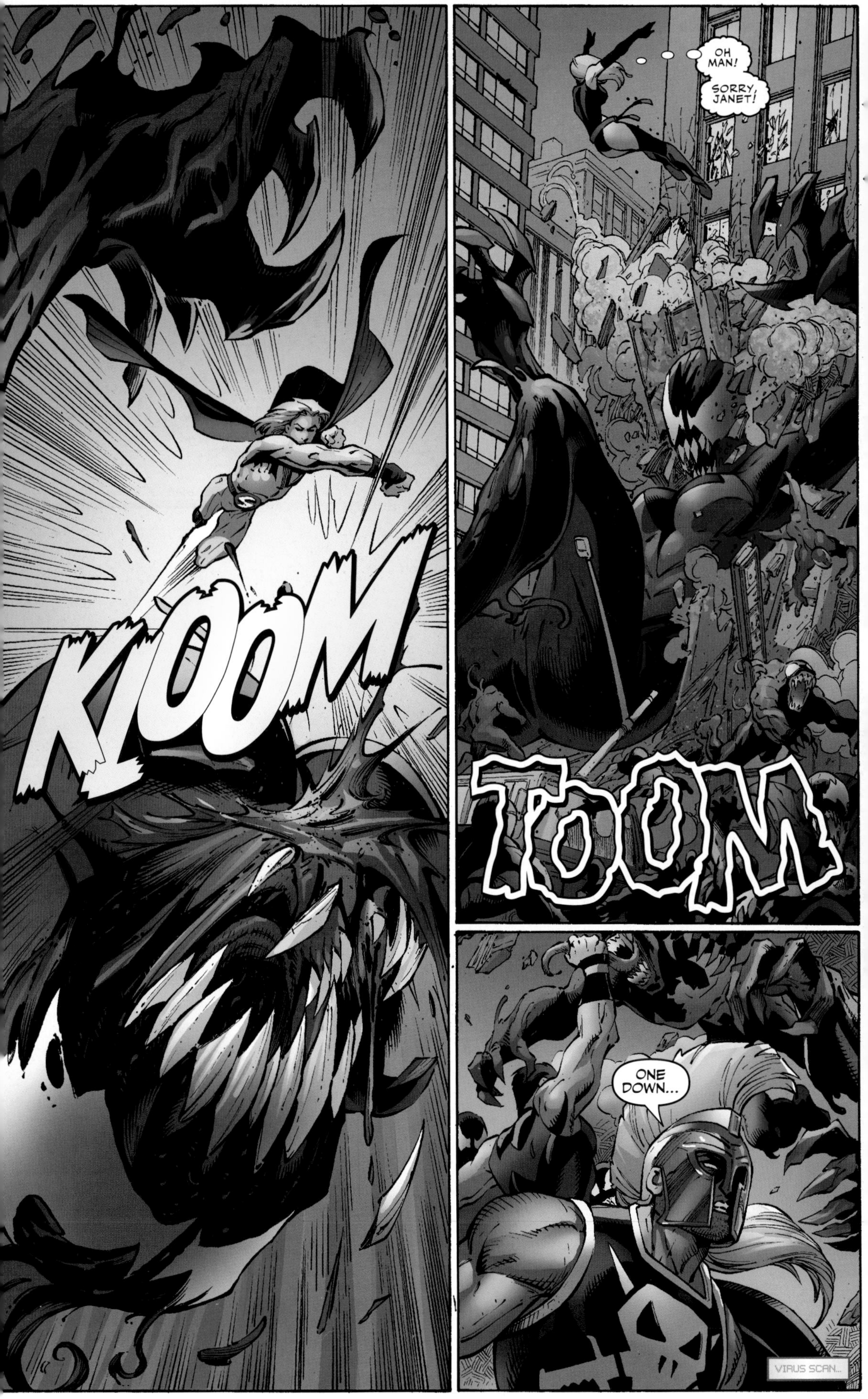
KLOOM
OH MAN!
SORRY, JANET!
TOOM
ONE DOWN...
VIRUS SCAN...

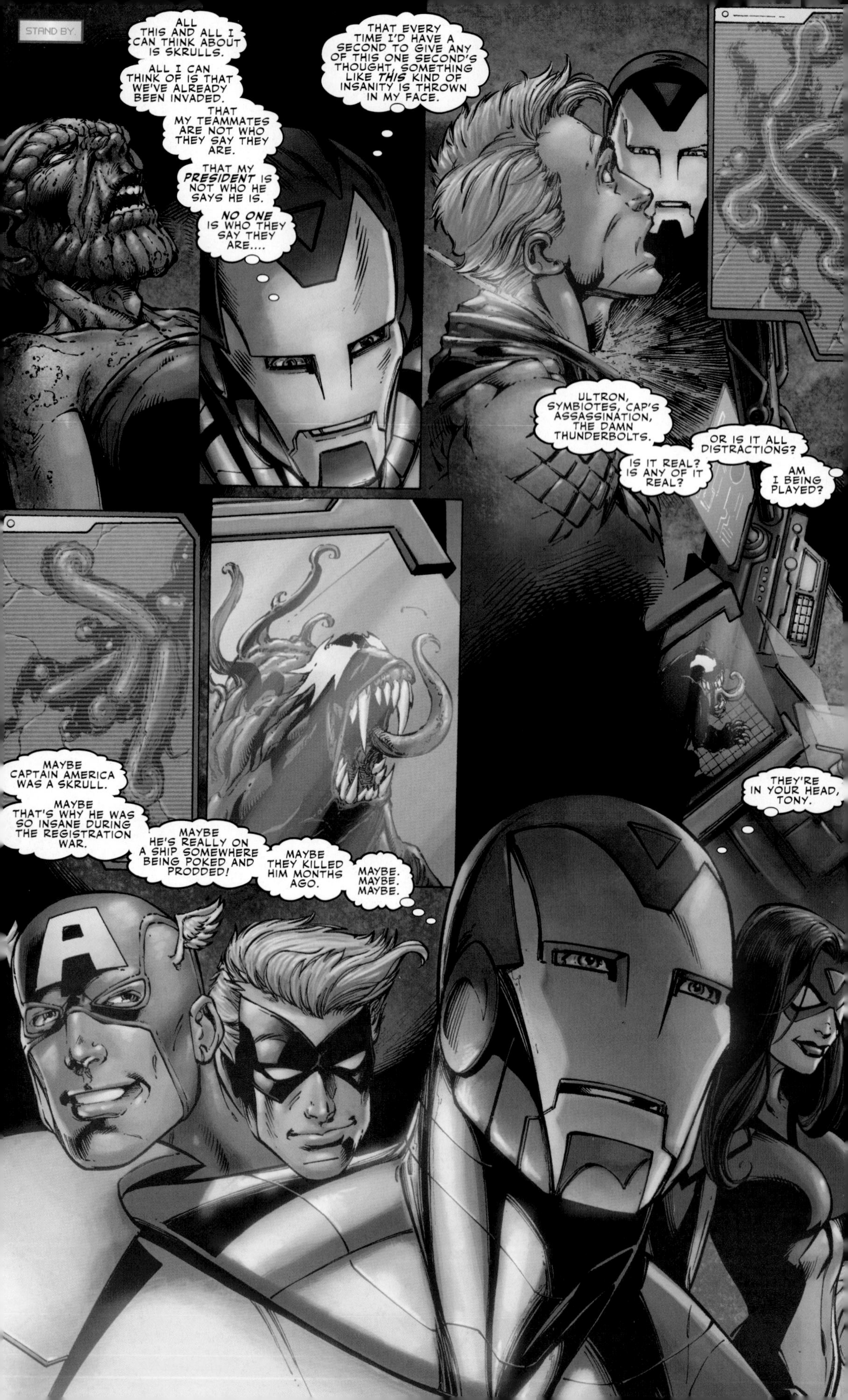
STAND BY.
ALL THIS AND ALL I CAN THINK ABOUT IS SKRULLS.
ALL I CAN THINK OF IS THAT WE'VE ALREADY BEEN INVADED.
THAT MY TEAMMATES ARE NOT WHO THEY SAY THEY ARE.
THAT MY *PRESIDENT* IS NOT WHO HE SAYS HE IS.
NO ONE IS WHO THEY SAY THEY ARE....
THAT EVERY TIME I'D HAVE A SECOND TO GIVE ANY OF THIS ONE SECOND'S THOUGHT, SOMETHING LIKE *THIS* KIND OF INSANITY IS THROWN IN MY FACE.
ULTRON, SYMBIOTES, CAP'S ASSASSINATION, THE DAMN THUNDERBOLTS.
IS IT REAL? IS ANY OF IT REAL?
OR IS IT ALL DISTRACTIONS?
AM I BEING PLAYED?
MAYBE CAPTAIN AMERICA WAS A SKRULL.
MAYBE THAT'S WHY HE WAS SO INSANE DURING THE REGISTRATION WAR.
MAYBE HE'S REALLY ON A SHIP SOMEWHERE BEING POKED AND PRODDED!
MAYBE THEY KILLED HIM MONTHS AGO.
MAYBE. MAYBE. MAYBE.
THEY'RE IN YOUR HEAD, TONY.

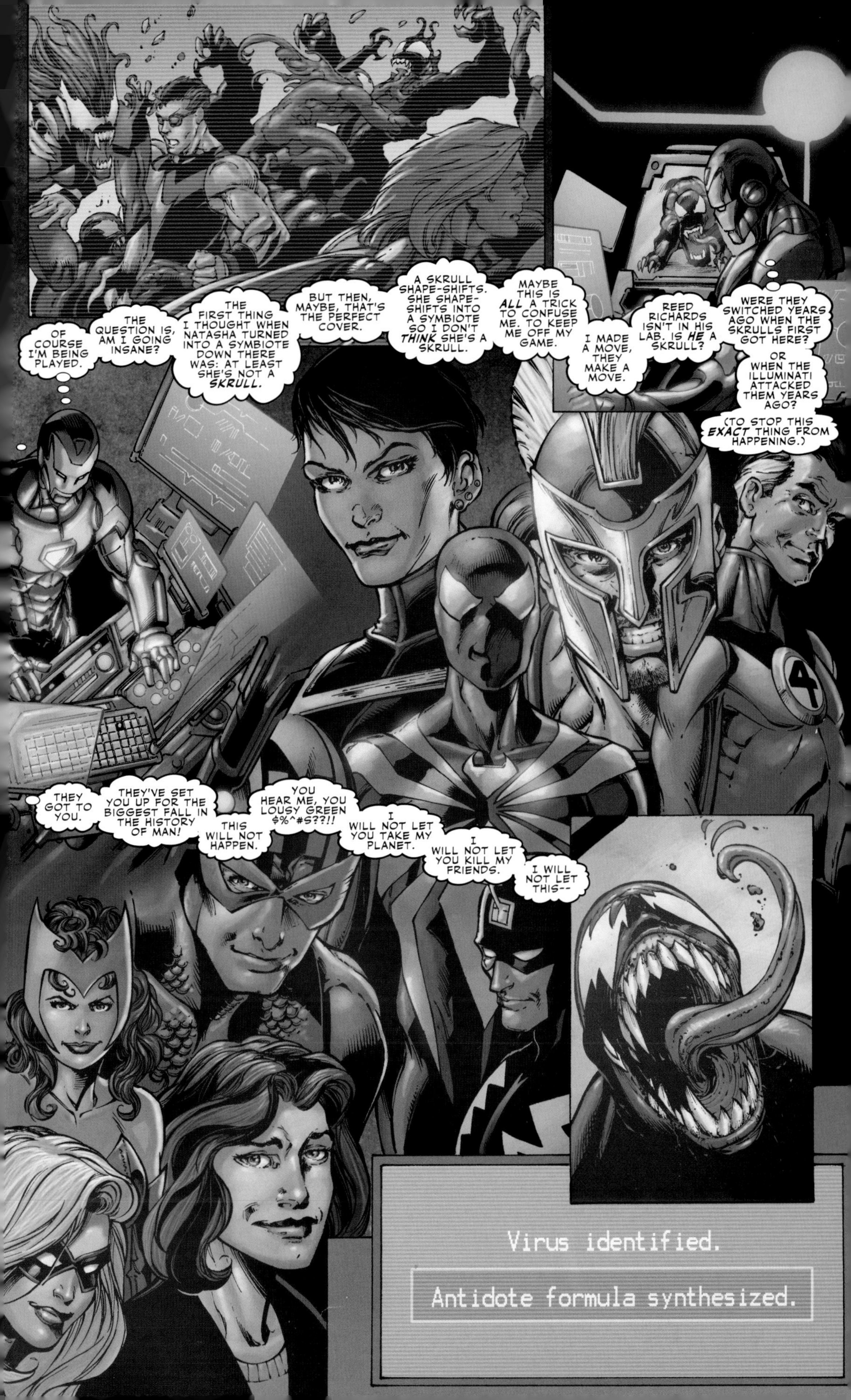

OF COURSE I'M BEING PLAYED.
THE QUESTION IS, AM I GOING INSANE?
THE FIRST THING I THOUGHT WHEN NATASHA TURNED INTO A SYMBIOTE DOWN THERE WAS: AT LEAST SHE'S NOT A SKRULL.
BUT THEN, MAYBE, THAT'S THE PERFECT COVER.
A SKRULL SHAPE-SHIFTS. SHE SHAPE-SHIFTS INTO A SYMBIOTE SO I DON'T THINK SHE'S A SKRULL.
MAYBE THIS IS ALL A TRICK TO CONFUSE ME. TO KEEP ME OFF MY GAME.
I MADE A MOVE, THEY MAKE A MOVE.
REED RICHARDS ISN'T IN HIS LAB. IS HE A SKRULL?
WERE THEY SWITCHED YEARS AGO WHEN THE SKRULLS FIRST GOT HERE?
OR WHEN THE ILLUMINATI ATTACKED THEM YEARS AGO?
(TO STOP THIS EXACT THING FROM HAPPENING.)
THEY GOT TO YOU.
THEY'VE SET YOU UP FOR THE BIGGEST FALL IN THE HISTORY OF MAN!
THIS WILL NOT HAPPEN.
YOU HEAR ME, YOU LOUSY GREEN $%^#S??!!
I WILL NOT LET YOU TAKE MY PLANET.
I WILL NOT LET YOU KILL MY FRIENDS.
I WILL NOT LET THIS--
Virus identified.
Antidote formula synthesized.

TESTING INSTITUTED. RESULTS POSITIVE.

FULL VIRAL REVERSAL.

ALL VITAL SIGNS NOMINAL.

CANINE BREED COCKER SPANIEL. VIRUS ELIMINATED.

AGH!

COME ON, DANNY!

IF I COULD OPEN UP THIS WOULD BE DONE IN A SECOND.

OF COURSE, EVERYONE WOULD BE DEAD...

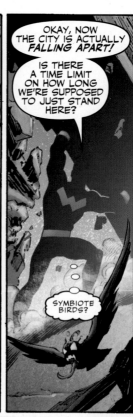

OKAY, NOW THE CITY IS ACTUALLY FALLING APART!

IS THERE A TIME LIMIT ON HOW LONG WE'RE SUPPOSED TO JUST STAND HERE?

SYMBIOTE BIRDS?

WHOA WHOA WHOA! DANNY!!

COME ON!

YOU CAN DO THIS! FOCUS!

ANTIDOTE LAUNCHED.

STAND BY...

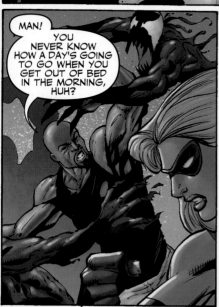

MAN! YOU NEVER KNOW HOW A DAY'S GOING TO GO WHEN YOU GET OUT OF BED IN THE MORNING, HUH?

ANTIDOTE ACTIVATED.

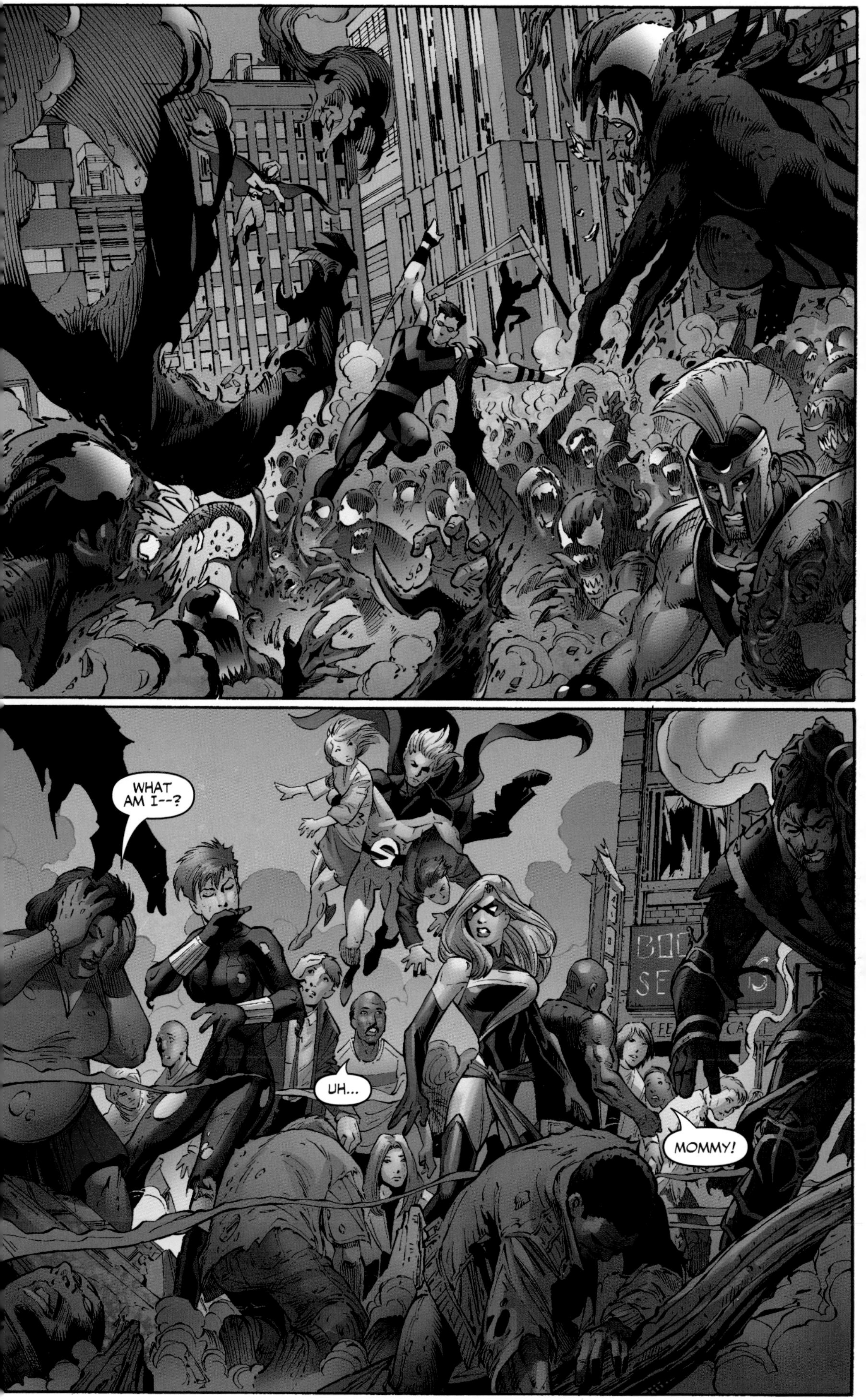
WHAT AM I--?
UH...
MOMMY!

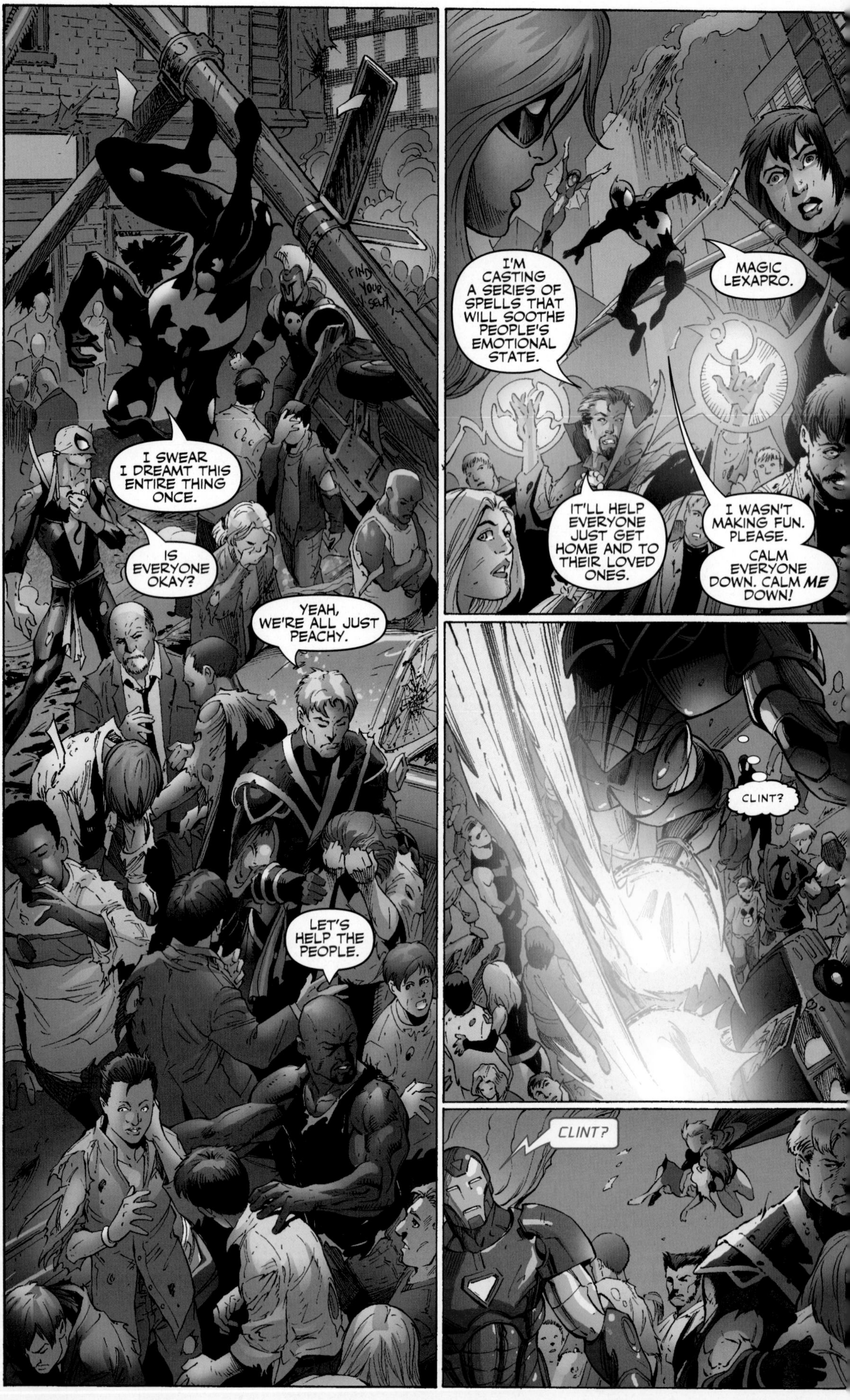

I SWEAR I DREAMT THIS ENTIRE THING ONCE.
IS EVERYONE OKAY?
YEAH, WE'RE ALL JUST PEACHY.
LET'S HELP THE PEOPLE.
I'M CASTING A SERIES OF SPELLS THAT WILL SOOTHE PEOPLE'S EMOTIONAL STATE.
MAGIC LEXAPRO.
IT'LL HELP EVERYONE JUST GET HOME AND TO THEIR LOVED ONES.
I WASN'T MAKING FUN. PLEASE.
CALM EVERYONE DOWN. CALM ME DOWN!
CLINT?
CLINT?

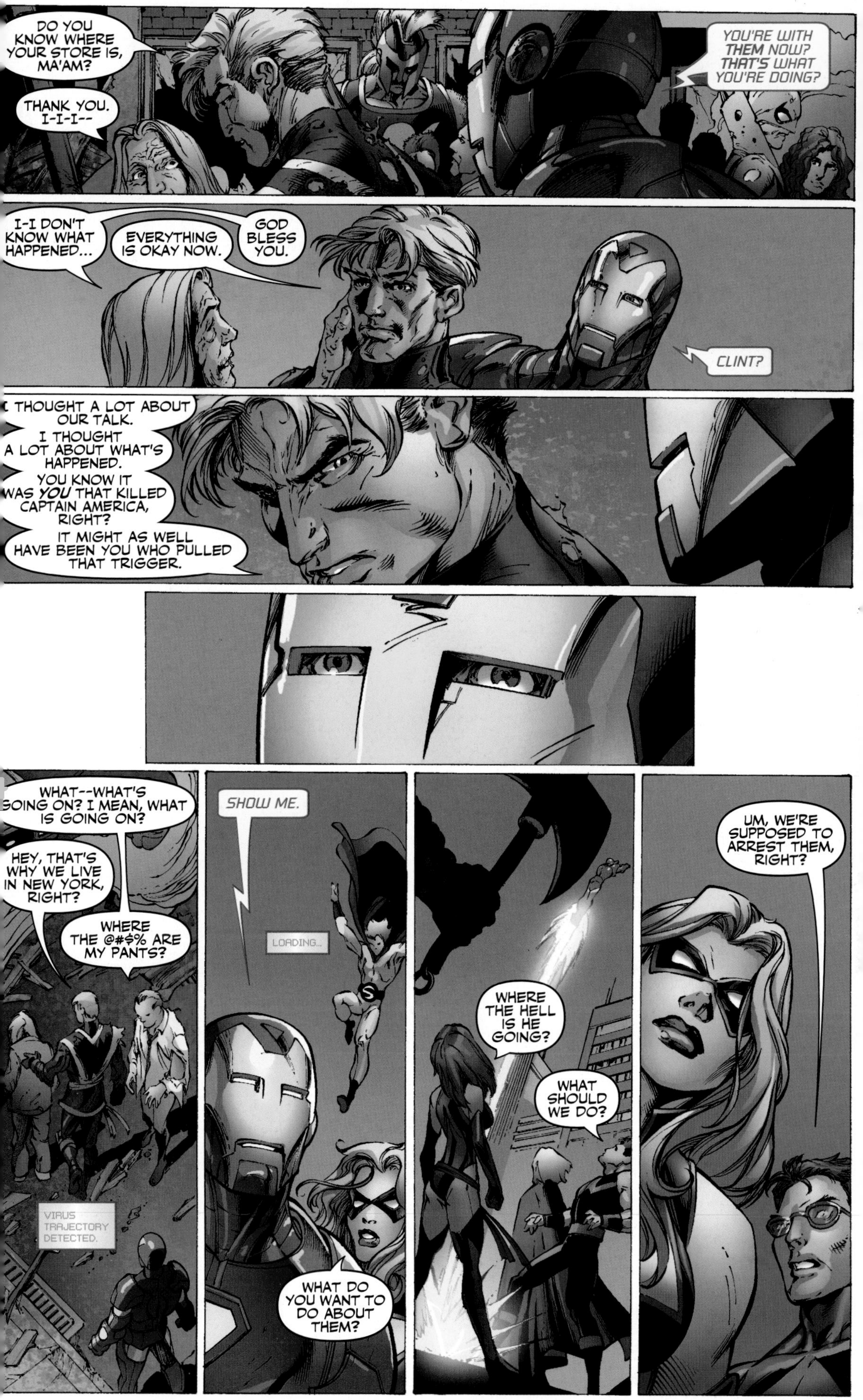
DO YOU KNOW WHERE YOUR STORE IS, MA'AM?
THANK YOU. I-I-I--
YOU'RE WITH THEM NOW? THAT'S WHAT YOU'RE DOING?
I-I DON'T KNOW WHAT HAPPENED...
EVERYTHING IS OKAY NOW.
GOD BLESS YOU.
CLINT?
I THOUGHT A LOT ABOUT OUR TALK.
I THOUGHT A LOT ABOUT WHAT'S HAPPENED.
YOU KNOW IT WAS YOU THAT KILLED CAPTAIN AMERICA, RIGHT?
IT MIGHT AS WELL HAVE BEEN YOU WHO PULLED THAT TRIGGER.
WHAT--WHAT'S GOING ON? I MEAN, WHAT IS GOING ON?
HEY, THAT'S WHY WE LIVE IN NEW YORK, RIGHT?
WHERE THE @#$% ARE MY PANTS?
VIRUS TRAJECTORY DETECTED.
SHOW ME.
LOADING...
WHAT DO YOU WANT TO DO ABOUT THEM?
WHERE THE HELL IS HE GOING?
WHAT SHOULD WE DO?
UM, WE'RE SUPPOSED TO ARREST THEM, RIGHT?

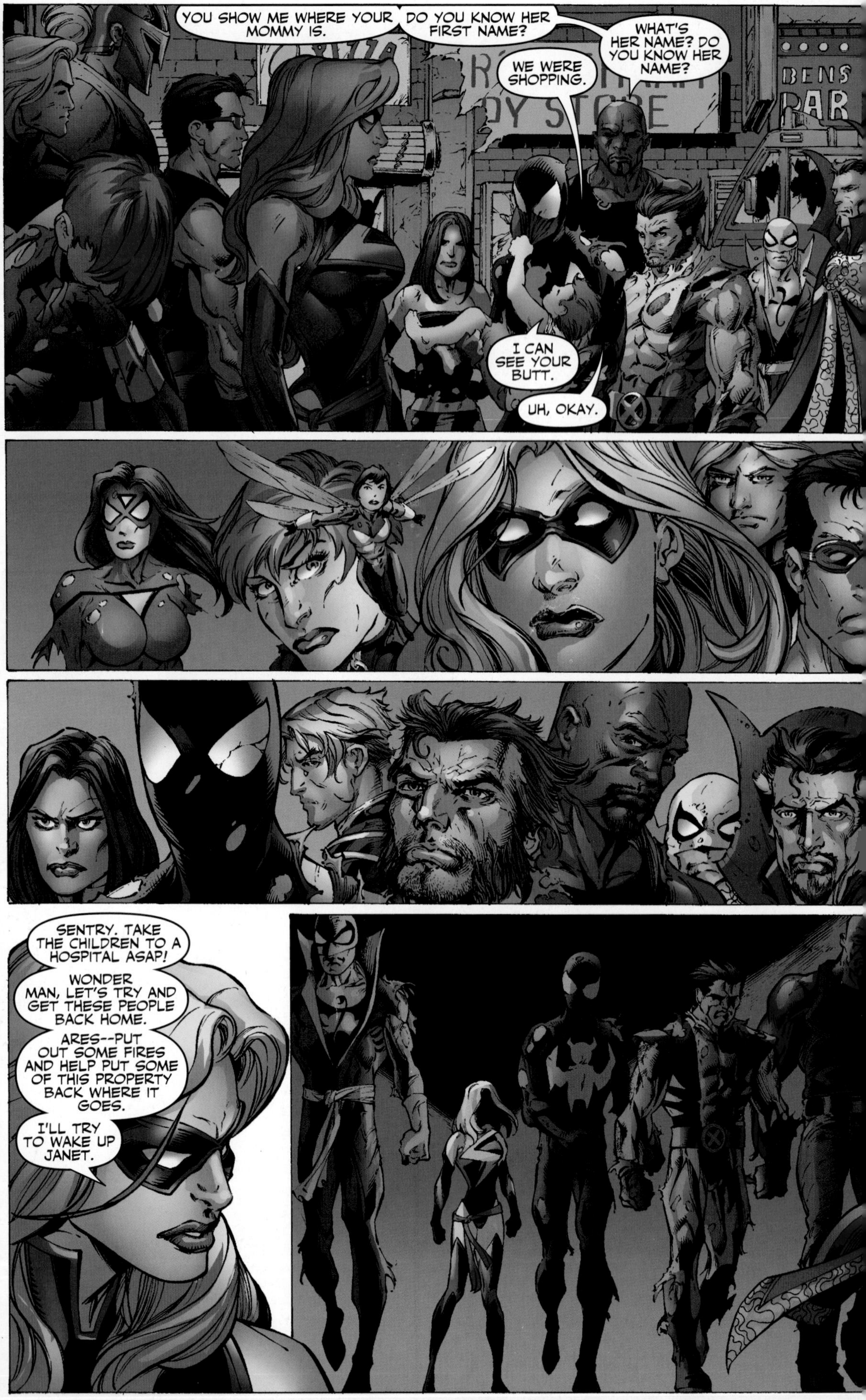
YOU SHOW ME WHERE YOUR MOMMY IS.
DO YOU KNOW HER FIRST NAME?
WHAT'S HER NAME? DO YOU KNOW HER NAME?
WE WERE SHOPPING.
I CAN SEE YOUR BUTT.
UH, OKAY.
SENTRY. TAKE THE CHILDREN TO A HOSPITAL ASAP!
WONDER MAN, LET'S TRY AND GET THESE PEOPLE BACK HOME.
ARES--PUT OUT SOME FIRES AND HELP PUT SOME OF THIS PROPERTY BACK WHERE IT GOES.
I'LL TRY TO WAKE UP JANET.

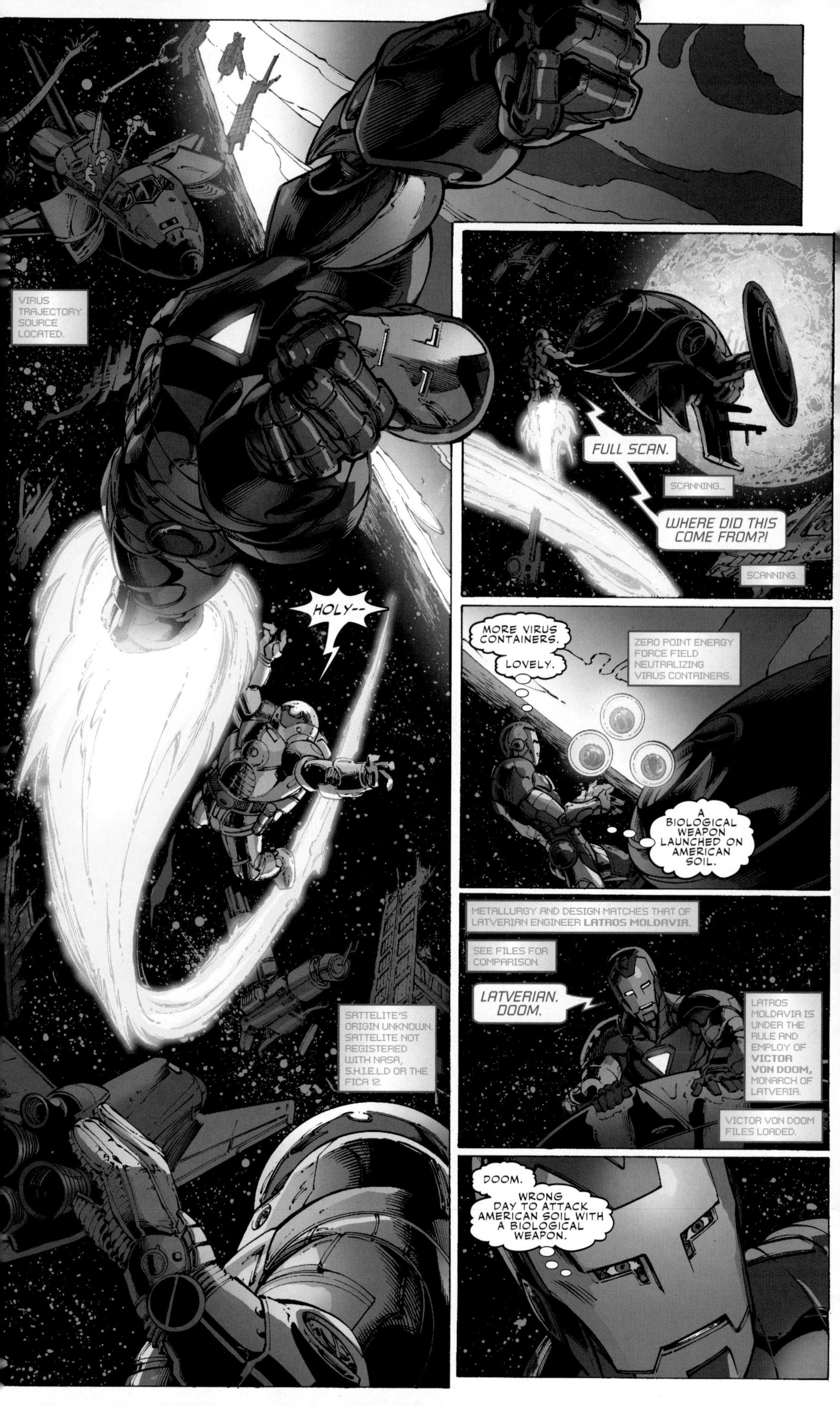

VIRUS TRAJECTORY SOURCE LOCATED.
HOLY--
SATTELITE'S ORIGIN UNKNOWN. SATTELITE NOT REGISTERED WITH NASA, S.H.I.E.L.D OR THE FICA 12.
FULL SCAN.
SCANNING...
WHERE DID THIS COME FROM?!
SCANNING.
MORE VIRUS CONTAINERS.
LOVELY.
ZERO POINT ENERGY FORCE FIELD NEUTRALIZING VIRUS CONTAINERS.
A BIOLOGICAL WEAPON LAUNCHED ON AMERICAN SOIL.
METALLURGY AND DESIGN MATCHES THAT OF LATVERIAN ENGINEER LATROS MOLDAVIA.
SEE FILES FOR COMPARISON.
LATVERIAN. DOOM.
LATROS MOLDAVIA IS UNDER THE RULE AND EMPLOY OF VICTOR VON DOOM, MONARCH OF LATVERIA.
VICTOR VON DOOM FILES LOADED.
DOOM.
WRONG DAY TO ATTACK AMERICAN SOIL WITH A BIOLOGICAL WEAPON.

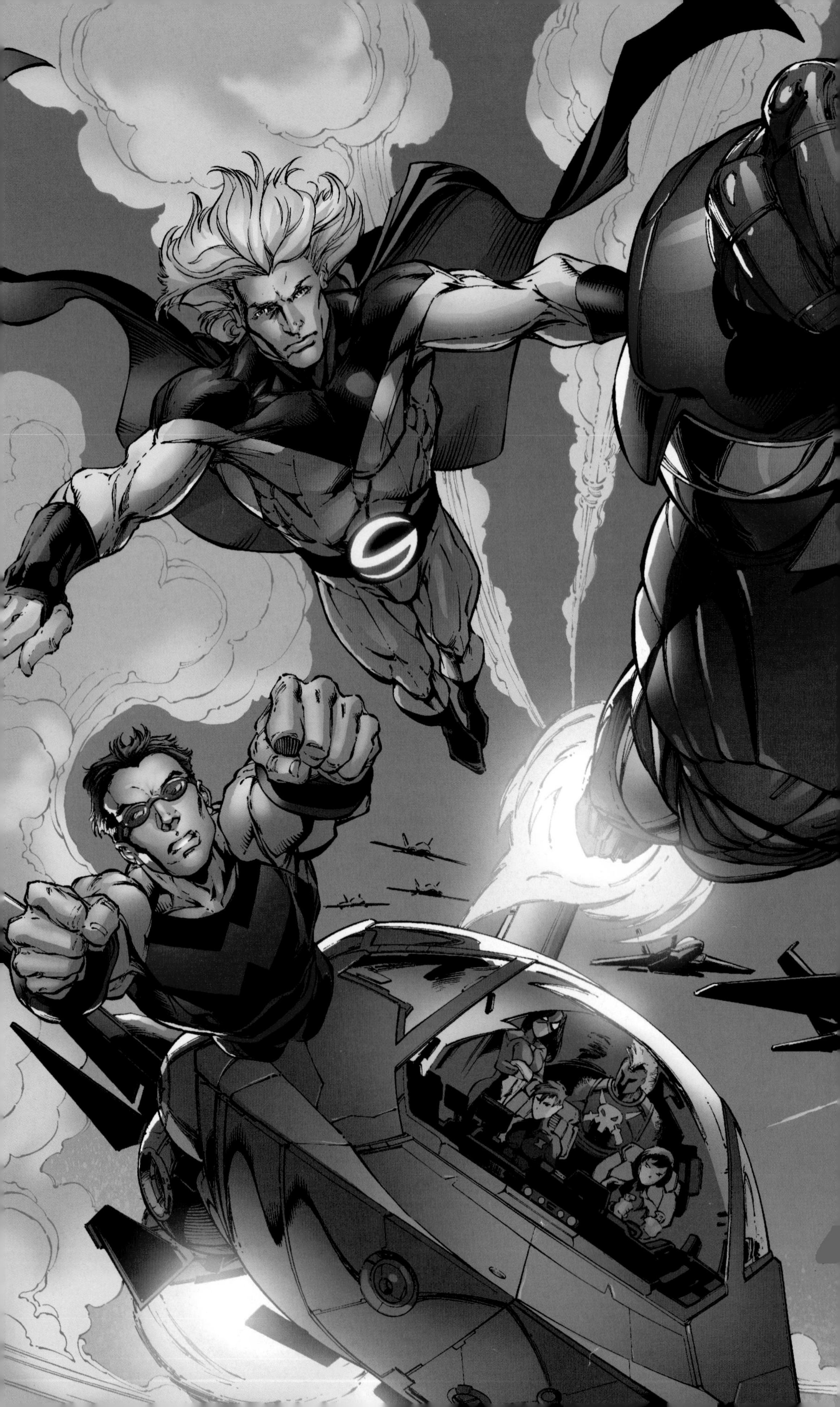

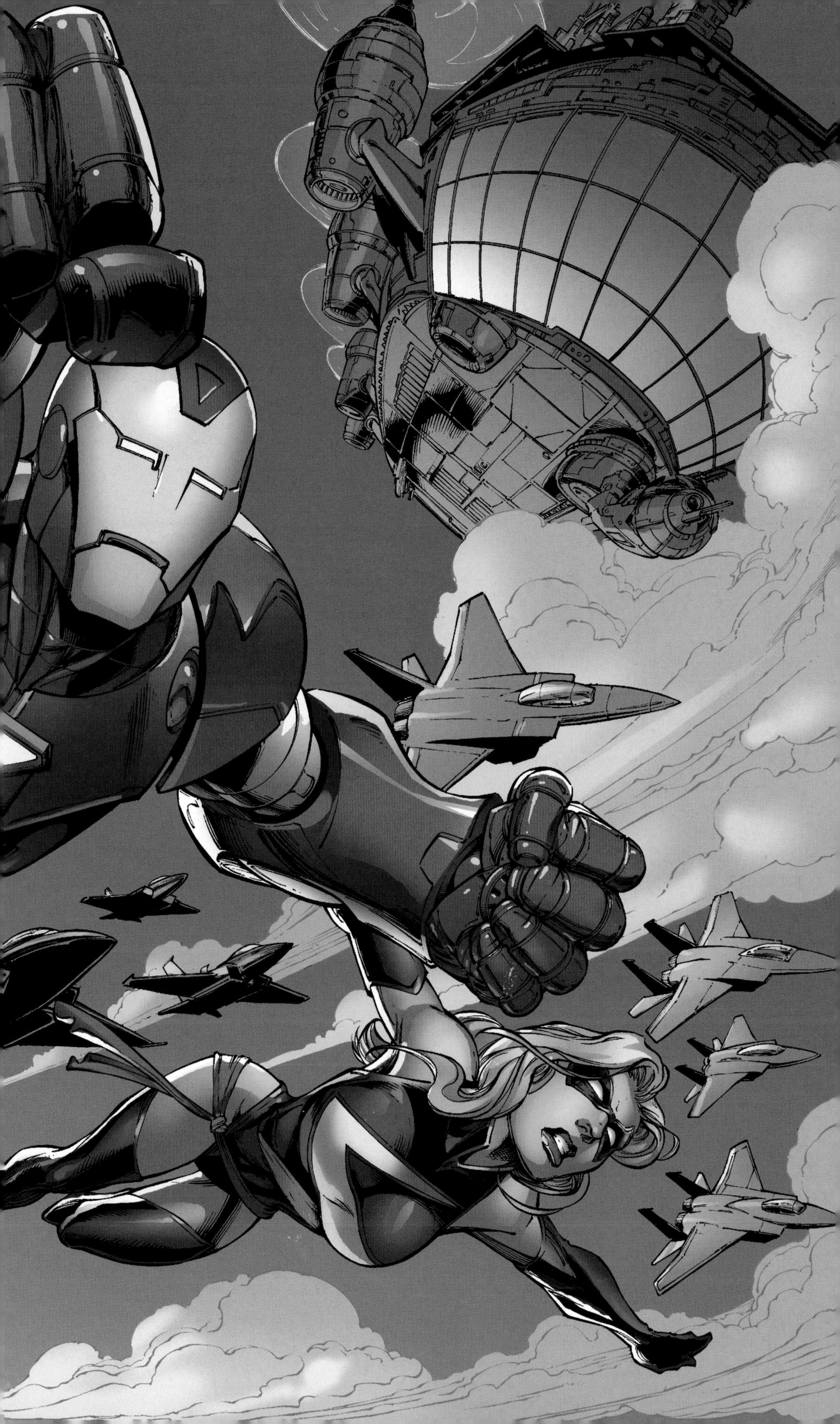

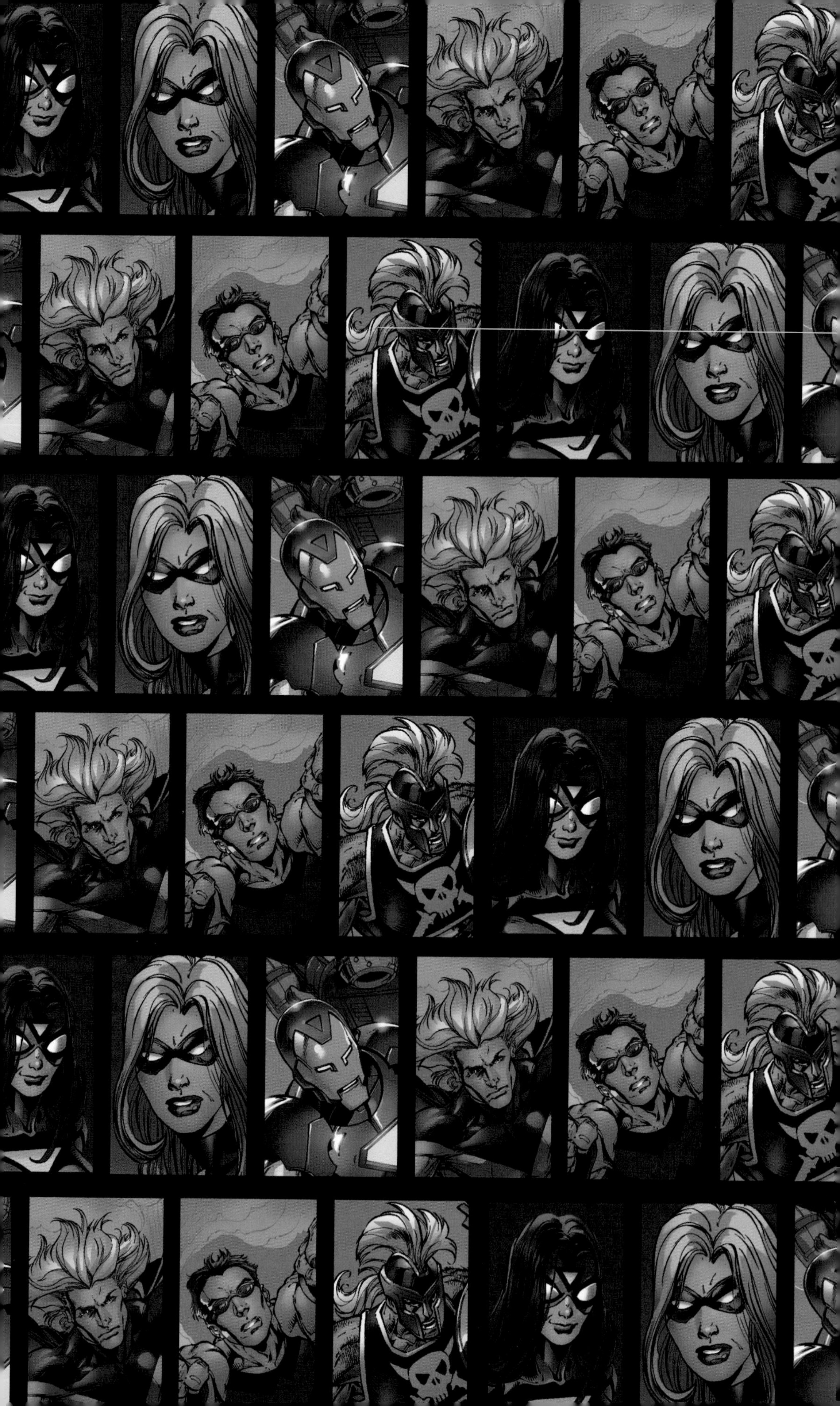

ISSUE #9

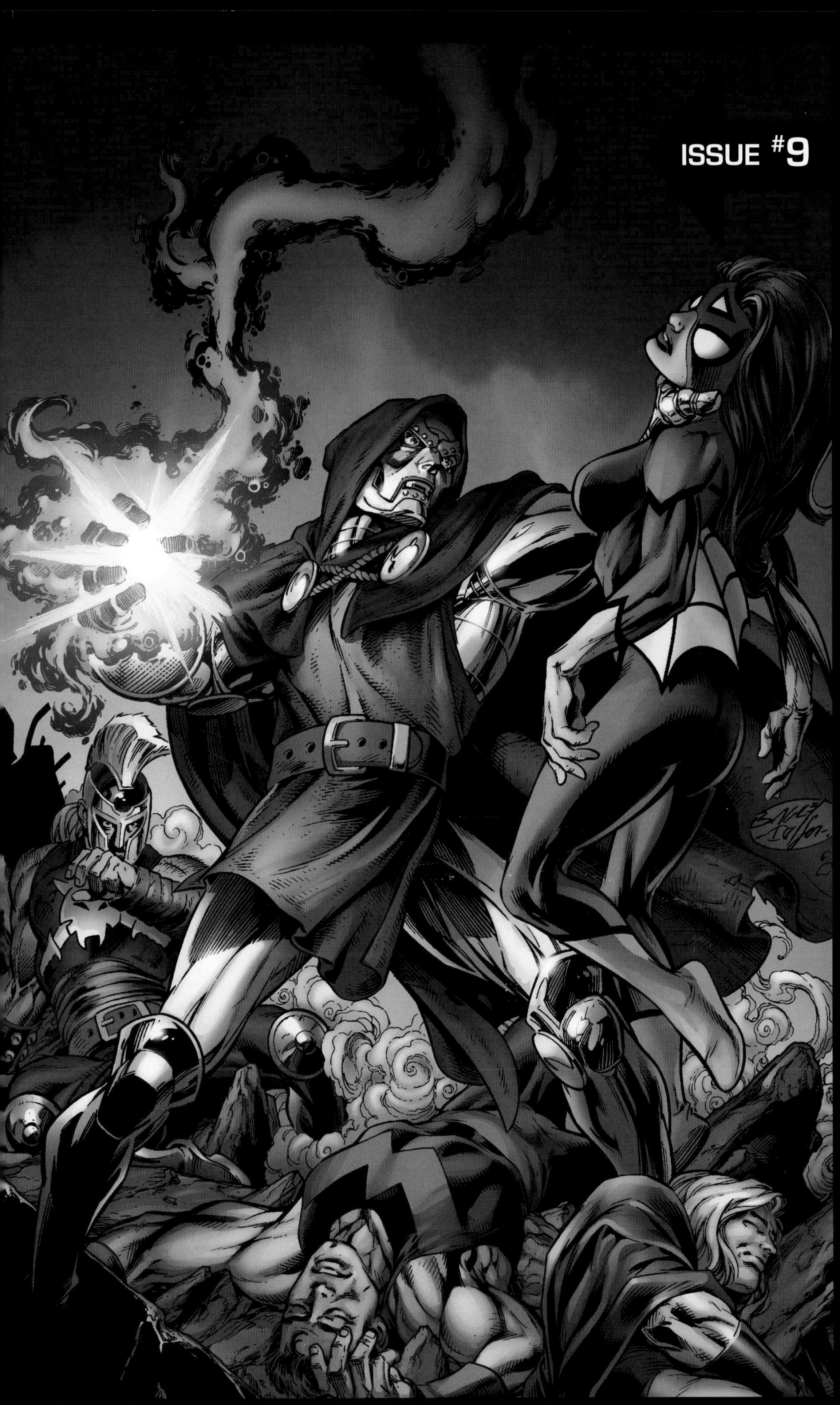

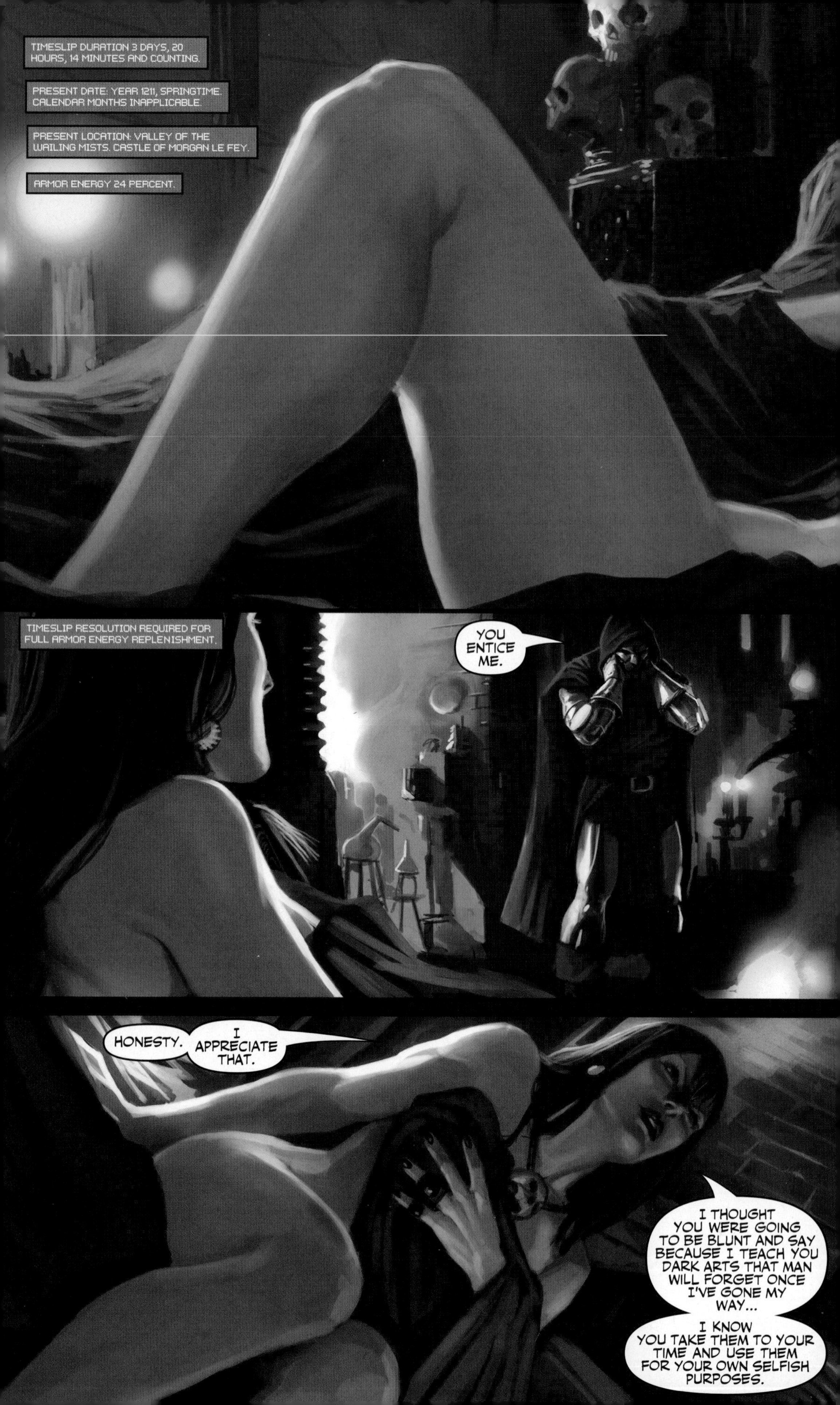

TIMESLIP DURATION 3 DAYS, 20 HOURS, 14 MINUTES AND COUNTING.
PRESENT DATE: YEAR 1211, SPRINGTIME. CALENDAR MONTHS INAPPLICABLE.
PRESENT LOCATION: VALLEY OF THE WAILING MISTS. CASTLE OF MORGAN LE FEY.
ARMOR ENERGY 24 PERCENT.
TIMESLIP RESOLUTION REQUIRED FOR FULL ARMOR ENERGY REPLENISHMENT.
YOU ENTICE ME.
HONESTY.
I APPRECIATE THAT.
I THOUGHT YOU WERE GOING TO BE BLUNT AND SAY BECAUSE I TEACH YOU DARK ARTS THAT MAN WILL FORGET ONCE I'VE GONE MY WAY...
I KNOW YOU TAKE THEM TO YOUR TIME AND USE THEM FOR YOUR OWN SELFISH PURPOSES.

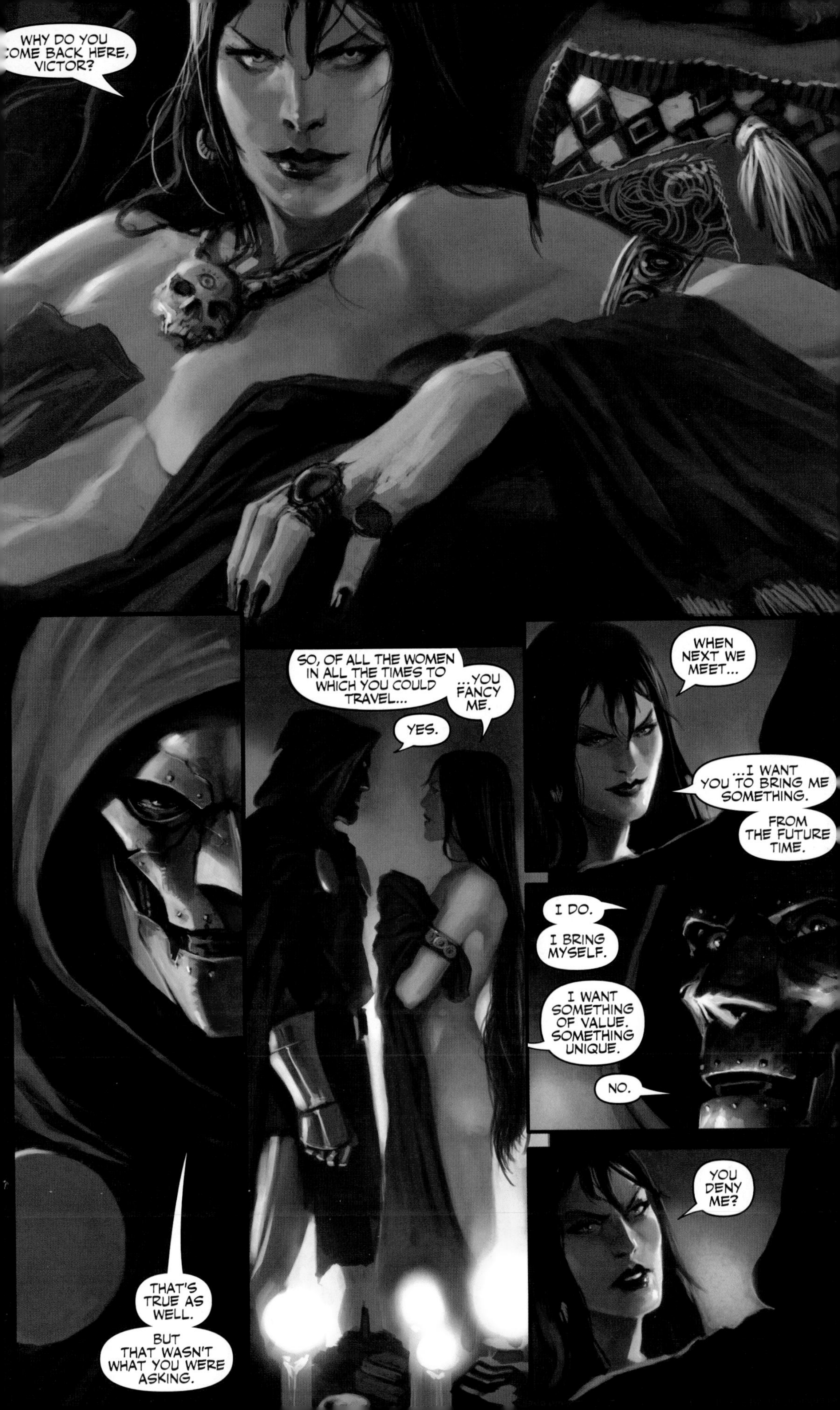
WHY DO YOU COME BACK HERE, VICTOR?
SO, OF ALL THE WOMEN IN ALL THE TIMES TO WHICH YOU COULD TRAVEL...
...YOU FANCY ME.
YES.
THAT'S TRUE AS WELL.
BUT THAT WASN'T WHAT YOU WERE ASKING.
WHEN NEXT WE MEET...
...I WANT YOU TO BRING ME SOMETHING.
FROM THE FUTURE TIME.
I DO.
I BRING MYSELF.
I WANT SOMETHING OF VALUE. SOMETHING UNIQUE.
NO.
YOU DENY ME?

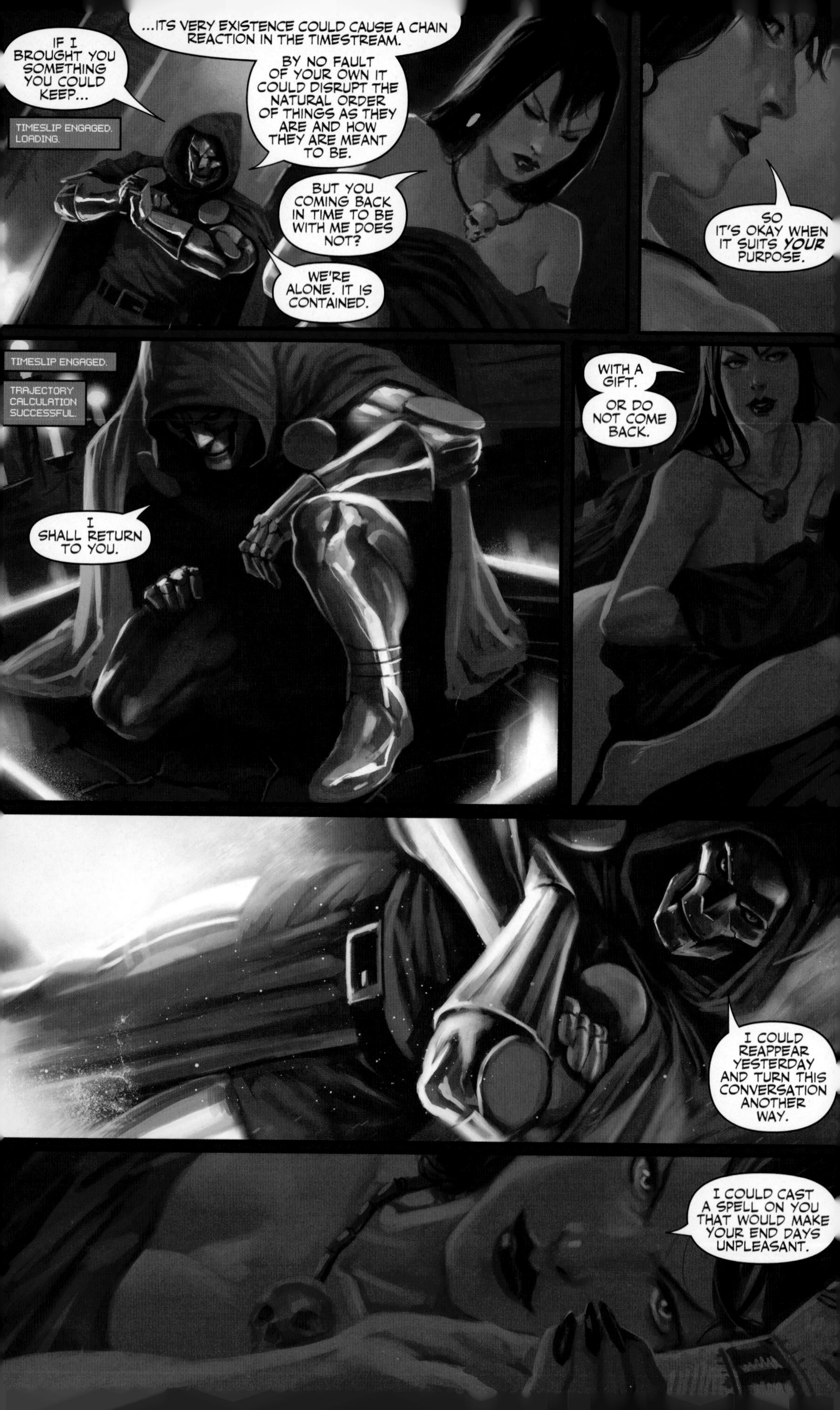
IF I BROUGHT YOU SOMETHING YOU COULD KEEP...
...ITS VERY EXISTENCE COULD CAUSE A CHAIN REACTION IN THE TIMESTREAM.
TIMESLIP ENGAGED. LOADING.
BY NO FAULT OF YOUR OWN IT COULD DISRUPT THE NATURAL ORDER OF THINGS AS THEY ARE AND HOW THEY ARE MEANT TO BE.
BUT YOU COMING BACK IN TIME TO BE WITH ME DOES NOT?
WE'RE ALONE. IT IS CONTAINED.
SO IT'S OKAY WHEN IT SUITS YOUR PURPOSE.
TIMESLIP ENGAGED.
TRAJECTORY CALCULATION SUCCESSFUL.
I SHALL RETURN TO YOU.
WITH A GIFT.
OR DO NOT COME BACK.
I COULD REAPPEAR YESTERDAY AND TURN THIS CONVERSATION ANOTHER WAY.
I COULD CAST A SPELL ON YOU THAT WOULD MAKE YOUR END DAYS UNPLEASANT.

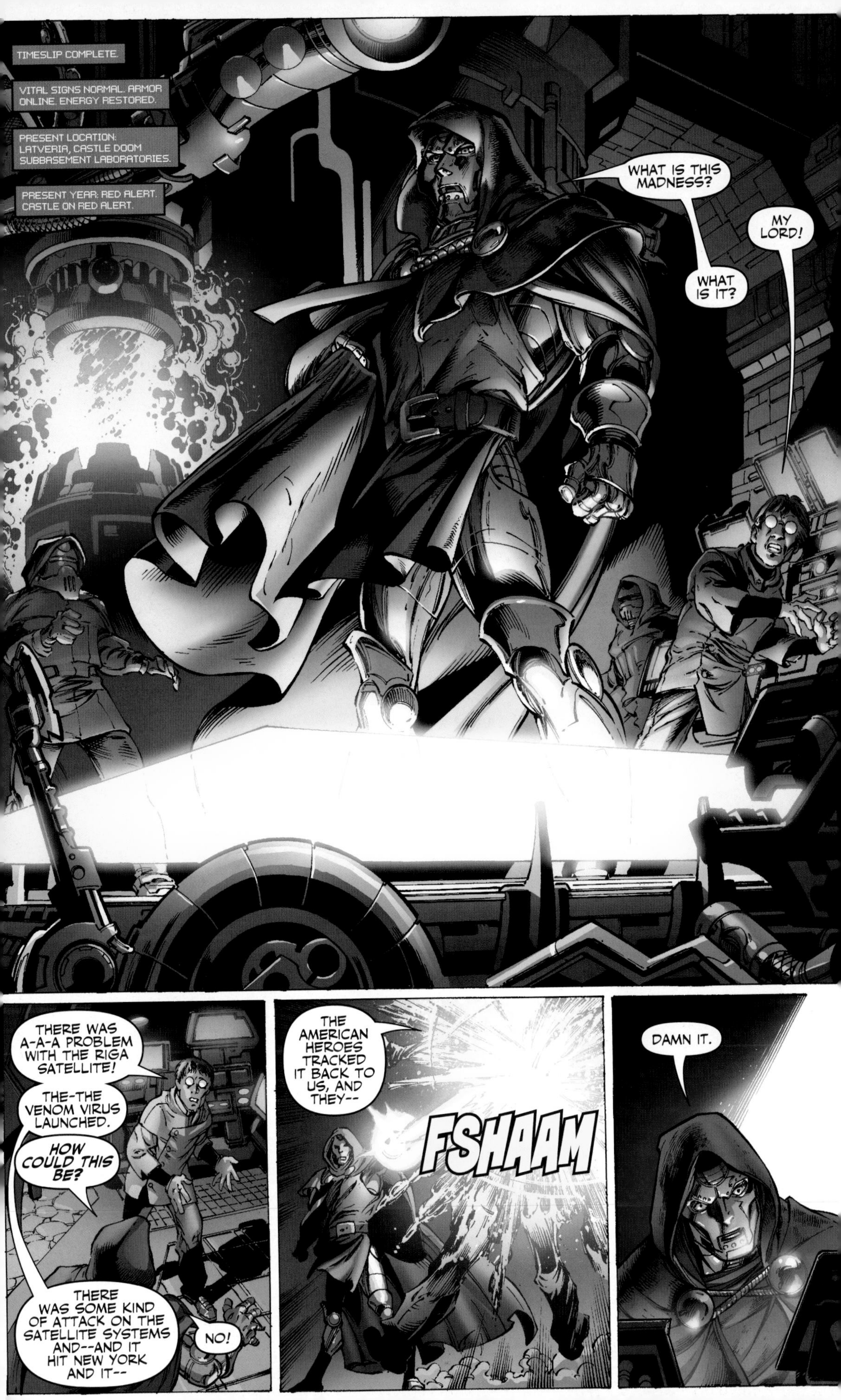

TIMESLIP COMPLETE.
VITAL SIGNS NORMAL. ARMOR ONLINE. ENERGY RESTORED.
PRESENT LOCATION: LATVERIA, CASTLE DOOM SUBBASEMENT LABORATORIES.
PRESENT YEAR: RED ALERT. CASTLE ON RED ALERT.
WHAT IS THIS MADNESS?
WHAT IS IT?
MY LORD!
THERE WAS A-A-A PROBLEM WITH THE RIGA SATELLITE!
THE-THE VENOM VIRUS LAUNCHED.
HOW COULD THIS BE?
THERE WAS SOME KIND OF ATTACK ON THE SATELLITE SYSTEMS AND--AND IT HIT NEW YORK AND IT--
NO!
THE AMERICAN HEROES TRACKED IT BACK TO US, AND THEY--
FSHAAM
DAMN IT.

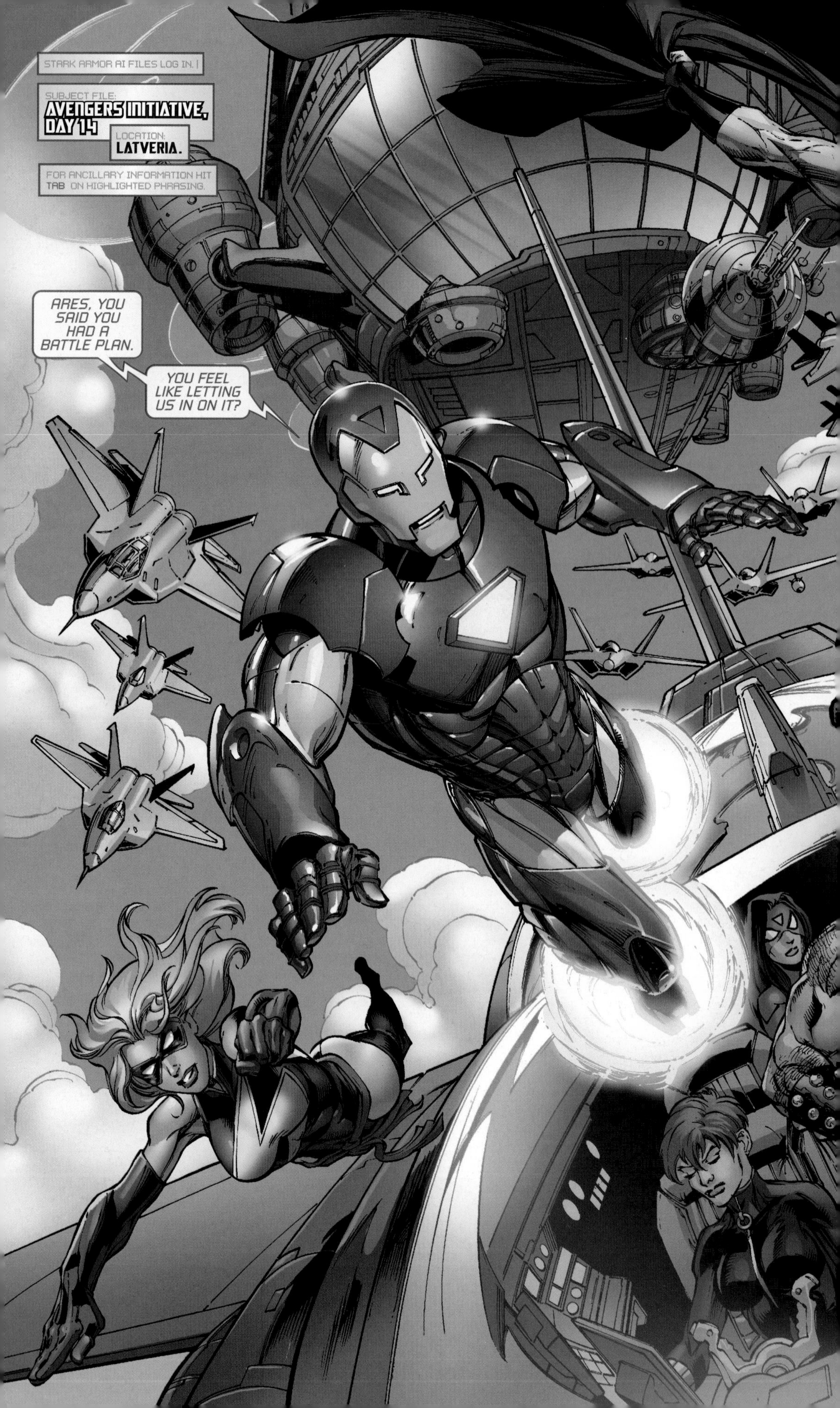
STARK ARMOR AI FILES LOG IN. |
SUBJECT FILE:
AVENGERS INITIATIVE, DAY 14
LOCATION:
LATVERIA.
FOR ANCILLARY INFORMATION HIT TAB ON HIGHLIGHTED PHRASING.
ARES, YOU SAID YOU HAD A BATTLE PLAN.
YOU FEEL LIKE LETTING US IN ON IT?

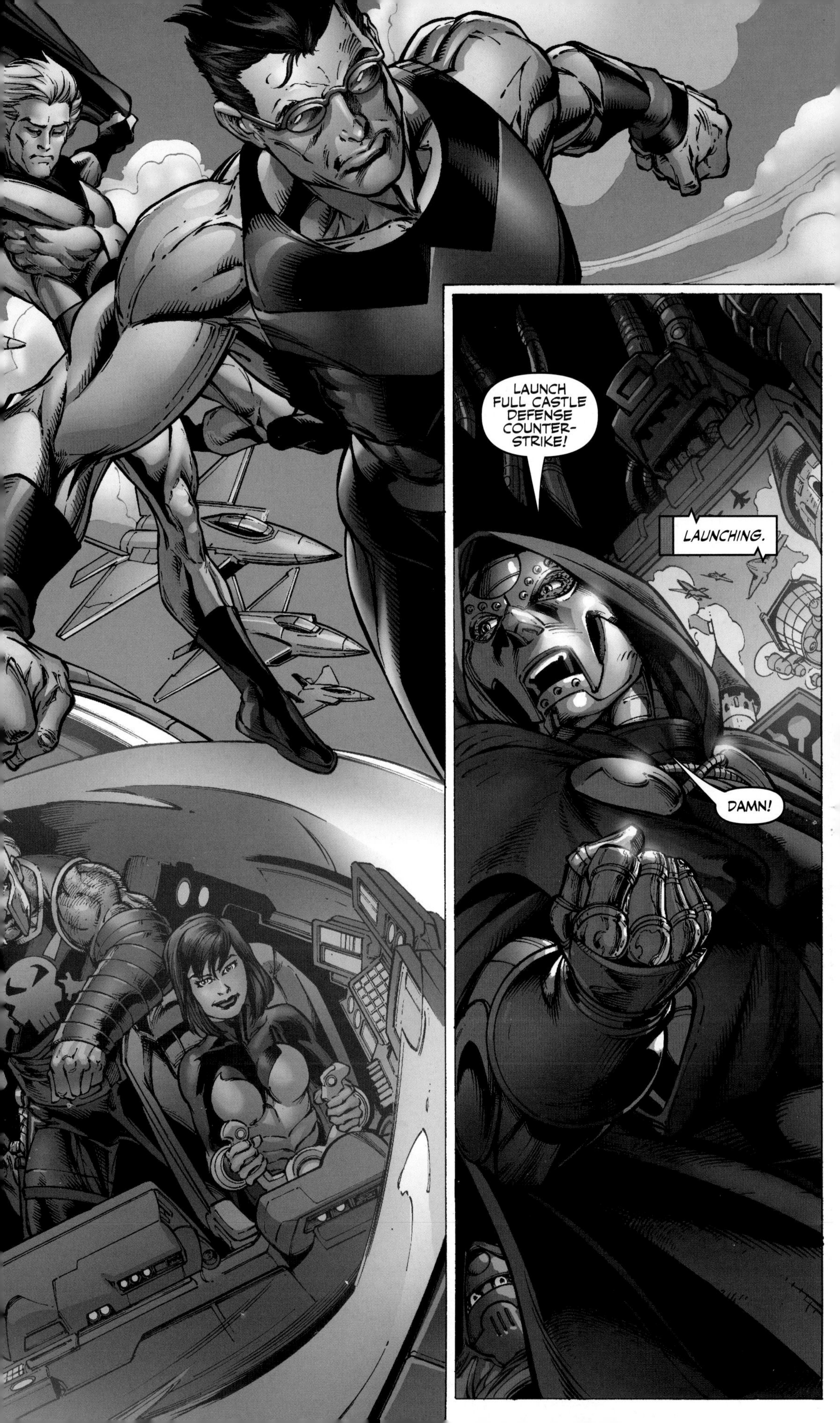
LAUNCH FULL CASTLE DEFENSE COUNTER-STRIKE!
LAUNCHING.
DAMN!

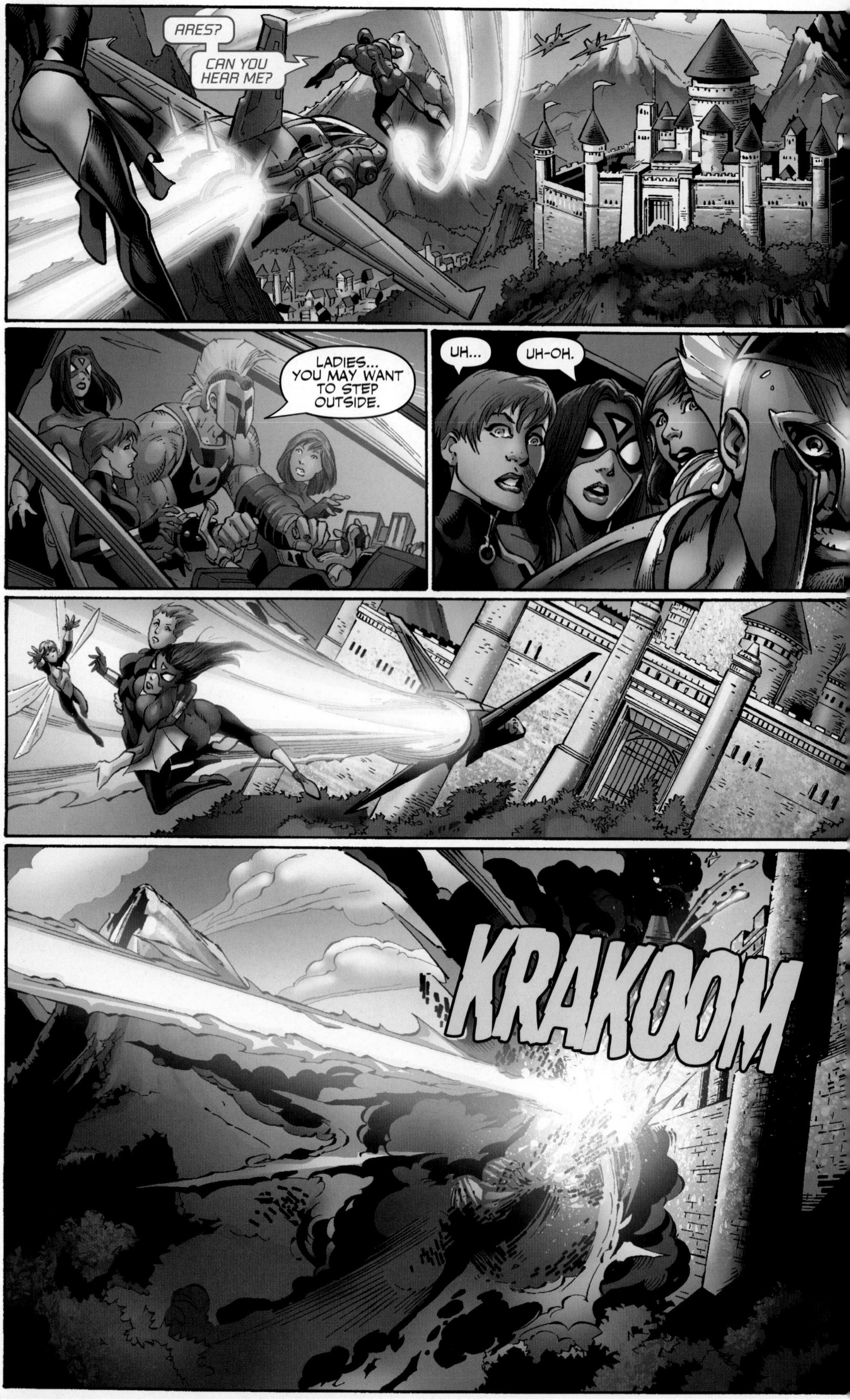
ARES?
CAN YOU HEAR ME?
LADIES... YOU MAY WANT TO STEP OUTSIDE.
UH...
UH-OH.
KRAKOOM

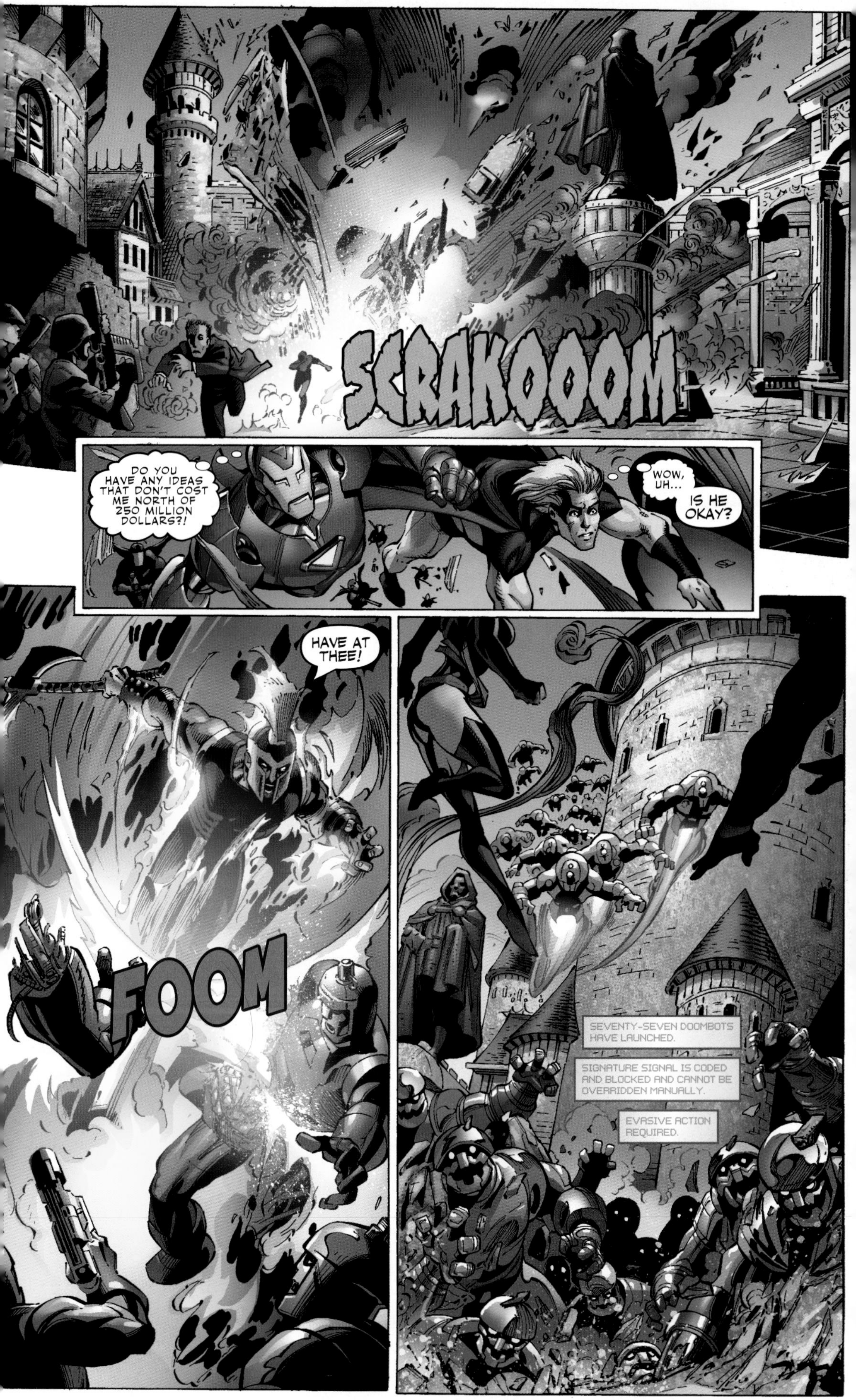
SCRAKOOOM
DO YOU HAVE ANY IDEAS THAT DON'T COST ME NORTH OF 250 MILLION DOLLARS?!
WOW, UH...
IS HE OKAY?
HAVE AT THEE!
FOOM
SEVENTY-SEVEN DOOMBOTS HAVE LAUNCHED.
SIGNATURE SIGNAL IS CODED AND BLOCKED AND CANNOT BE OVERRIDDEN MANUALLY.
EVASIVE ACTION REQUIRED.

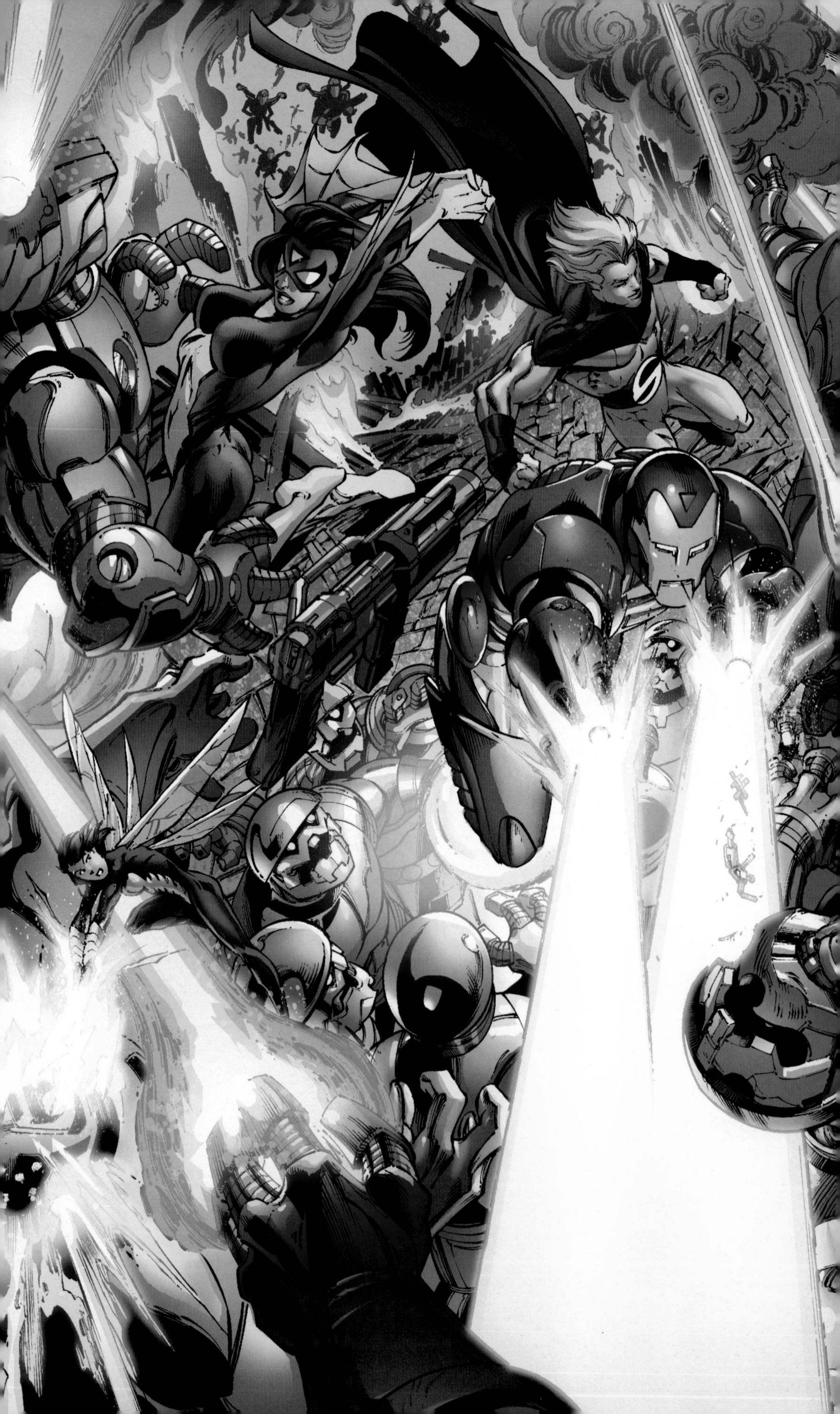

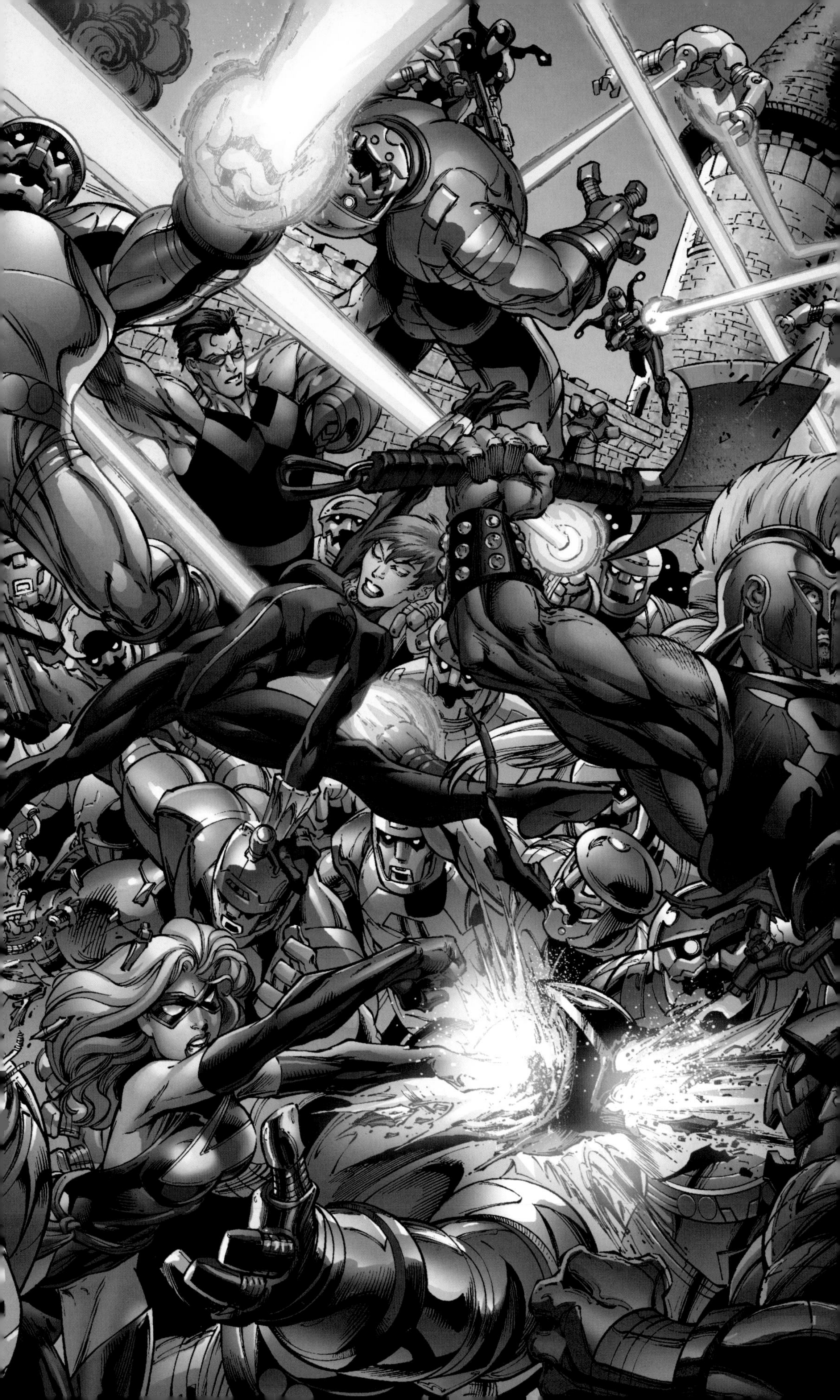

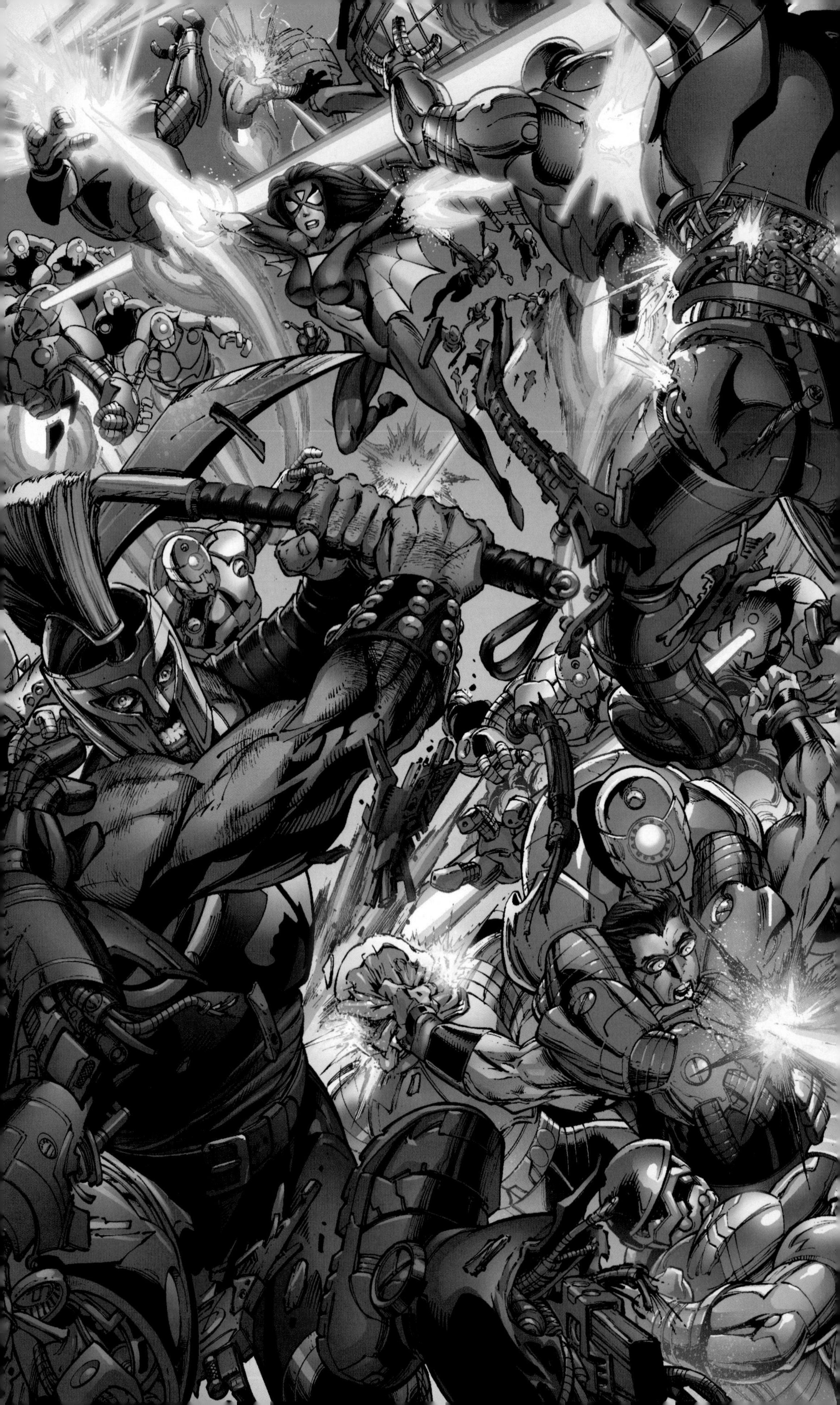

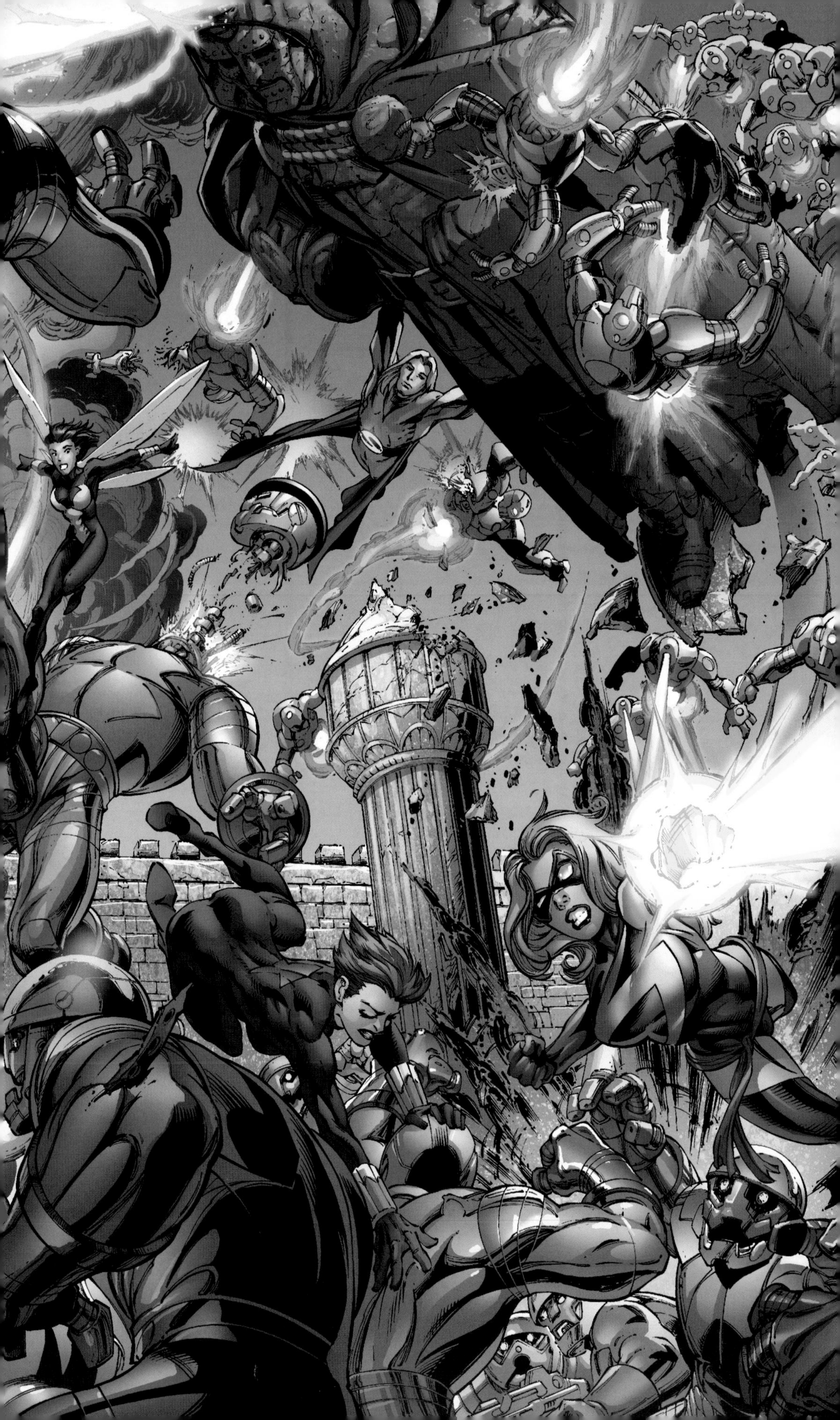

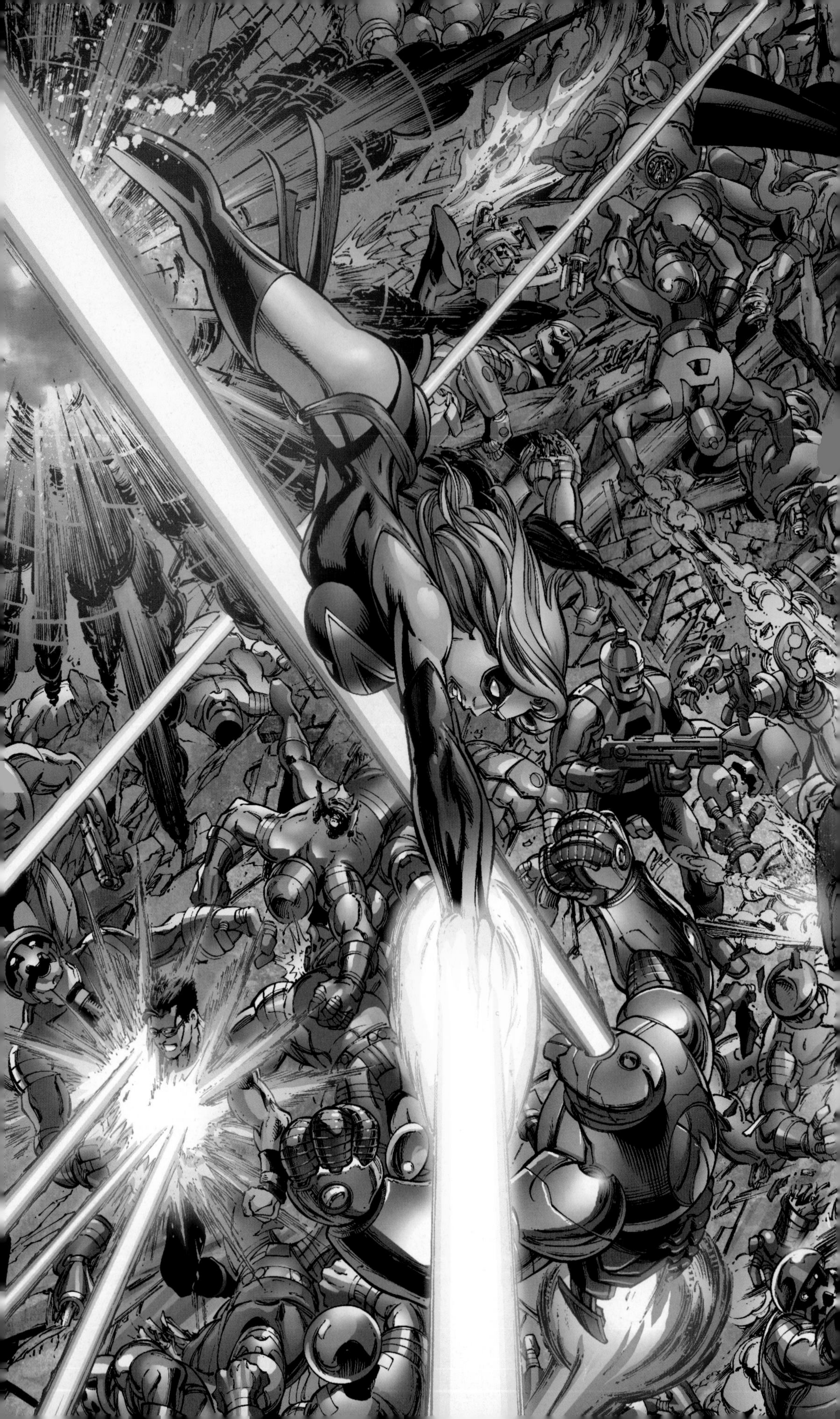

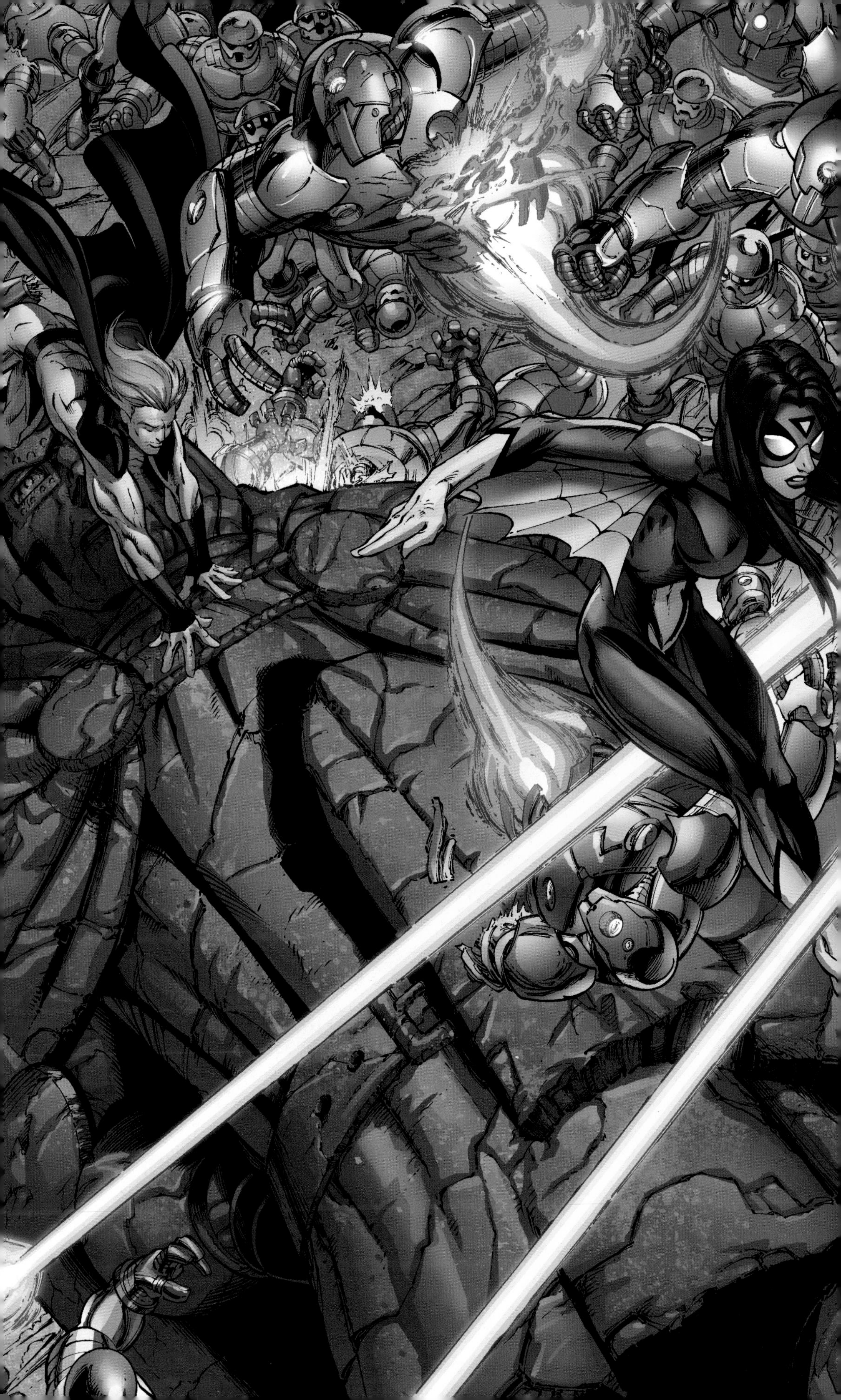

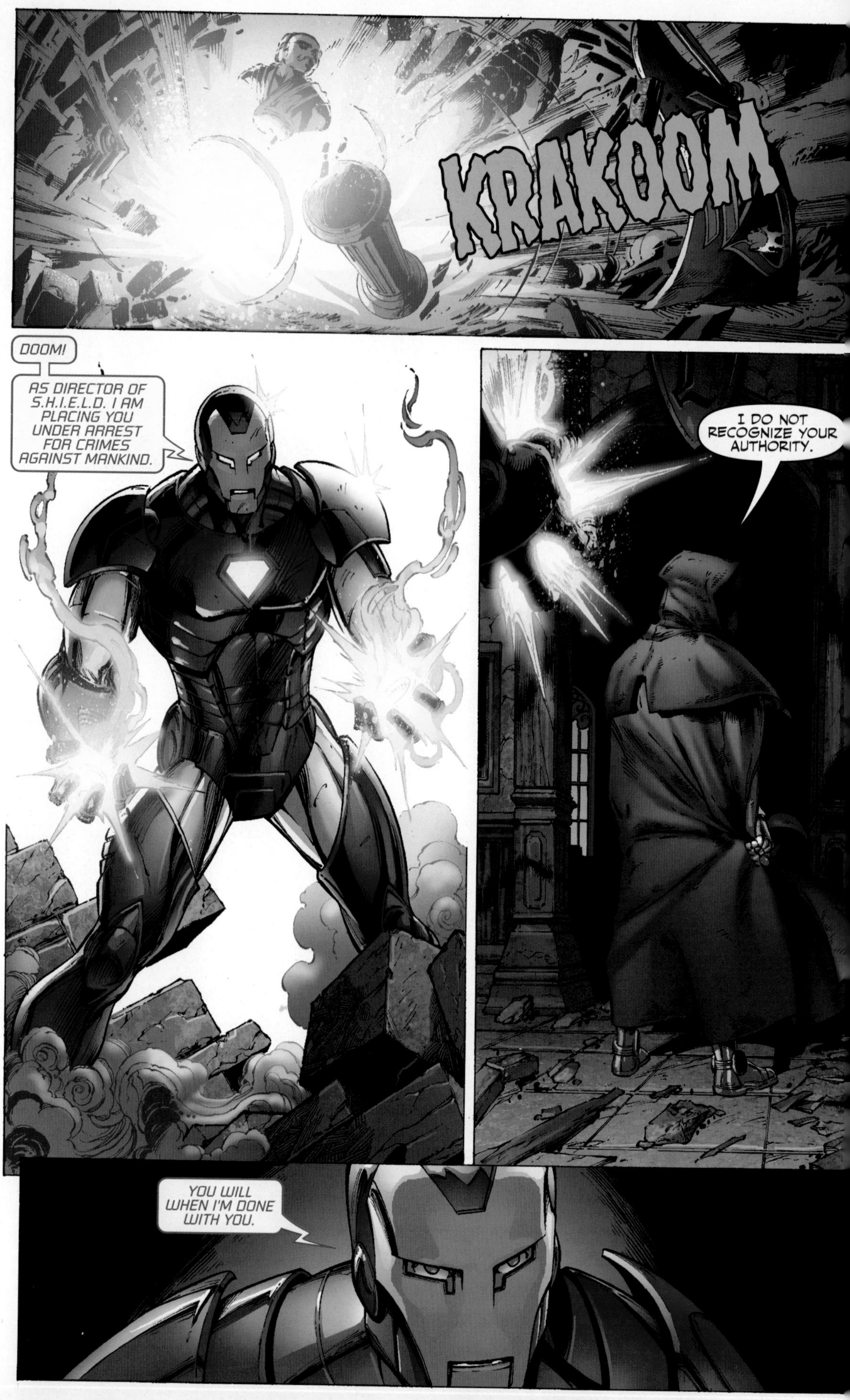
KRAKOOM
DOOM!
AS DIRECTOR OF S.H.I.E.L.D. I AM PLACING YOU UNDER ARREST FOR CRIMES AGAINST MANKIND.
I DO NOT RECOGNIZE YOUR AUTHORITY.
YOU WILL WHEN I'M DONE WITH YOU.

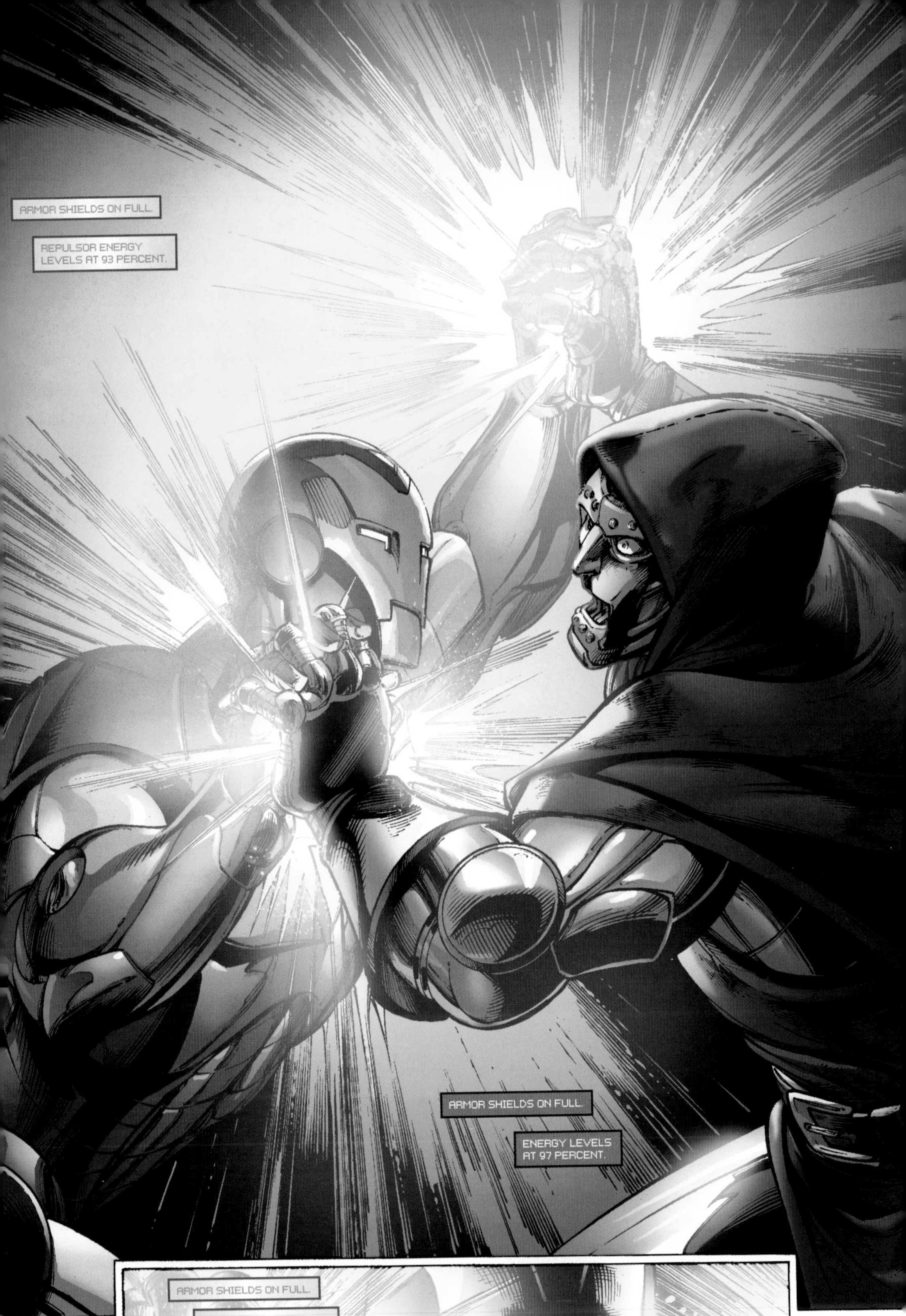
ARMOR SHIELDS ON FULL.
REPULSOR ENERGY LEVELS AT 93 PERCENT.
ARMOR SHIELDS ON FULL.
ENERGY LEVELS AT 97 PERCENT.

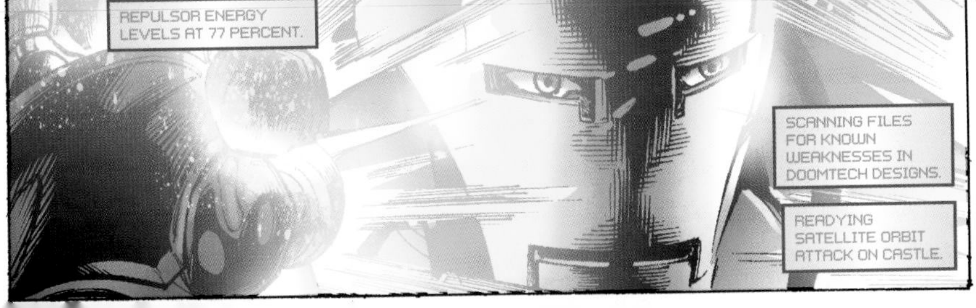
ARMOR SHIELDS ON FULL.
REPULSOR ENERGY LEVELS AT 77 PERCENT.
SCANNING FILES FOR KNOWN WEAKNESSES IN DOOMTECH DESIGNS.
READYING SATELLITE ORBIT ATTACK ON CASTLE.

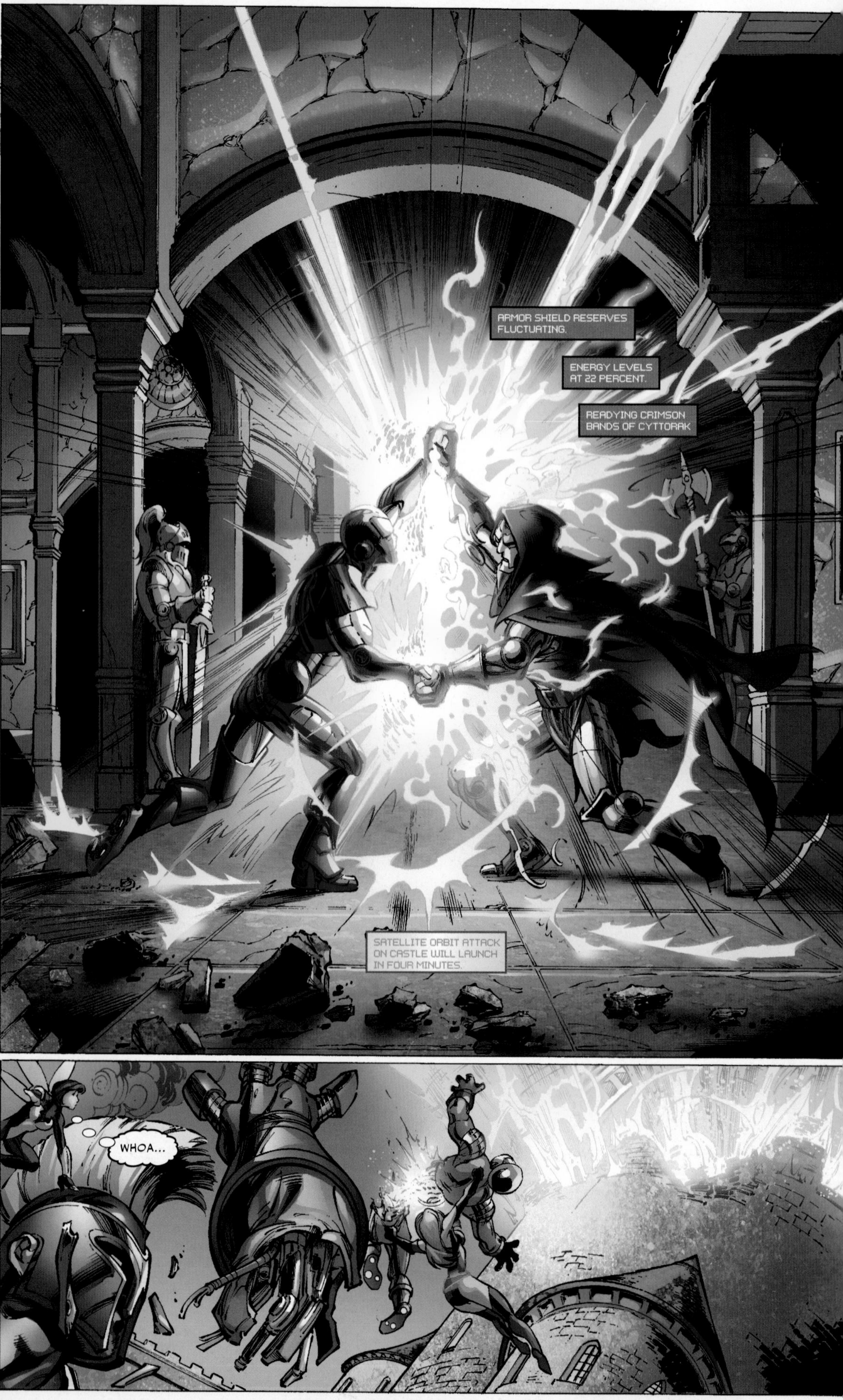
ARMOR SHIELD RESERVES FLUCTUATING.
ENERGY LEVELS AT 22 PERCENT.
READYING CRIMSON BANDS OF CYTTORAK
SATELLITE ORBIT ATTACK ON CASTLE WILL LAUNCH IN FOUR MINUTES.
WHOA...

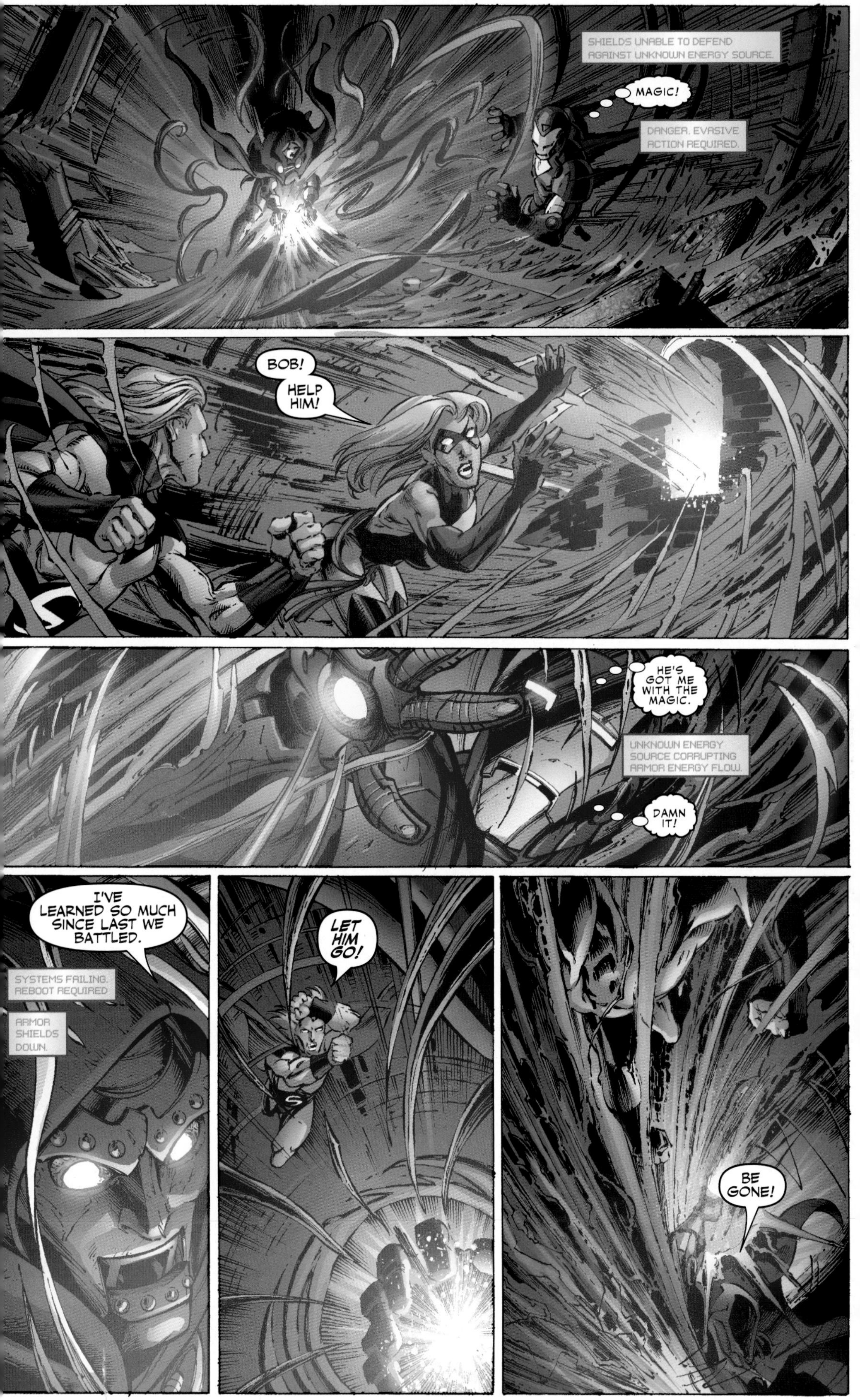

SHIELDS UNABLE TO DEFEND AGAINST UNKNOWN ENERGY SOURCE.
MAGIC!
DANGER. EVASIVE ACTION REQUIRED.
BOB! HELP HIM!
HE'S GOT ME WITH THE MAGIC.
UNKNOWN ENERGY SOURCE CORRUPTING ARMOR ENERGY FLOW.
DAMN IT!
I'VE LEARNED SO MUCH SINCE LAST WE BATTLED.
SYSTEMS FAILING. REBOOT REQUIRED
ARMOR SHIELDS DOWN.
LET HIM GO!
BE GONE!

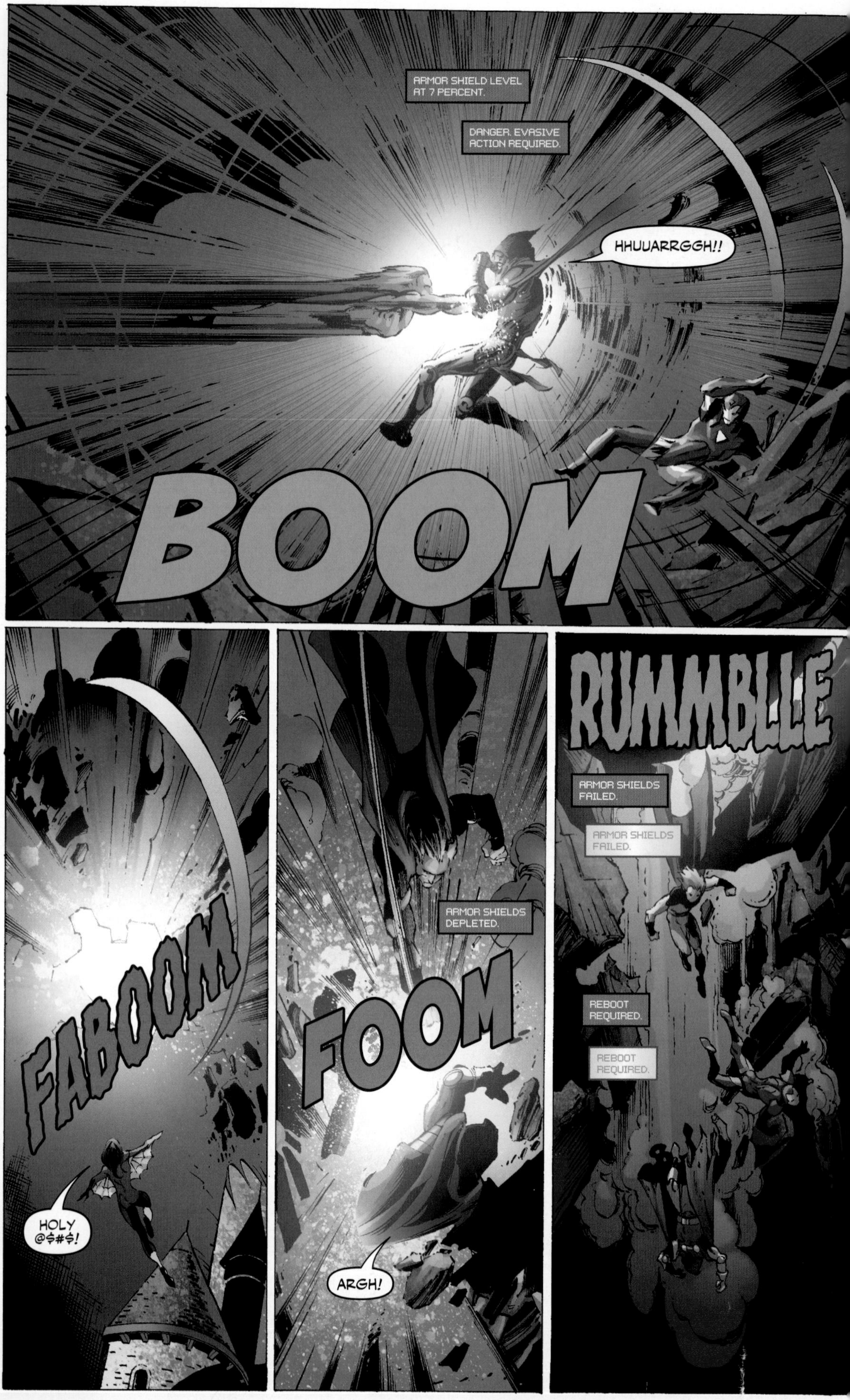
ARMOR SHIELD LEVEL AT 7 PERCENT.
DANGER. EVASIVE ACTION REQUIRED.
HHUUARRGGH!!
BOOM
FABOOM
HOLY @$#$!
ARMOR SHIELDS DEPLETED.
FOOM
ARGH!
RUMMBLLE
ARMOR SHIELDS FAILED.
ARMOR SHIELDS FAILED.
REBOOT REQUIRED.
REBOOT REQUIRED.

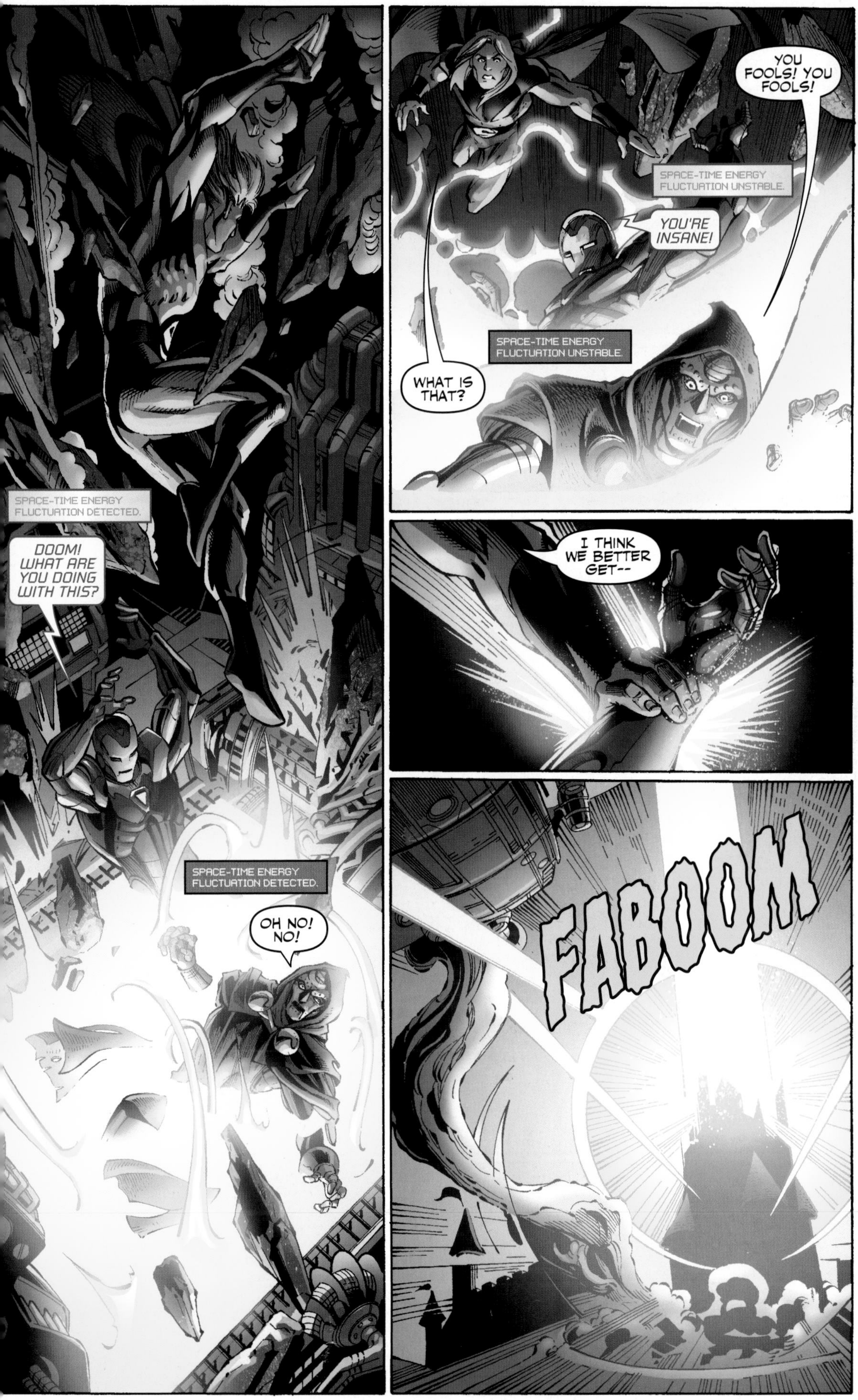
SPACE-TIME ENERGY FLUCTUATION DETECTED.
DOOM! WHAT ARE YOU DOING WITH THIS?
SPACE-TIME ENERGY FLUCTUATION DETECTED.
OH NO! NO!
YOU FOOLS! YOU FOOLS!
SPACE-TIME ENERGY FLUCTUATION UNSTABLE.
YOU'RE INSANE!
SPACE-TIME ENERGY FLUCTUATION UNSTABLE.
WHAT IS THAT?
I THINK WE BETTER GET--
FABOOM

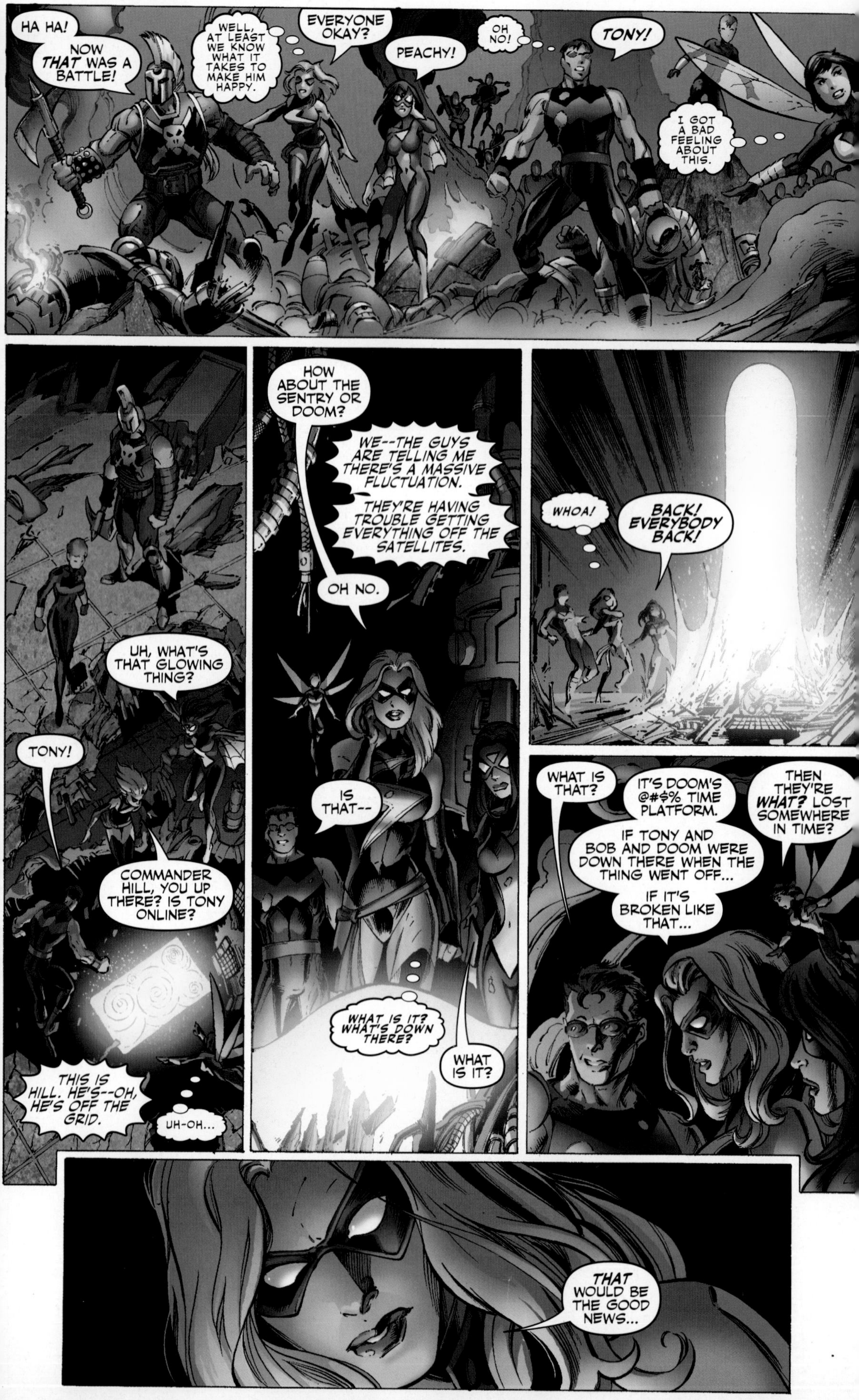

HA HA! NOW *THAT* WAS A BATTLE!
WELL, AT LEAST WE KNOW WHAT IT TAKES TO MAKE HIM HAPPY.
EVERYONE OKAY?
PEACHY!
OH NO!
TONY!
I GOT A BAD FEELING ABOUT THIS.
UH, WHAT'S THAT GLOWING THING?
TONY!
COMMANDER HILL, YOU UP THERE? IS TONY ONLINE?
THIS IS HILL. HE'S--OH, HE'S OFF THE GRID.
UH-OH...
HOW ABOUT THE SENTRY OR DOOM?
WE--THE GUYS ARE TELLING ME THERE'S A MASSIVE FLUCTUATION.
THEY'RE HAVING TROUBLE GETTING EVERYTHING OFF THE SATELLITES.
OH NO.
IS THAT--
WHAT IS IT? WHAT'S DOWN THERE?
WHAT IS IT?
WHOA!
BACK! EVERYBODY BACK!
WHAT IS THAT?
IT'S DOOM'S @#$% TIME PLATFORM.
IF TONY AND BOB AND DOOM WERE DOWN THERE WHEN THE THING WENT OFF...
IF IT'S BROKEN LIKE THAT...
THEN THEY'RE *WHAT?* LOST SOMEWHERE IN TIME?
THAT WOULD BE THE GOOD NEWS...

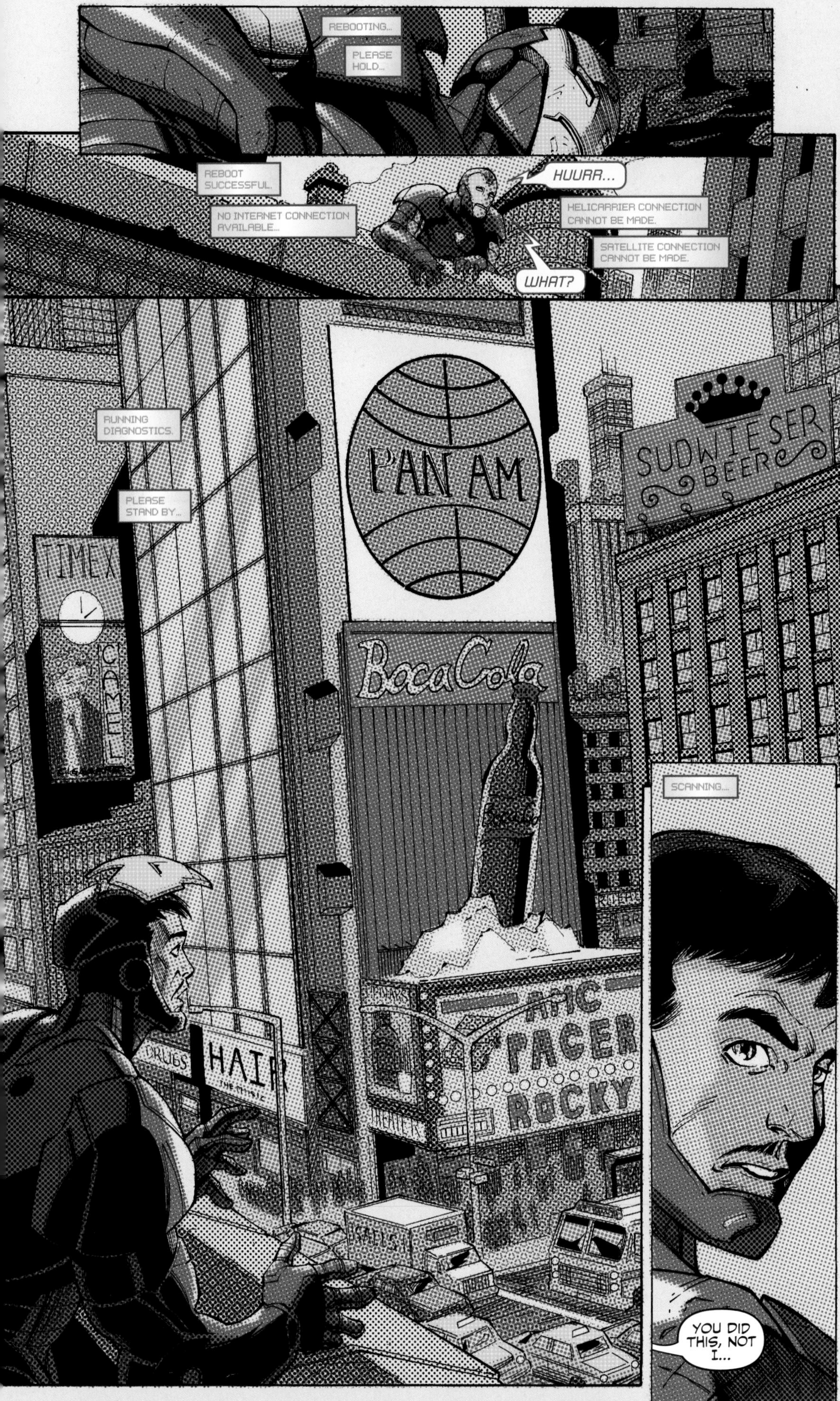
REBOOTING...
PLEASE HOLD...
REBOOT SUCCESSFUL.
NO INTERNET CONNECTION AVAILABLE...
HUURR...
HELICARRIER CONNECTION CANNOT BE MADE.
SATELLITE CONNECTION CANNOT BE MADE.
WHAT?
RUNNING DIAGNOSTICS.
PLEASE STAND BY...
PAN AM
SUDWIESER BEER
TIMEX
CAMEL
BocaCola
DRUGS
HAIR
AMC PACER
ROCKY
SCANNING...
YOU DID THIS, NOT I...

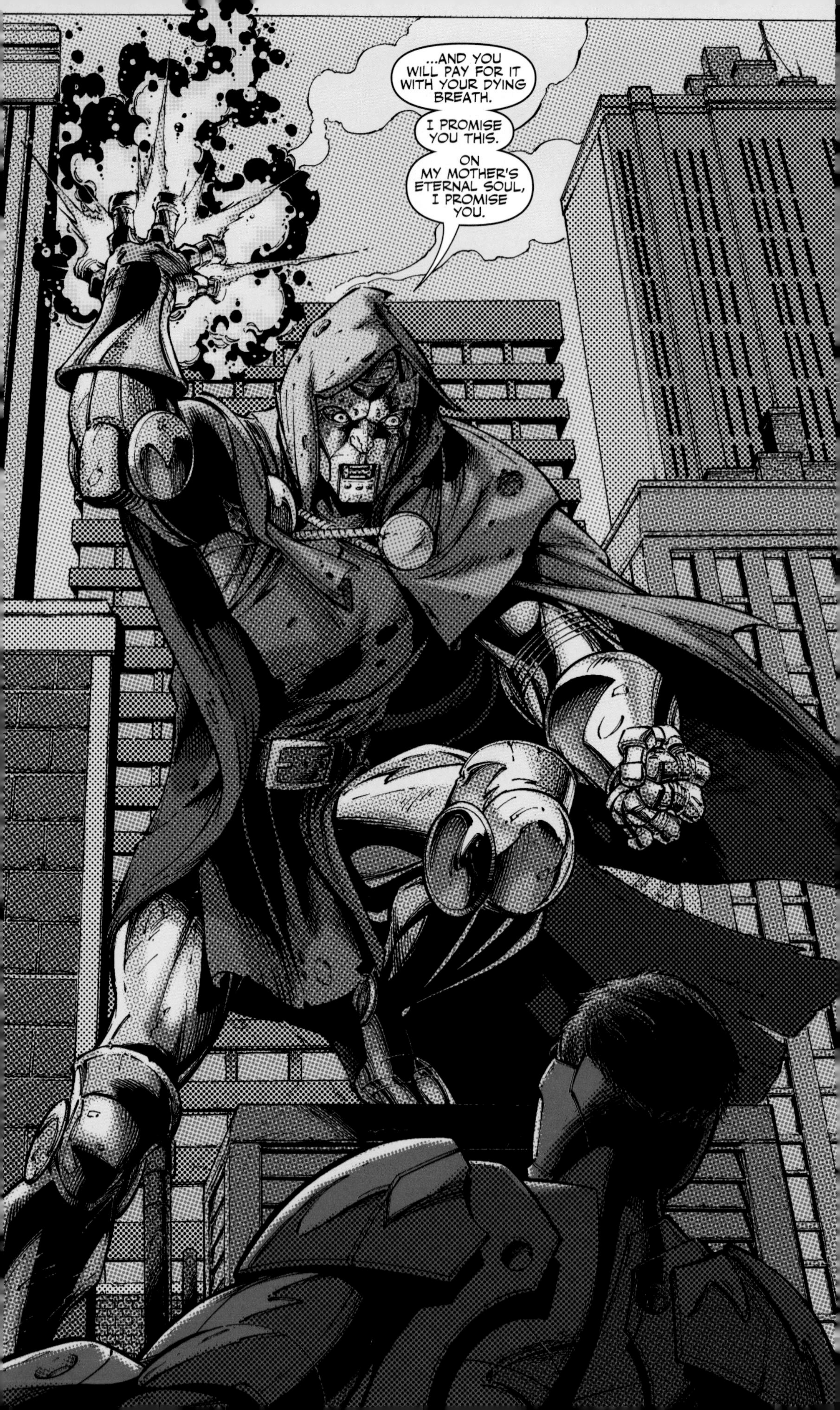
...AND YOU WILL PAY FOR IT WITH YOUR DYING BREATH.
I PROMISE YOU THIS.
ON MY MOTHER'S ETERNAL SOUL, I PROMISE YOU.

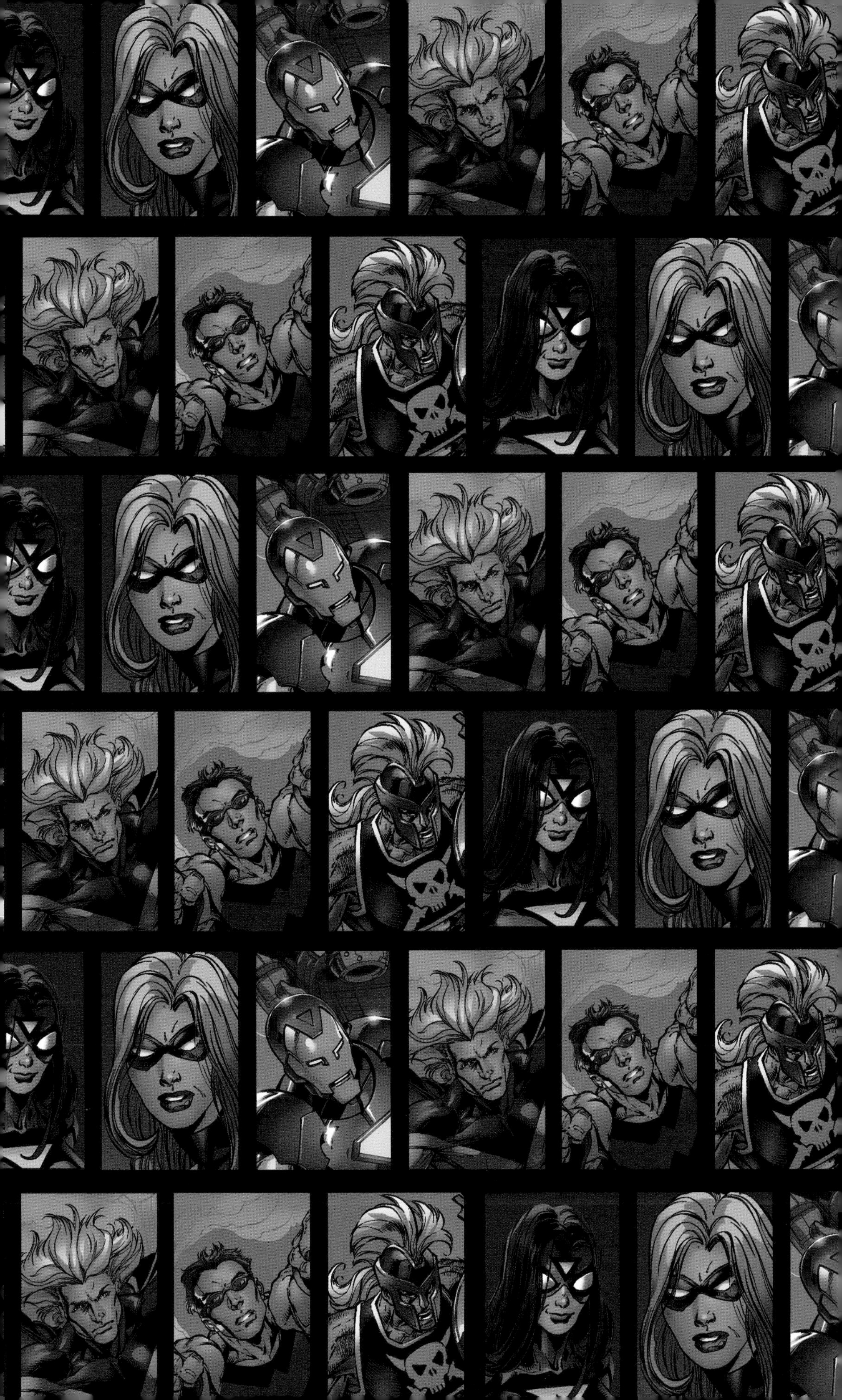

ISSUE #10

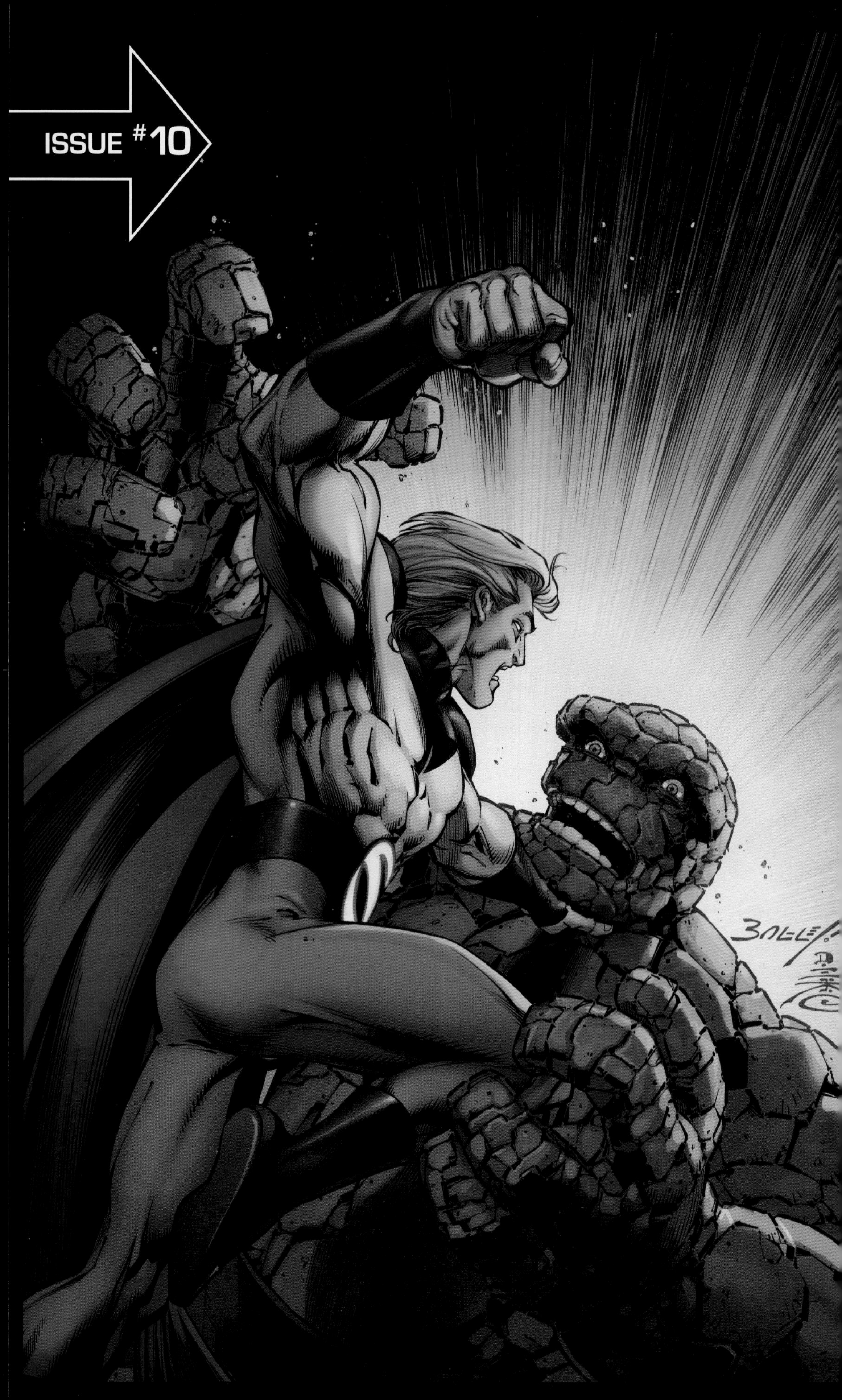

And there came a *day*, a day unlike any *other*, when *Earth's mightiest heroes and heroines* found themselves *united* against a common threat. On that day, the *Avengers* were born — to fight the foes no *single* super hero could withstand! Through the years, their roster has *prospered*, changing *many times*, but their *glory* has never been denied! Heed the *call*, then — for now, the *Avengers Assemble!*

THE MIGHTY AVENGERS!™

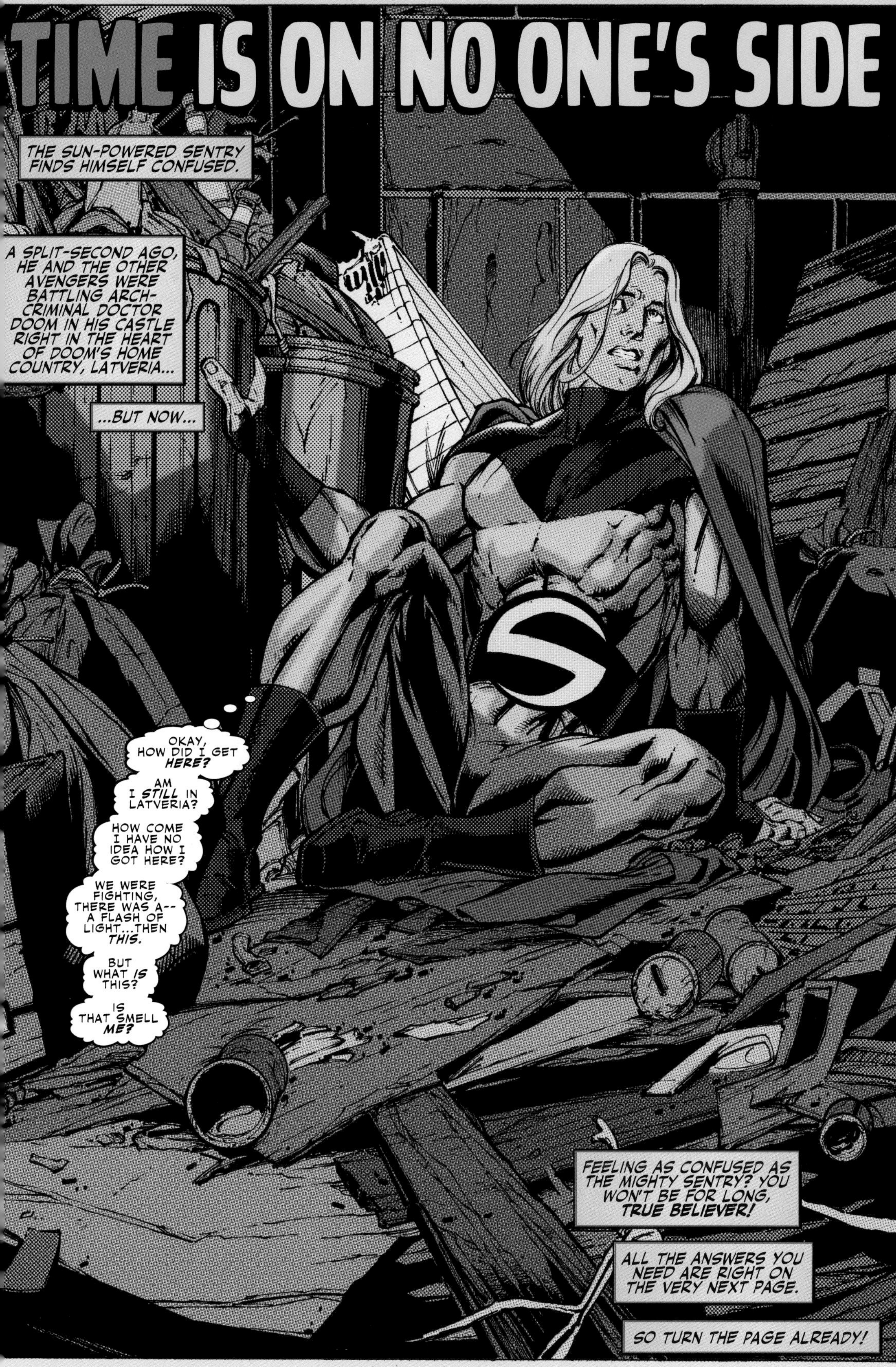
TIME IS ON NO ONE'S SIDE
THE SUN-POWERED SENTRY FINDS HIMSELF CONFUSED.
A SPLIT-SECOND AGO, HE AND THE OTHER AVENGERS WERE BATTLING ARCH-CRIMINAL DOCTOR DOOM IN HIS CASTLE RIGHT IN THE HEART OF DOOM'S HOME COUNTRY, LATVERIA...
...BUT NOW...
OKAY, HOW DID I GET HERE?
AM I STILL IN LATVERIA?
HOW COME I HAVE NO IDEA HOW I GOT HERE?
WE WERE FIGHTING, THERE WAS A-- A FLASH OF LIGHT...THEN THIS.
BUT WHAT IS THIS?
IS THAT SMELL ME?
FEELING AS CONFUSED AS THE MIGHTY SENTRY? YOU WON'T BE FOR LONG, TRUE BELIEVER!
ALL THE ANSWERS YOU NEED ARE RIGHT ON THE VERY NEXT PAGE.
SO TURN THE PAGE ALREADY!

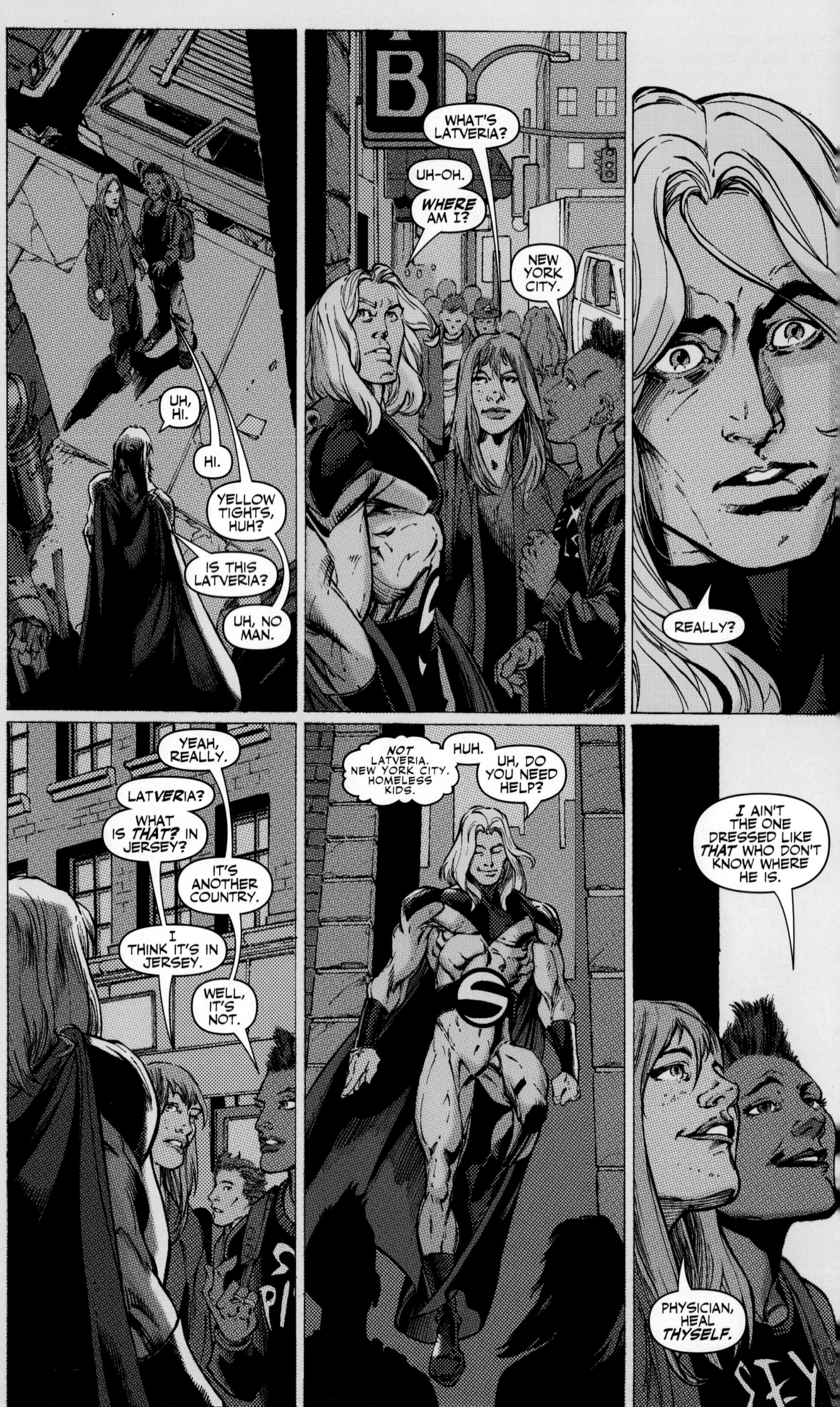
UH, HI.
HI.
YELLOW TIGHTS, HUH?
IS THIS LATVERIA?
UH, NO MAN.
WHAT'S LATVERIA?
UH-OH. WHERE AM I?
NEW YORK CITY.
REALLY?
YEAH, REALLY.
LATVERIA?
WHAT IS THAT? IN JERSEY?
IT'S ANOTHER COUNTRY.
I THINK IT'S IN JERSEY.
WELL, IT'S NOT.
NOT LATVERIA. NEW YORK CITY. HOMELESS KIDS.
HUH.
UH, DO YOU NEED HELP?
I AIN'T THE ONE DRESSED LIKE THAT WHO DON'T KNOW WHERE HE IS.
PHYSICIAN, HEAL THYSELF.

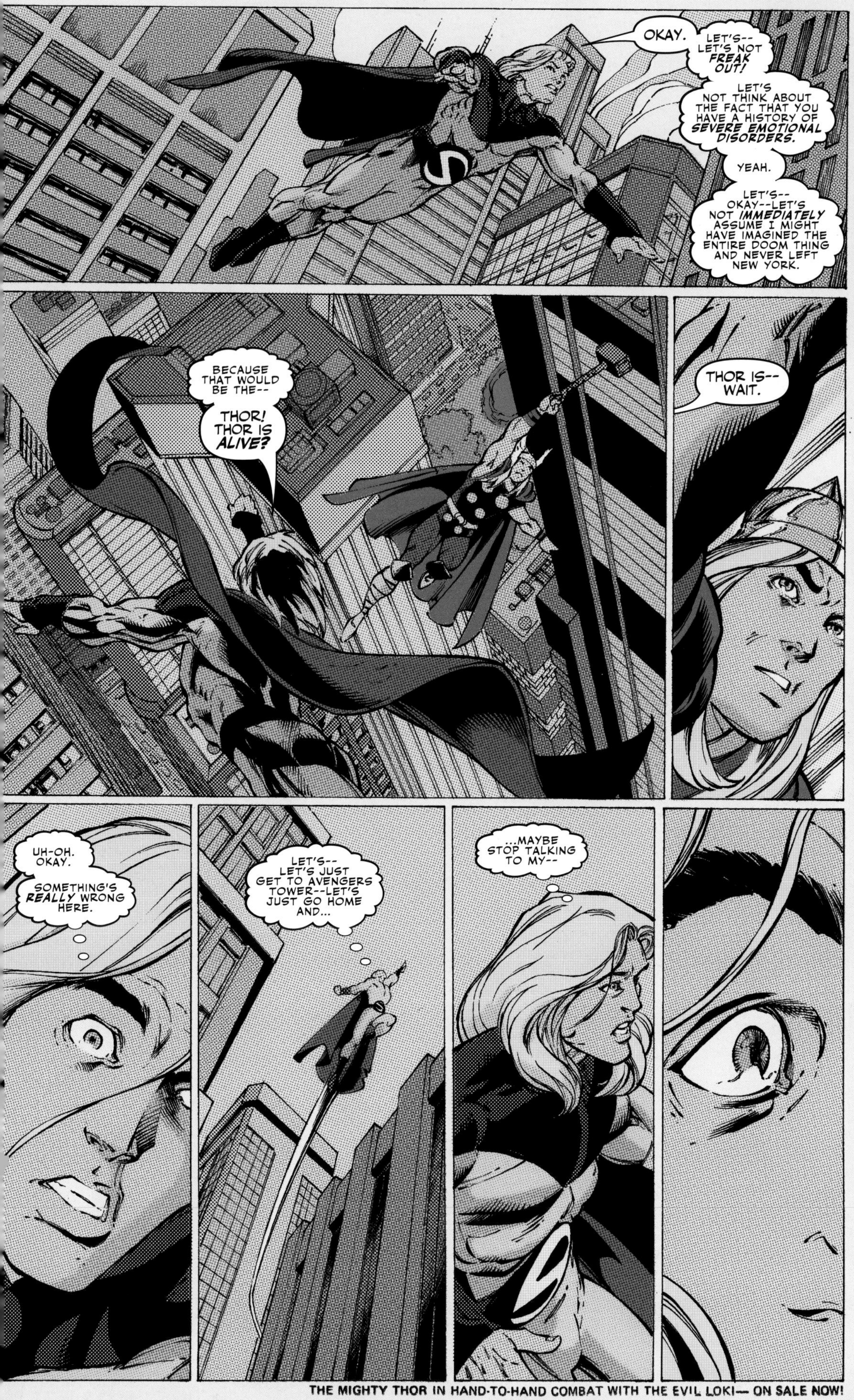
OKAY.
LET'S-- LET'S NOT FREAK OUT!
NOT THINK ABOUT THE FACT THAT YOU HAVE A HISTORY OF SEVERE EMOTIONAL DISORDERS.
YEAH.
LET'S-- OKAY--LET'S NOT IMMEDIATELY ASSUME I MIGHT HAVE IMAGINED THE ENTIRE DOOM THING AND NEVER LEFT NEW YORK.
BECAUSE THAT WOULD BE THE--
THOR! THOR IS ALIVE?
THOR IS-- WAIT.
UH-OH. OKAY.
SOMETHING'S REALLY WRONG HERE.
LET'S-- LET'S JUST GET TO AVENGERS TOWER--LET'S JUST GO HOME AND...
...MAYBE STOP TALKING TO MY--

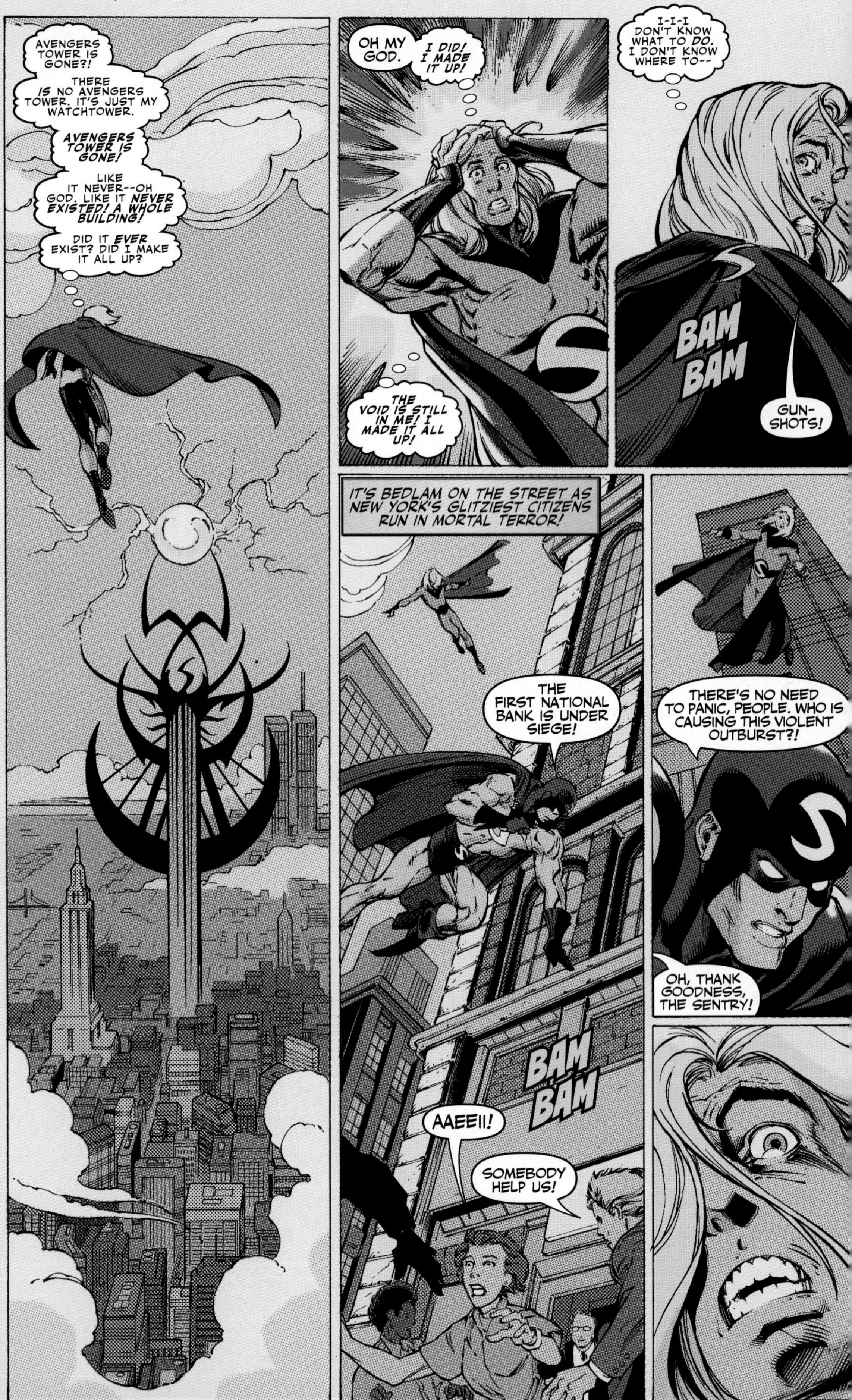
AVENGERS TOWER IS GONE?!
THERE IS NO AVENGERS TOWER. IT'S JUST MY WATCHTOWER.
AVENGERS TOWER IS GONE!
LIKE IT NEVER--OH GOD. LIKE IT NEVER EXISTED! A WHOLE BUILDING!
DID IT EVER EXIST? DID I MAKE IT ALL UP?
OH MY GOD.
I DID! I MADE IT UP!
THE VOID IS STILL IN ME! I MADE IT ALL UP!
I-I-I DON'T KNOW WHAT TO DO. I DON'T KNOW WHERE TO--
BAM BAM
GUN-SHOTS!
IT'S BEDLAM ON THE STREET AS NEW YORK'S GLITZIEST CITIZENS RUN IN MORTAL TERROR!
THE FIRST NATIONAL BANK IS UNDER SIEGE!
BAM BAM
AAEEII!
SOMEBODY HELP US!
THERE'S NO NEED TO PANIC, PEOPLE. WHO IS CAUSING THIS VIOLENT OUTBURST?!
OH, THANK GOODNESS, THE SENTRY!

CONTINUED AFTER NEXT PA

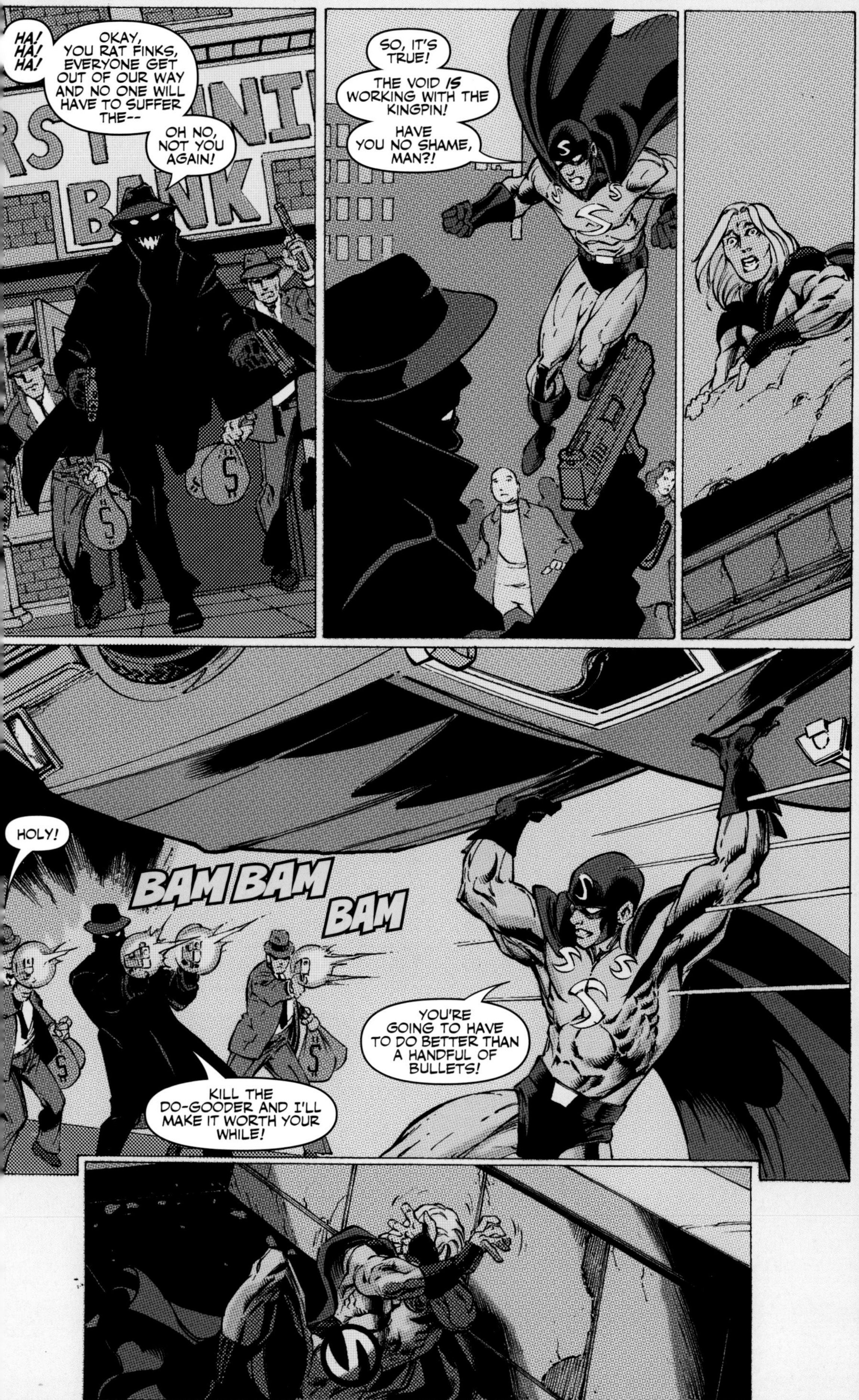
HA! HA! HA!
OKAY, YOU RAT FINKS, EVERYONE GET OUT OF OUR WAY AND NO ONE WILL HAVE TO SUFFER THE--
OH NO, NOT YOU AGAIN!
SO, IT'S TRUE!
THE VOID *IS* WORKING WITH THE KINGPIN!
HAVE YOU NO SHAME, MAN?!
HOLY!
BAM BAM BAM
YOU'RE GOING TO HAVE TO DO BETTER THAN A HANDFUL OF BULLETS!
KILL THE DO-GOODER AND I'LL MAKE IT WORTH YOUR WHILE!

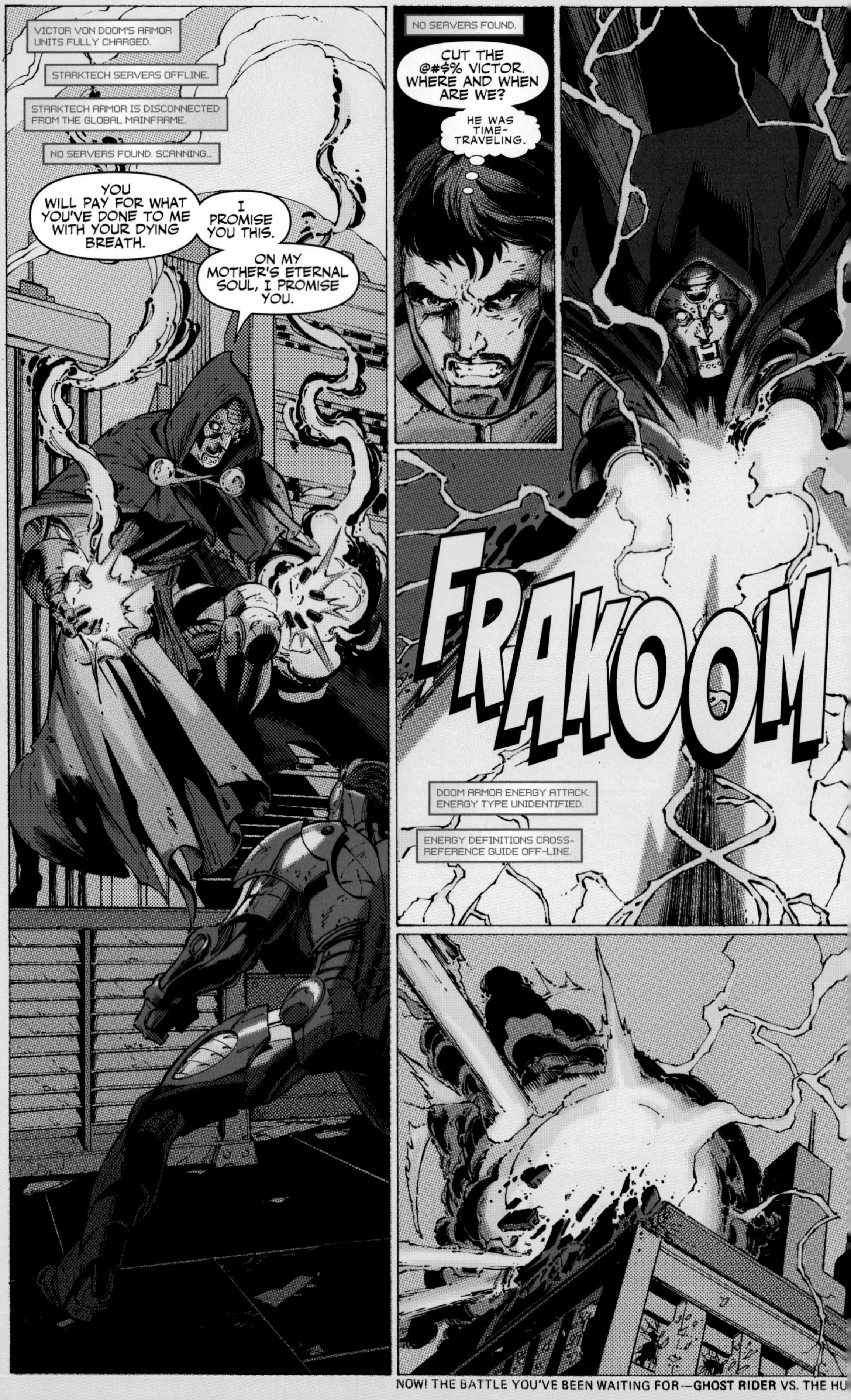
VICTOR VON DOOM'S ARMOR UNITS FULLY CHARGED.
STARKTECH SERVERS OFFLINE.
STARKTECH ARMOR IS DISCONNECTED FROM THE GLOBAL MAINFRAME.
NO SERVERS FOUND. SCANNING...
YOU WILL PAY FOR WHAT YOU'VE DONE TO ME WITH YOUR DYING BREATH.
I PROMISE YOU THIS.
ON MY MOTHER'S ETERNAL SOUL, I PROMISE YOU.
NO SERVERS FOUND.
CUT THE @#$% VICTOR. WHERE AND WHEN ARE WE?
HE WAS TIME-TRAVELING.
FRAKOOM
DOOM ARMOR ENERGY ATTACK. ENERGY TYPE UNIDENTIFIED.
ENERGY DEFINITIONS CROSS-REFERENCE GUIDE OFF-LINE.

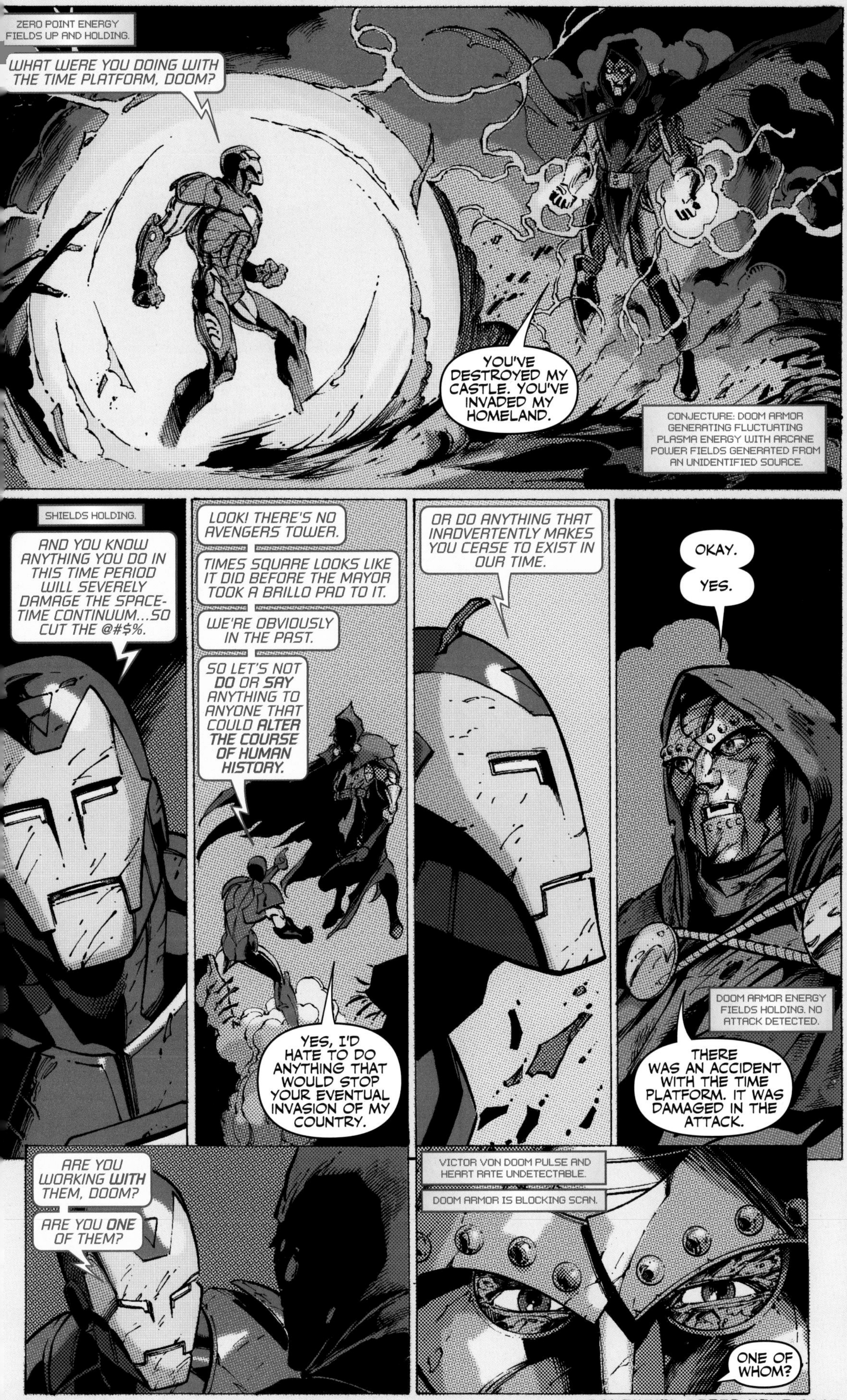
ZERO POINT ENERGY FIELDS UP AND HOLDING.
WHAT WERE YOU DOING WITH THE TIME PLATFORM, DOOM?
YOU'VE DESTROYED MY CASTLE. YOU'VE INVADED MY HOMELAND.
CONJECTURE: DOOM ARMOR GENERATING FLUCTUATING PLASMA ENERGY WITH ARCANE POWER FIELDS GENERATED FROM AN UNIDENTIFIED SOURCE.
SHIELDS HOLDING.
AND YOU KNOW ANYTHING YOU DO IN THIS TIME PERIOD WILL SEVERELY DAMAGE THE SPACE-TIME CONTINUUM...SO CUT THE @#$%.
LOOK! THERE'S NO AVENGERS TOWER.
TIMES SQUARE LOOKS LIKE IT DID BEFORE THE MAYOR TOOK A BRILLO PAD TO IT.
WE'RE OBVIOUSLY IN THE PAST.
SO LET'S NOT **DO** OR **SAY** ANYTHING TO ANYONE THAT COULD **ALTER THE COURSE OF HUMAN HISTORY.**
YES, I'D HATE TO DO ANYTHING THAT WOULD STOP YOUR EVENTUAL INVASION OF MY COUNTRY.
OR DO ANYTHING THAT INADVERTENTLY MAKES YOU CEASE TO EXIST IN OUR TIME.
OKAY.
YES.
DOOM ARMOR ENERGY FIELDS HOLDING. NO ATTACK DETECTED.
THERE WAS AN ACCIDENT WITH THE TIME PLATFORM. IT WAS DAMAGED IN THE ATTACK.
ARE YOU WORKING **WITH** THEM, DOOM?
ARE YOU **ONE** OF THEM?
VICTOR VON DOOM PULSE AND HEART RATE UNDETECTABLE.
DOOM ARMOR IS BLOCKING SCAN.
ONE OF WHOM?

CONTINUED AFTER NEXT PAGE

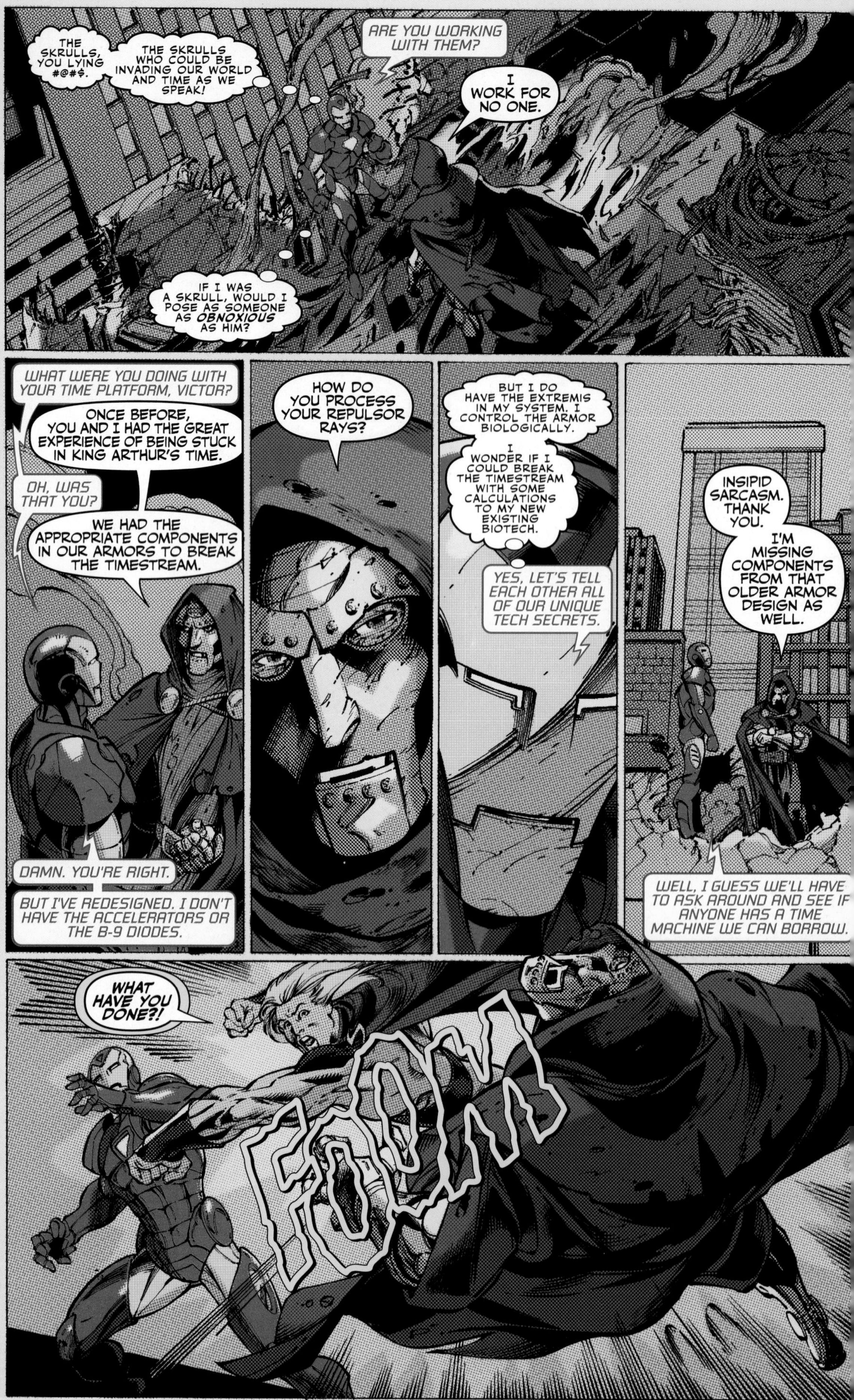

THE SKRULLS, YOU LYING #@#$.
THE SKRULLS WHO COULD BE INVADING OUR WORLD AND TIME AS WE SPEAK!
ARE YOU WORKING WITH THEM?
I WORK FOR NO ONE.
IF I WAS A SKRULL, WOULD I POSE AS SOMEONE AS OBNOXIOUS AS HIM?
WHAT WERE YOU DOING WITH YOUR TIME PLATFORM, VICTOR?
ONCE BEFORE, YOU AND I HAD THE GREAT EXPERIENCE OF BEING STUCK IN KING ARTHUR'S TIME.
OH, WAS THAT YOU?
WE HAD THE APPROPRIATE COMPONENTS IN OUR ARMORS TO BREAK THE TIMESTREAM.
DAMN. YOU'RE RIGHT.
BUT I'VE REDESIGNED. I DON'T HAVE THE ACCELERATORS OR THE B-9 DIODES.
HOW DO YOU PROCESS YOUR REPULSOR RAYS?
BUT I DO HAVE THE EXTREMIS IN MY SYSTEM. I CONTROL THE ARMOR BIOLOGICALLY.
I WONDER IF I COULD BREAK THE TIMESTREAM WITH SOME CALCULATIONS TO MY NEW EXISTING BIOTECH.
YES, LET'S TELL EACH OTHER ALL OF OUR UNIQUE TECH SECRETS.
INSIPID SARCASM. THANK YOU.
I'M MISSING COMPONENTS FROM THAT OLDER ARMOR DESIGN AS WELL.
WELL, I GUESS WE'LL HAVE TO ASK AROUND AND SEE IF ANYONE HAS A TIME MACHINE WE CAN BORROW.
WHAT HAVE YOU DONE?!
FOOM

CONTINUED AFTER NEXT PAG

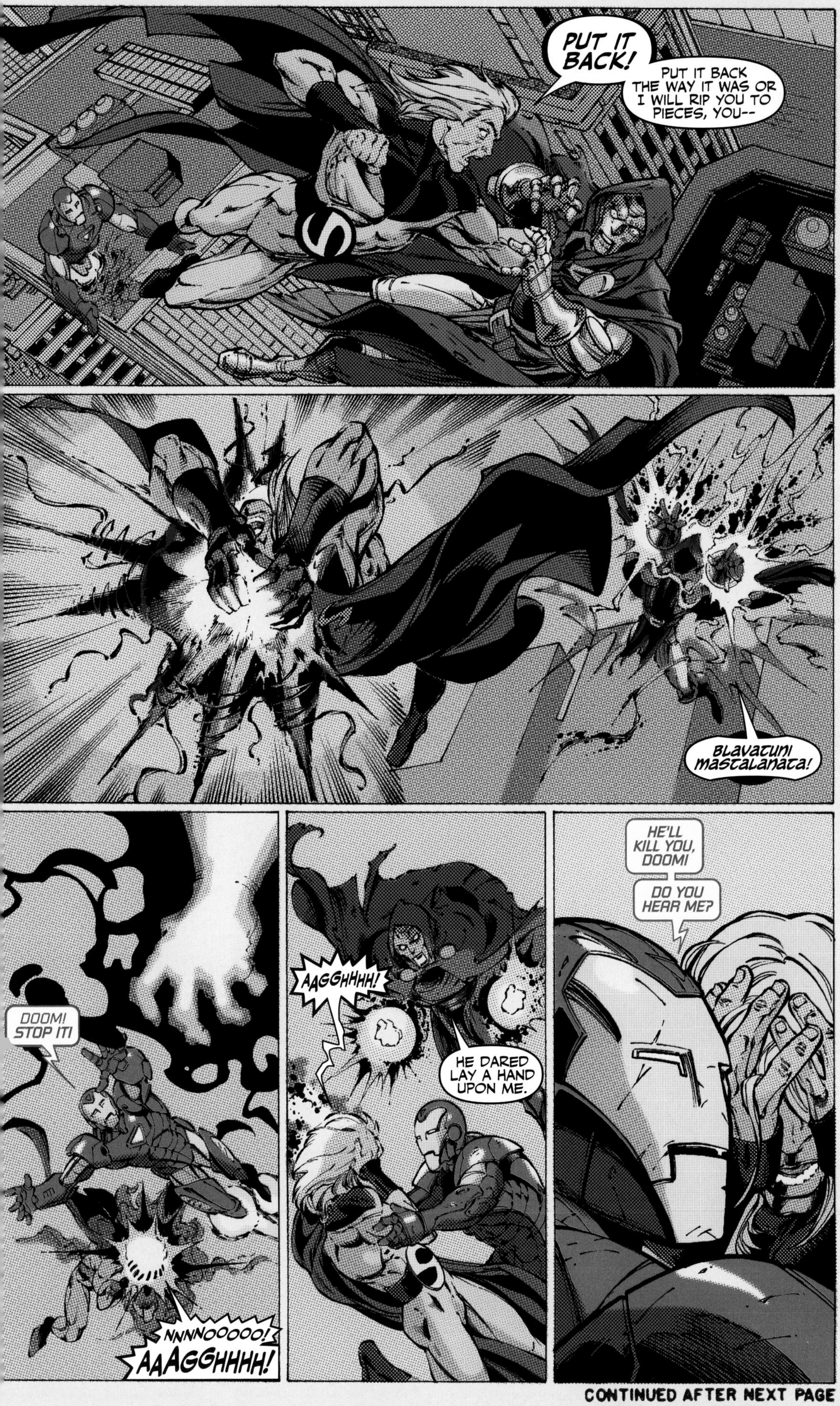
PUT IT BACK!
PUT IT BACK THE WAY IT WAS OR I WILL RIP YOU TO PIECES, YOU--
BLAVATUNI MASTALANATA!
DOOM! STOP IT!
NNNOOOOO! AAAGGHHHH!
AAGGHHHH!
HE DARED LAY A HAND UPON ME.
HE'LL KILL YOU, DOOM!
DO YOU HEAR ME?

CONTINUED AFTER NEXT PAGE

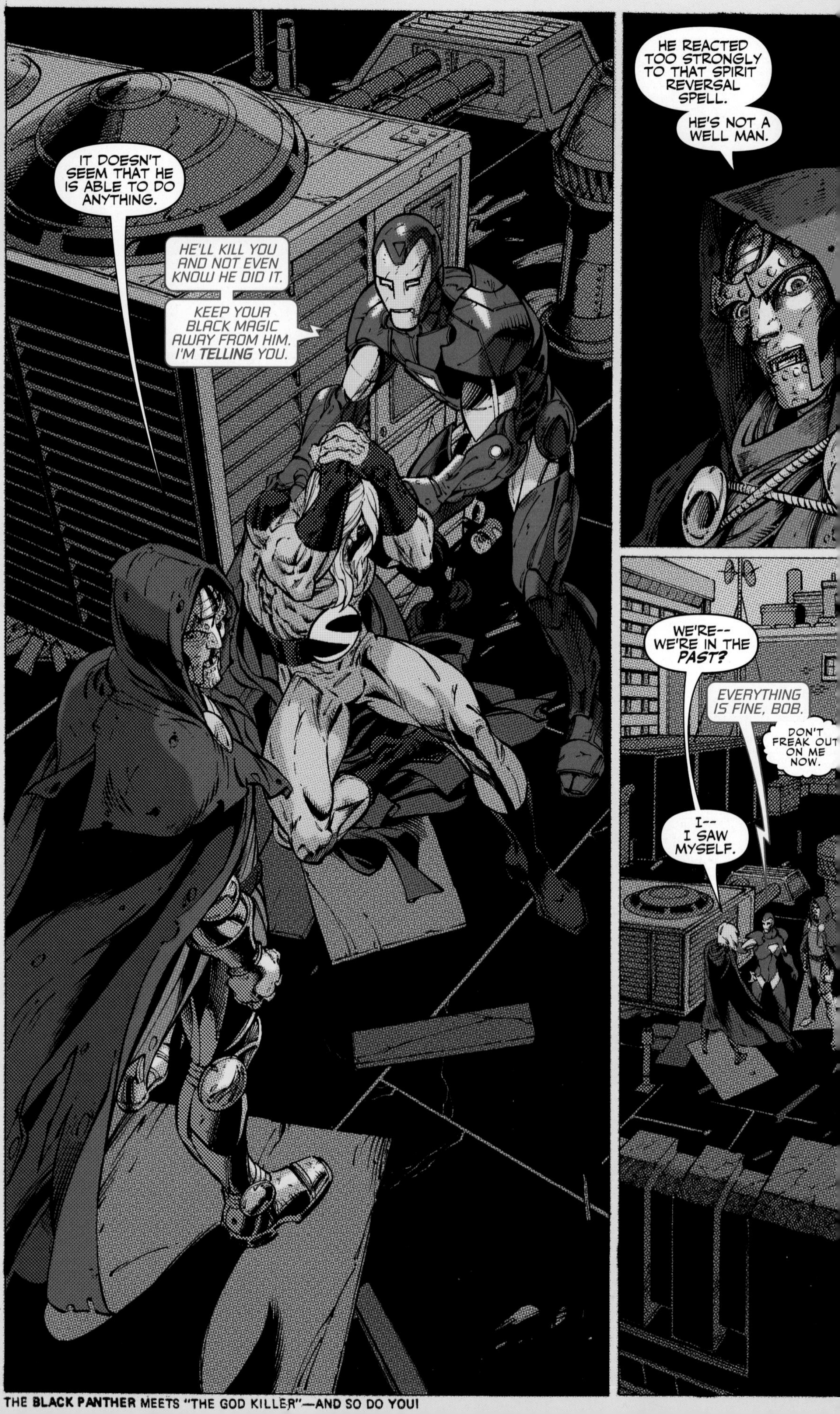
IT DOESN'T SEEM THAT HE IS ABLE TO DO ANYTHING.
HE'LL KILL YOU AND NOT EVEN KNOW HE DID IT.
KEEP YOUR BLACK MAGIC AWAY FROM HIM. I'M TELLING YOU.
HE REACTED TOO STRONGLY TO THAT SPIRIT REVERSAL SPELL.
HE'S NOT A WELL MAN.
WE'RE-- WE'RE IN THE PAST?
EVERYTHING IS FINE, BOB.
DON'T FREAK OUT ON ME NOW.
I-- I SAW MYSELF.

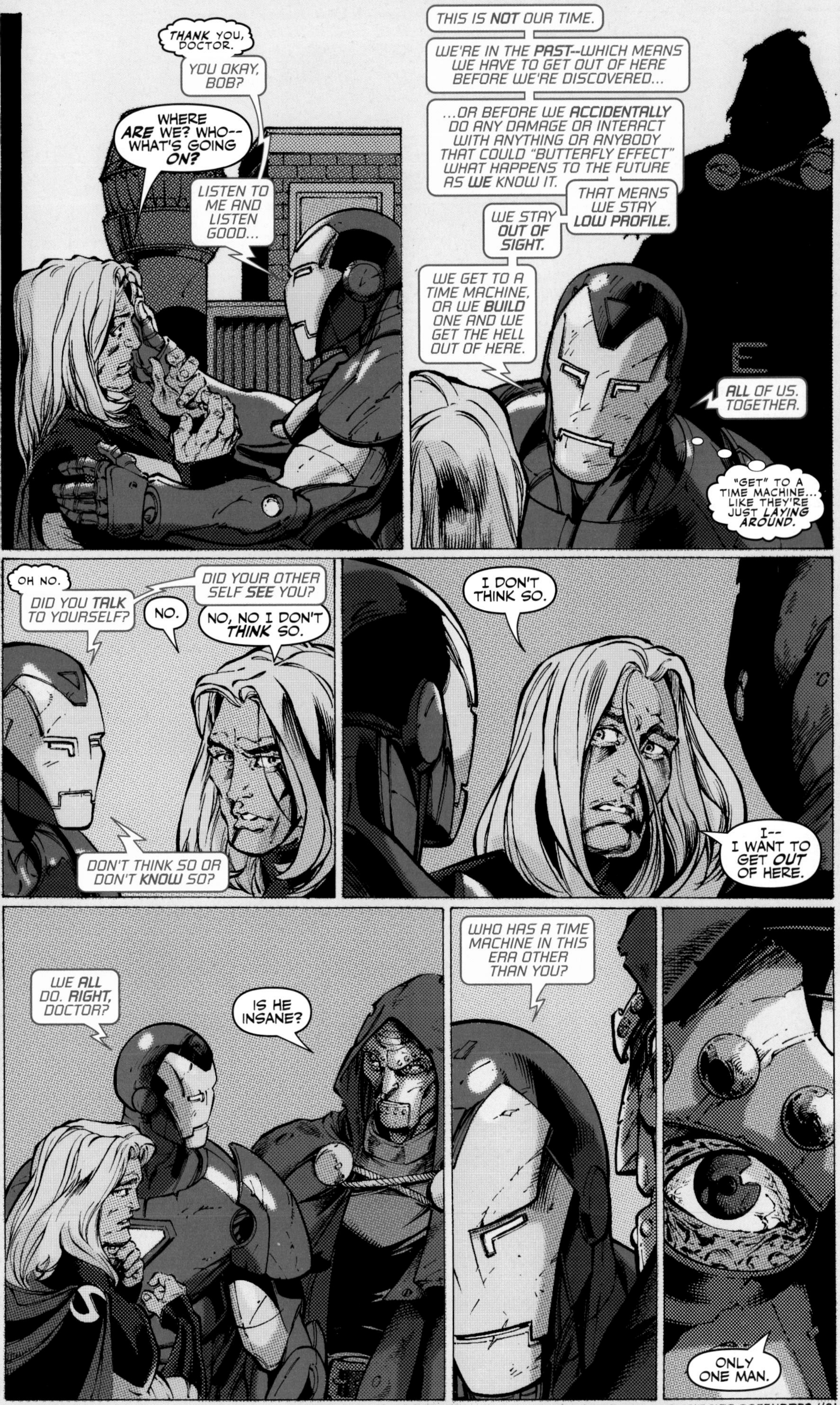
THANK YOU, DOCTOR.
YOU OKAY, BOB?
WHERE ARE WE? WHO-- WHAT'S GOING ON?
LISTEN TO ME AND LISTEN GOOD...
THIS IS NOT OUR TIME.
WE'RE IN THE PAST--WHICH MEANS WE HAVE TO GET OUT OF HERE BEFORE WE'RE DISCOVERED...
...OR BEFORE WE ACCIDENTALLY DO ANY DAMAGE OR INTERACT WITH ANYTHING OR ANYBODY THAT COULD "BUTTERFLY EFFECT" WHAT HAPPENS TO THE FUTURE AS WE KNOW IT.
THAT MEANS WE STAY LOW PROFILE.
WE STAY OUT OF SIGHT.
WE GET TO A TIME MACHINE, OR WE BUILD ONE AND WE GET THE HELL OUT OF HERE.
ALL OF US. TOGETHER.
"GET" TO A TIME MACHINE... LIKE THEY'RE JUST LAYING AROUND.
OH NO.
DID YOU TALK TO YOURSELF?
NO.
DID YOUR OTHER SELF SEE YOU?
NO, NO I DON'T THINK SO.
DON'T THINK SO OR DON'T KNOW SO?
I DON'T THINK SO.
I-- I WANT TO GET OUT OF HERE.
WE ALL DO. RIGHT, DOCTOR?
IS HE INSANE?
WHO HAS A TIME MACHINE IN THIS ERA OTHER THAN YOU?
ONLY ONE MAN.
DAREDEVIL JOINS THE WORLD'S GREATEST NON-TEAM—IN GIANT-SIZE DEFENDERS #3!

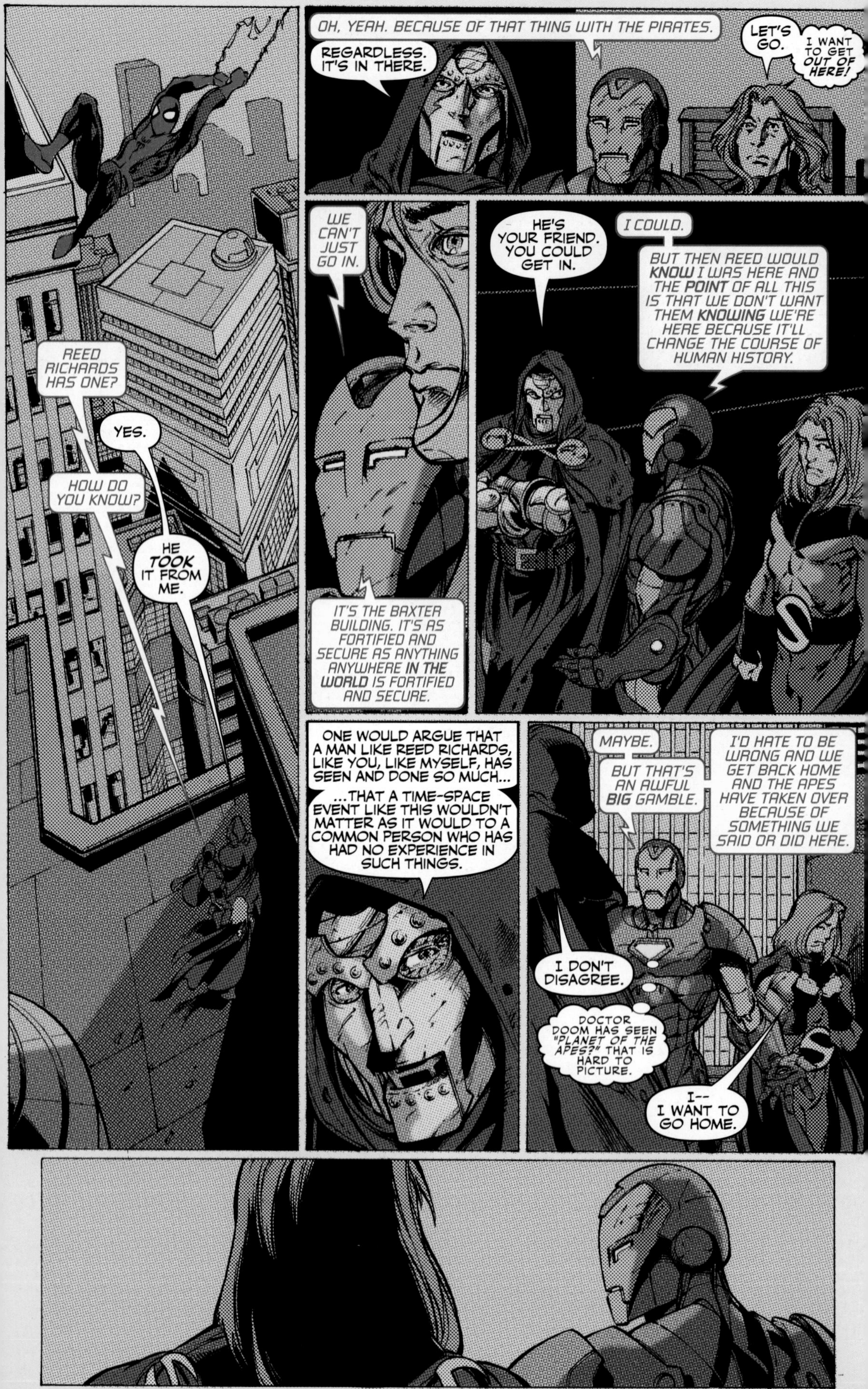

OH, YEAH. BECAUSE OF THAT THING WITH THE PIRATES.
REGARDLESS. IT'S IN THERE.
LET'S GO.
I WANT TO GET OUT OF HERE!
REED RICHARDS HAS ONE?
YES.
HOW DO YOU KNOW?
HE TOOK IT FROM ME.
WE CAN'T JUST GO IN.
IT'S THE BAXTER BUILDING. IT'S AS FORTIFIED AND SECURE AS ANYTHING ANYWHERE IN THE WORLD IS FORTIFIED AND SECURE.
HE'S YOUR FRIEND. YOU COULD GET IN.
I COULD.
BUT THEN REED WOULD KNOW I WAS HERE AND THE POINT OF ALL THIS IS THAT WE DON'T WANT THEM KNOWING WE'RE HERE BECAUSE IT'LL CHANGE THE COURSE OF HUMAN HISTORY.
ONE WOULD ARGUE THAT A MAN LIKE REED RICHARDS, LIKE YOU, LIKE MYSELF, HAS SEEN AND DONE SO MUCH...
...THAT A TIME-SPACE EVENT LIKE THIS WOULDN'T MATTER AS IT WOULD TO A COMMON PERSON WHO HAS HAD NO EXPERIENCE IN SUCH THINGS.
MAYBE.
BUT THAT'S AN AWFUL BIG GAMBLE.
I'D HATE TO BE WRONG AND WE GET BACK HOME AND THE APES HAVE TAKEN OVER BECAUSE OF SOMETHING WE SAID OR DID HERE.
I DON'T DISAGREE.
DOCTOR DOOM HAS SEEN "PLANET OF THE APES?" THAT IS HARD TO PICTURE.
I-- I WANT TO GO HOME.

CONTINUED AFTER NEXT PAGE

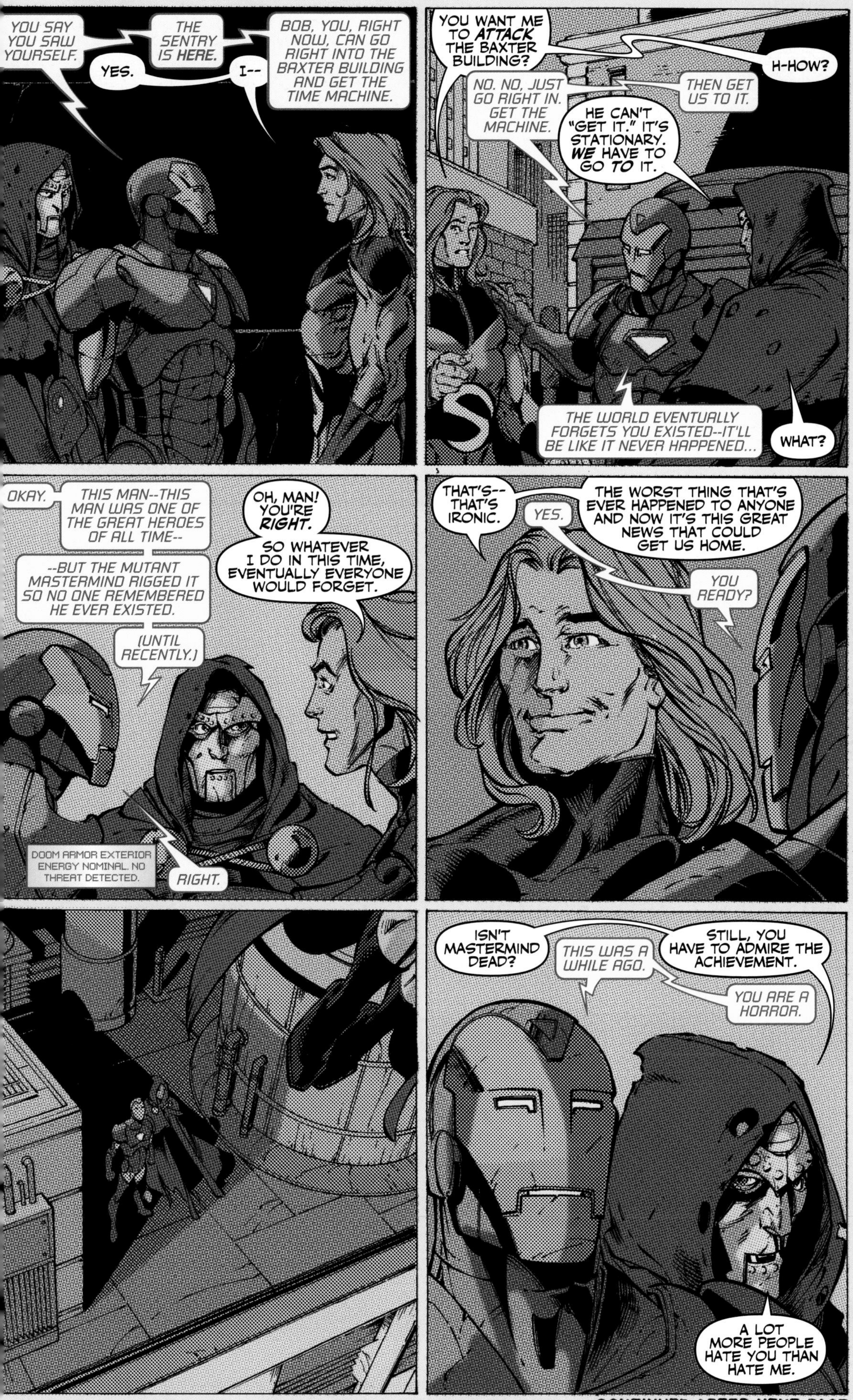
YOU SAY YOU SAW YOURSELF.
YES.
THE SENTRY IS HERE.
I--
BOB, YOU, RIGHT NOW, CAN GO RIGHT INTO THE BAXTER BUILDING AND GET THE TIME MACHINE.
YOU WANT ME TO ATTACK THE BAXTER BUILDING?
H-HOW?
NO. NO, JUST GO RIGHT IN. GET THE MACHINE.
THEN GET US TO IT.
HE CAN'T "GET IT." IT'S STATIONARY. WE HAVE TO GO TO IT.
THE WORLD EVENTUALLY FORGETS YOU EXISTED--IT'LL BE LIKE IT NEVER HAPPENED...
WHAT?
OKAY.
THIS MAN--THIS MAN WAS ONE OF THE GREAT HEROES OF ALL TIME--
--BUT THE MUTANT MASTERMIND RIGGED IT SO NO ONE REMEMBERED HE EVER EXISTED.
(UNTIL RECENTLY.)
OH, MAN! YOU'RE RIGHT.
SO WHATEVER I DO IN THIS TIME, EVENTUALLY EVERYONE WOULD FORGET.
DOOM ARMOR EXTERIOR ENERGY NOMINAL. NO THREAT DETECTED.
RIGHT.
THAT'S-- THAT'S IRONIC.
YES.
THE WORST THING THAT'S EVER HAPPENED TO ANYONE AND NOW IT'S THIS GREAT NEWS THAT COULD GET US HOME.
YOU READY?
ISN'T MASTERMIND DEAD?
THIS WAS A WHILE AGO.
STILL, YOU HAVE TO ADMIRE THE ACHIEVEMENT.
YOU ARE A HORROR.
A LOT MORE PEOPLE HATE YOU THAN HATE ME.

CONTINUED AFTER NEXT PAGE

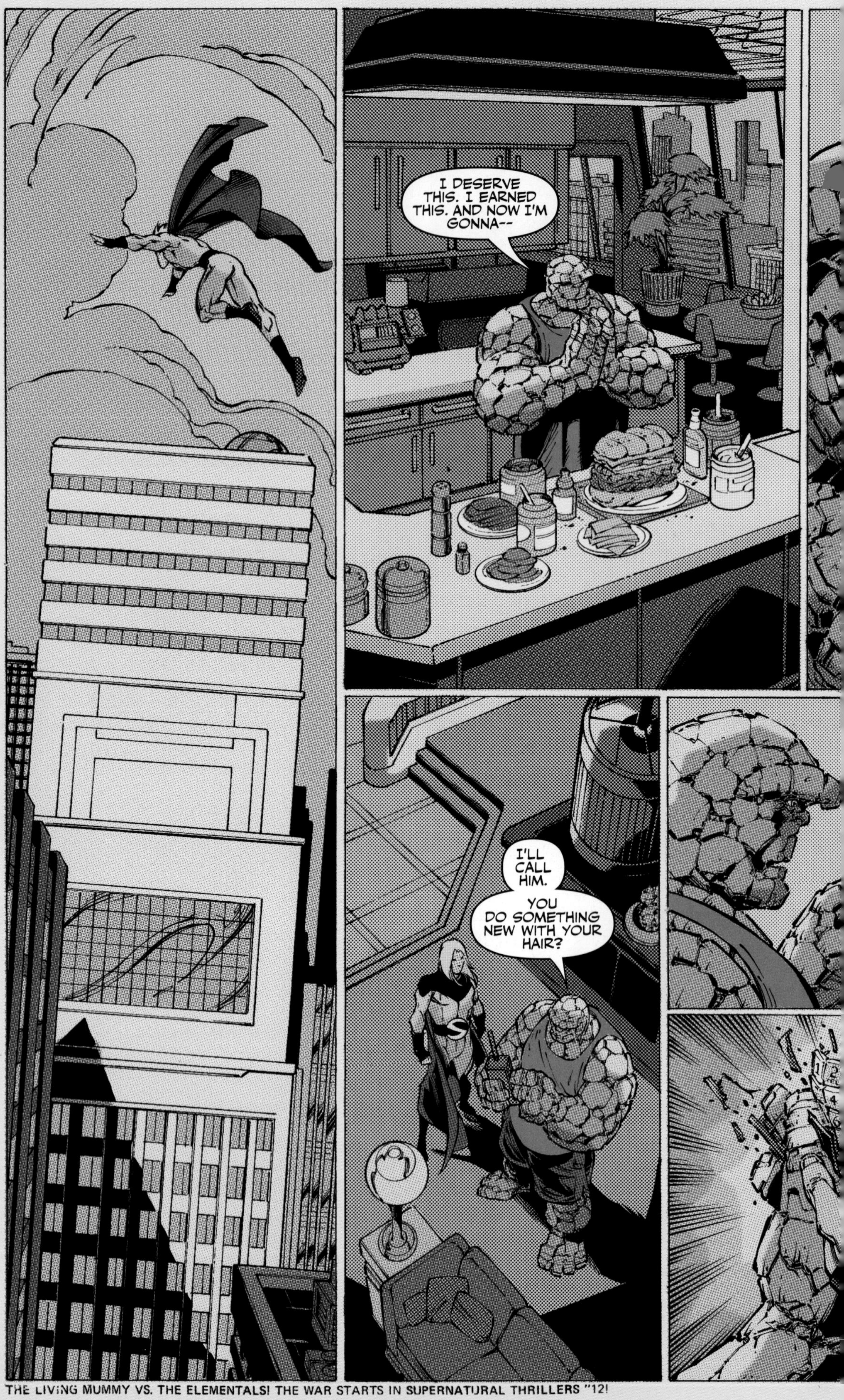
I DESERVE THIS. I EARNED THIS. AND NOW I'M GONNA--
I'LL CALL HIM.
YOU DO SOMETHING NEW WITH YOUR HAIR?

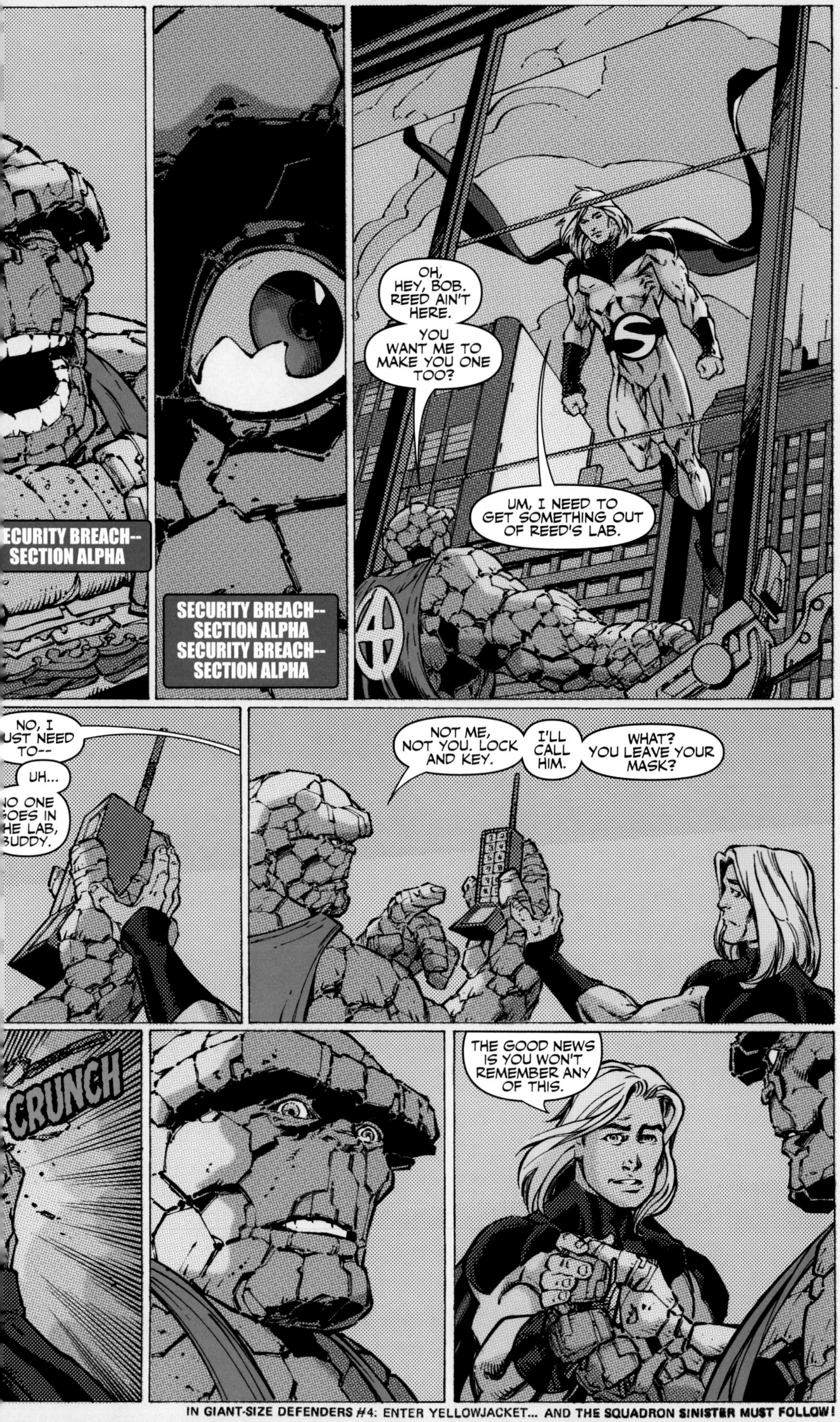
ECURITY BREACH--
SECTION ALPHA
SECURITY BREACH--
SECTION ALPHA
SECURITY BREACH--
SECTION ALPHA
OH, HEY, BOB. REED AIN'T HERE.
YOU WANT ME TO MAKE YOU ONE TOO?
UM, I NEED TO GET SOMETHING OUT OF REED'S LAB.
NO, I UST NEED TO--
UH...
NO ONE GOES IN HE LAB, BUDDY.
WHAT? YOU LEAVE YOUR MASK?
I'LL CALL HIM.
NOT ME, NOT YOU. LOCK AND KEY.
CRUNCH
THE GOOD NEWS IS YOU WON'T REMEMBER ANY OF THIS.

IN GIANT-SIZE DEFENDERS #4: ENTER YELLOWJACKET... AND THE SQUADRON SINISTER MUST FOLLOW!

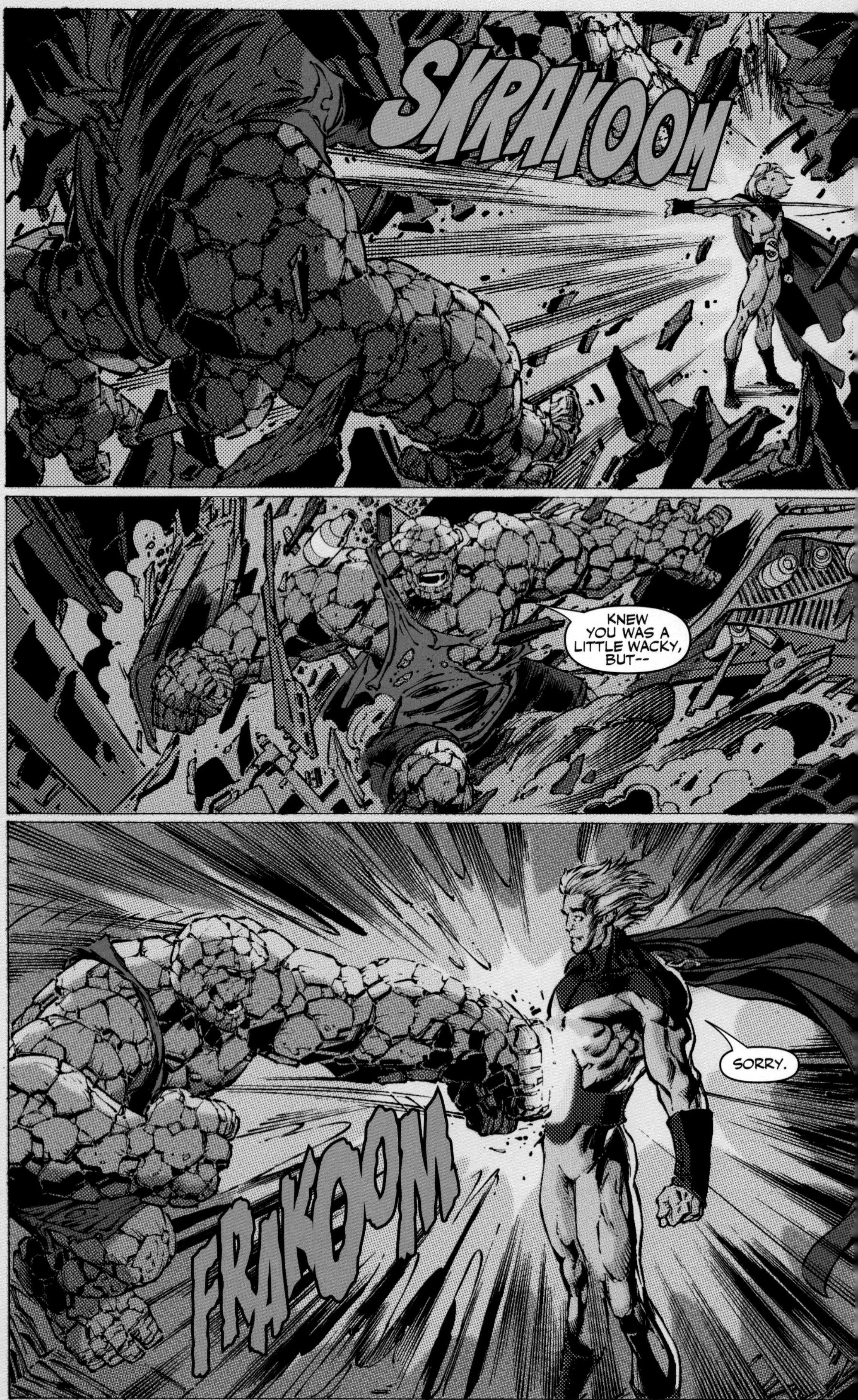
SKRAKOOM
KNEW YOU WAS A LITTLE WACKY, BUT--
SORRY.
FRAKOOM

CONTINUED AFTER NEXT PAG

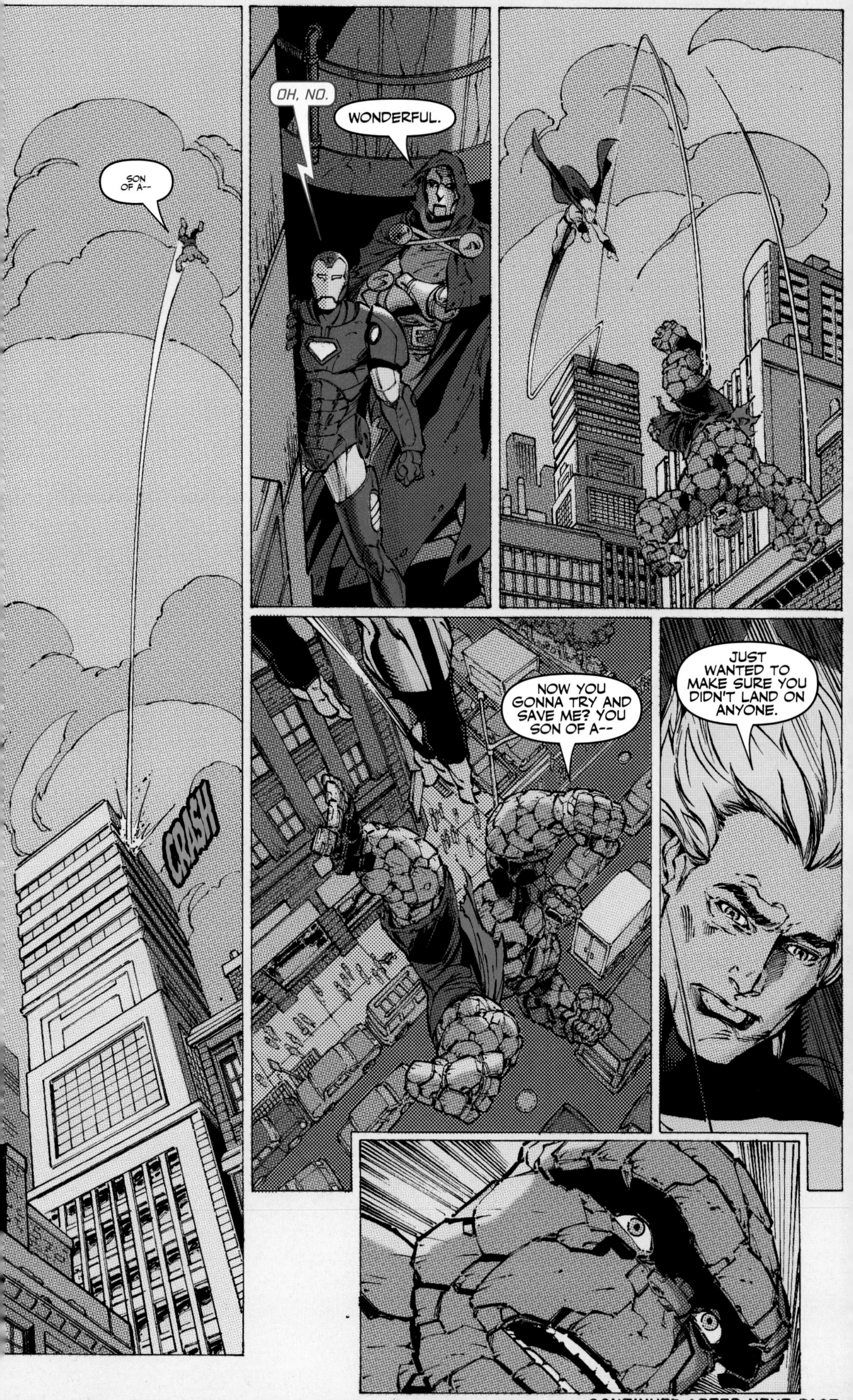
SON OF A--
OH, NO.
WONDERFUL.
NOW YOU GONNA TRY AND SAVE ME? YOU SON OF A--
JUST WANTED TO MAKE SURE YOU DIDN'T LAND ON ANYONE.
CRASH

CONTINUED AFTER NEXT PAGE

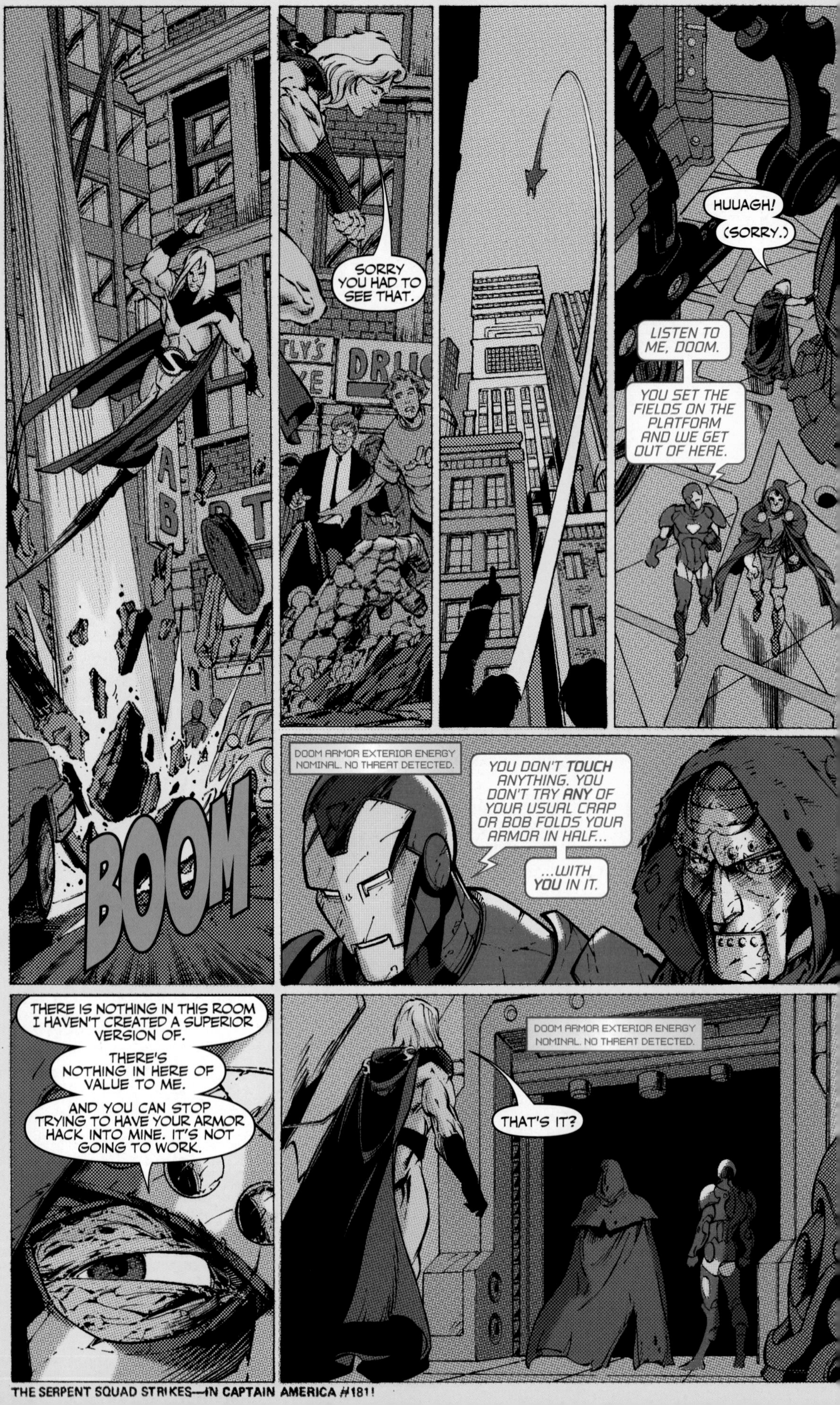

SORRY YOU HAD TO SEE THAT.
HUUAGH! (SORRY.)
LISTEN TO ME, DOOM.
YOU SET THE FIELDS ON THE PLATFORM AND WE GET OUT OF HERE.
BOOM
DOOM ARMOR EXTERIOR ENERGY NOMINAL. NO THREAT DETECTED.
YOU DON'T **TOUCH** ANYTHING. YOU DON'T TRY **ANY** OF YOUR USUAL CRAP OR BOB FOLDS YOUR ARMOR IN HALF...
...WITH **YOU** IN IT.
THERE IS NOTHING IN THIS ROOM I HAVEN'T CREATED A SUPERIOR VERSION OF.
THERE'S NOTHING IN HERE OF VALUE TO ME.
AND YOU CAN STOP TRYING TO HAVE YOUR ARMOR HACK INTO MINE. IT'S NOT GOING TO WORK.
DOOM ARMOR EXTERIOR ENERGY NOMINAL. NO THREAT DETECTED.
THAT'S IT?

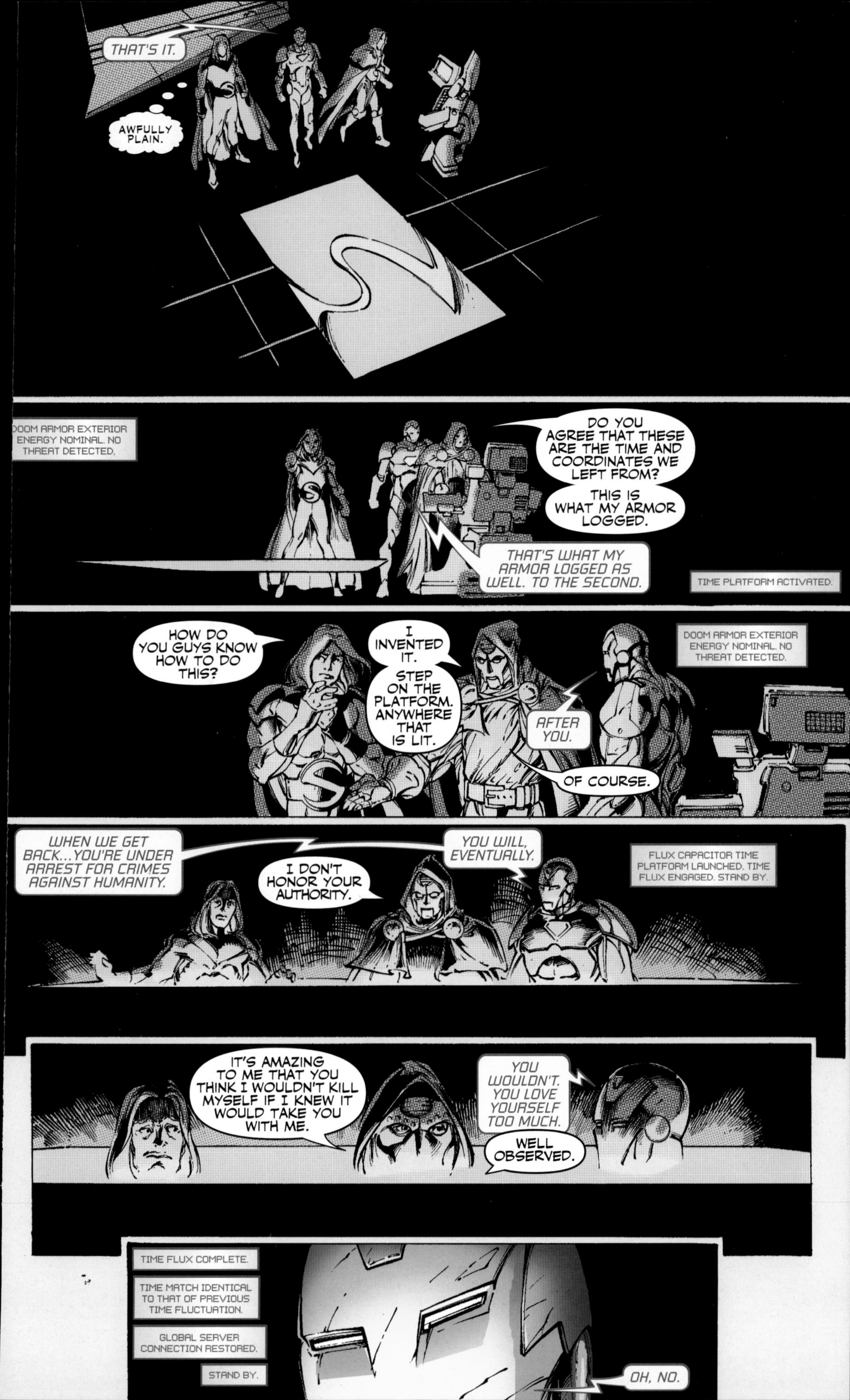

THAT'S IT.
AWFULLY PLAIN.
DOOM ARMOR EXTERIOR ENERGY NOMINAL. NO THREAT DETECTED.
DO YOU AGREE THAT THESE ARE THE TIME AND COORDINATES WE LEFT FROM?
THIS IS WHAT MY ARMOR LOGGED.
THAT'S WHAT MY ARMOR LOGGED AS WELL. TO THE SECOND.
TIME PLATFORM ACTIVATED.
HOW DO YOU GUYS KNOW HOW TO DO THIS?
I INVENTED IT.
STEP ON THE PLATFORM. ANYWHERE THAT IS LIT.
DOOM ARMOR EXTERIOR ENERGY NOMINAL. NO THREAT DETECTED.
AFTER YOU.
OF COURSE.
WHEN WE GET BACK...YOU'RE UNDER ARREST FOR CRIMES AGAINST HUMANITY.
I DON'T HONOR YOUR AUTHORITY.
YOU WILL, EVENTUALLY.
FLUX CAPACITOR TIME PLATFORM LAUNCHED. TIME FLUX ENGAGED. STAND BY.
IT'S AMAZING TO ME THAT YOU THINK I WOULDN'T KILL MYSELF IF I KNEW IT WOULD TAKE YOU WITH ME.
YOU WOULDN'T. YOU LOVE YOURSELF TOO MUCH.
WELL OBSERVED.
TIME FLUX COMPLETE.
TIME MATCH IDENTICAL TO THAT OF PREVIOUS TIME FLUCTUATION.
GLOBAL SERVER CONNECTION RESTORED.
STAND BY.
OH, NO.

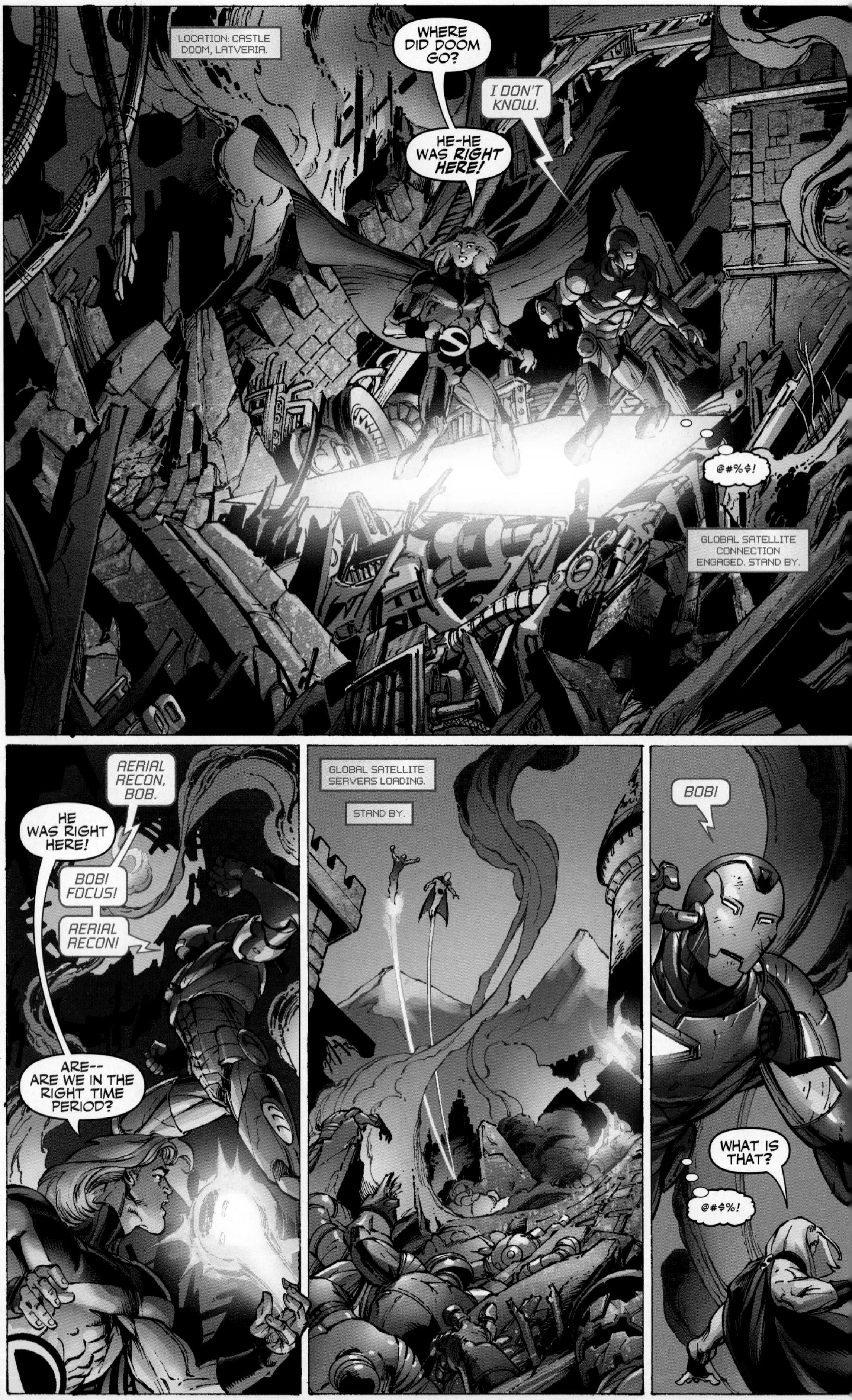

LOCATION: CASTLE DOOM, LATVERIA.
WHERE DID DOOM GO?
HE-HE WAS RIGHT HERE!
I DON'T KNOW.
@#%$!
GLOBAL SATELLITE CONNECTION ENGAGED. STAND BY.
AERIAL RECON, BOB.
HE WAS RIGHT HERE!
BOB! FOCUS!
AERIAL RECON!
ARE-- ARE WE IN THE RIGHT TIME PERIOD?
GLOBAL SATELLITE SERVERS LOADING.
STAND BY.
BOB!
WHAT IS THAT?
@#$%!

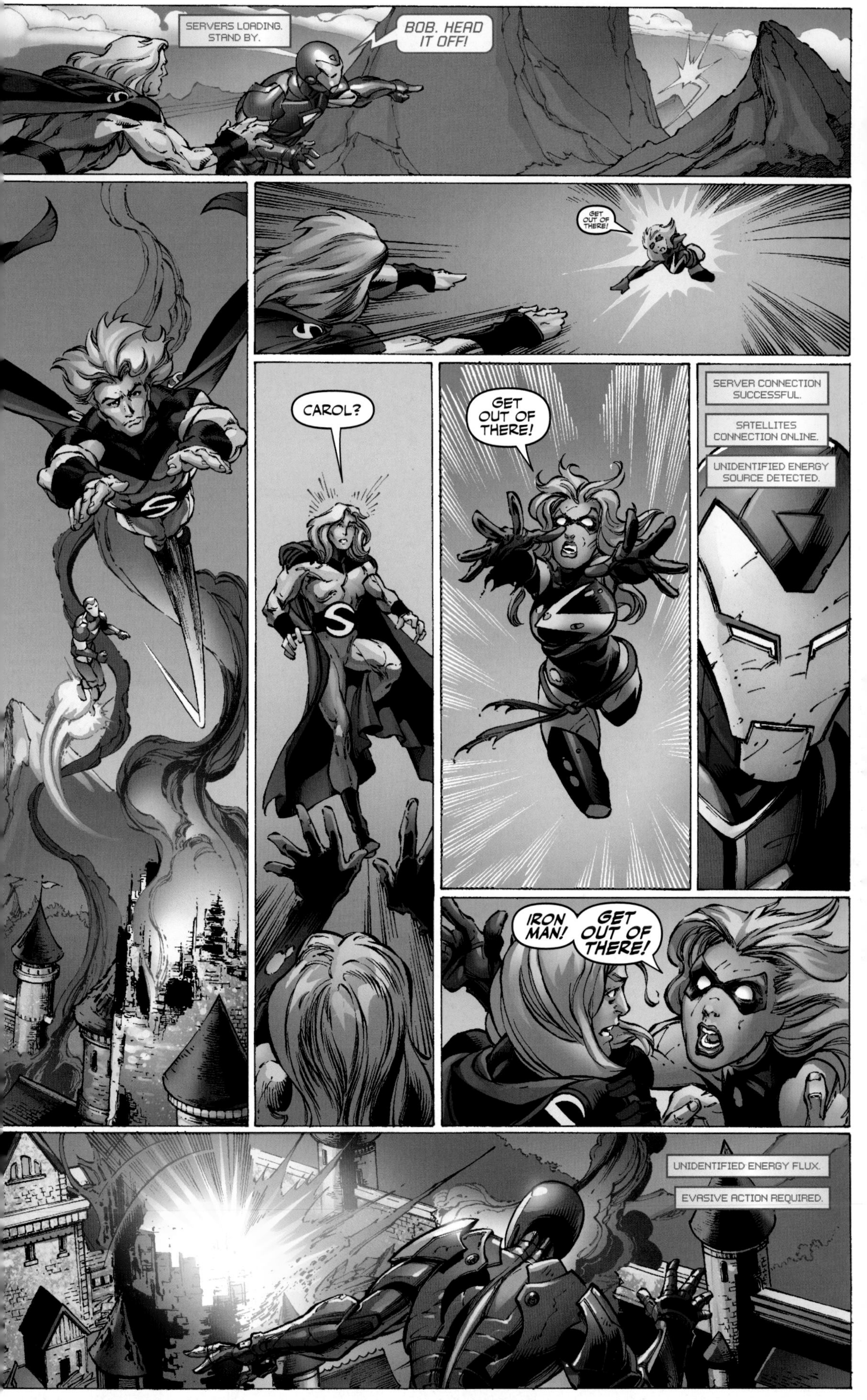
SERVERS LOADING. STAND BY.
BOB. HEAD IT OFF!
GET OUT OF THERE!
CAROL?
GET OUT OF THERE!
SERVER CONNECTION SUCCESSFUL.
SATELLITES CONNECTION ONLINE.
UNIDENTIFIED ENERGY SOURCE DETECTED.
IRON MAN!
GET OUT OF THERE!
UNIDENTIFIED ENERGY FLUX.
EVASIVE ACTION REQUIRED.

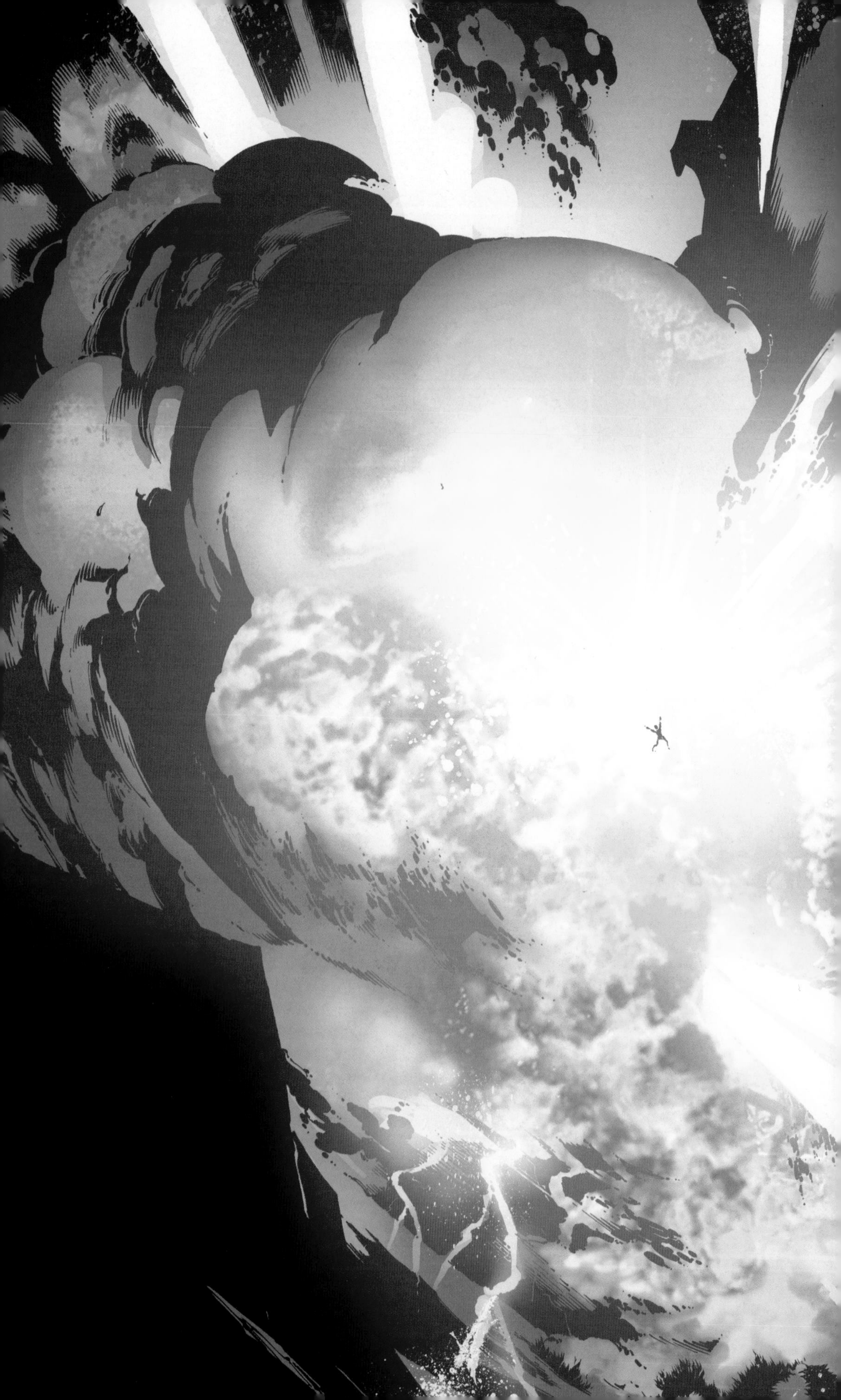

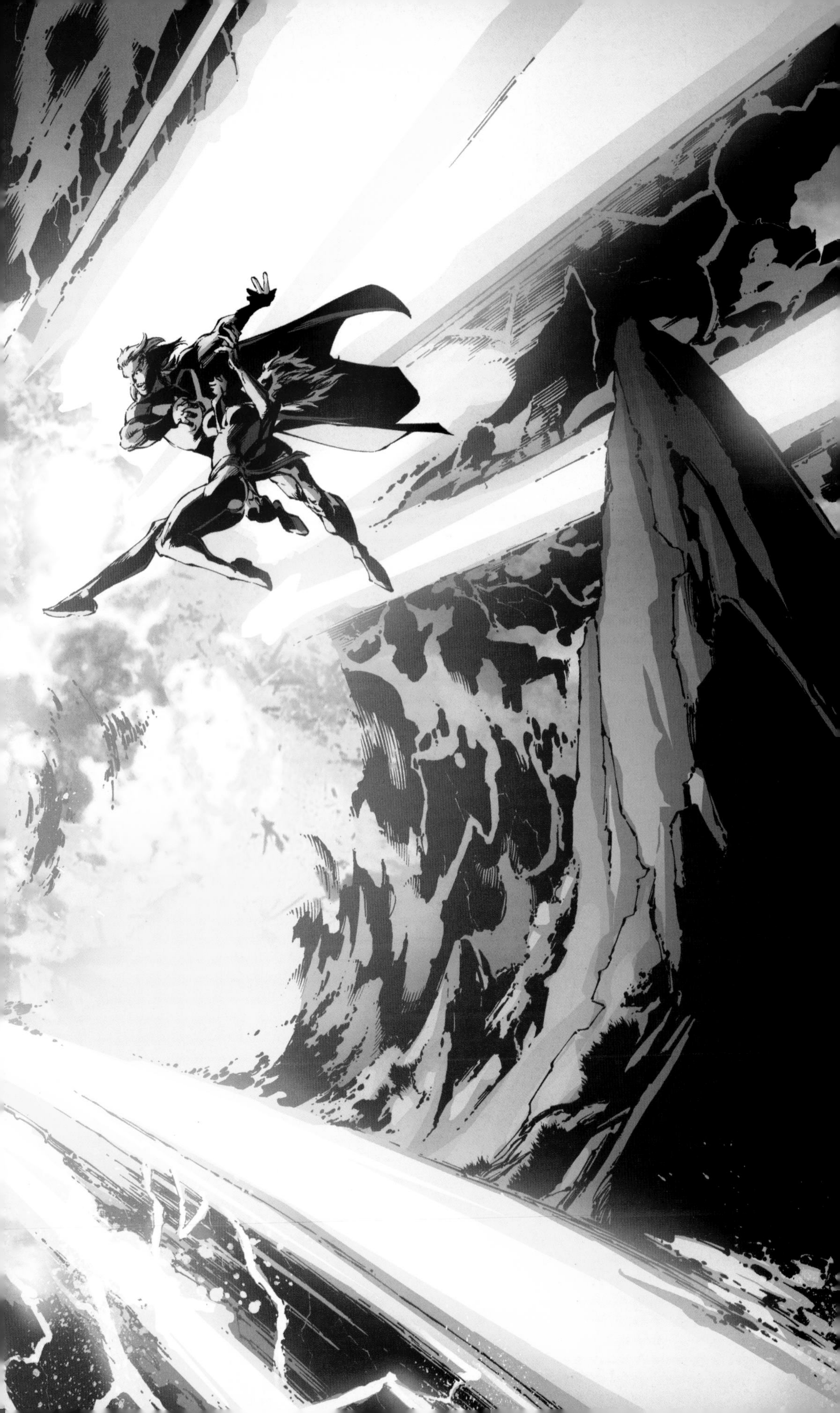

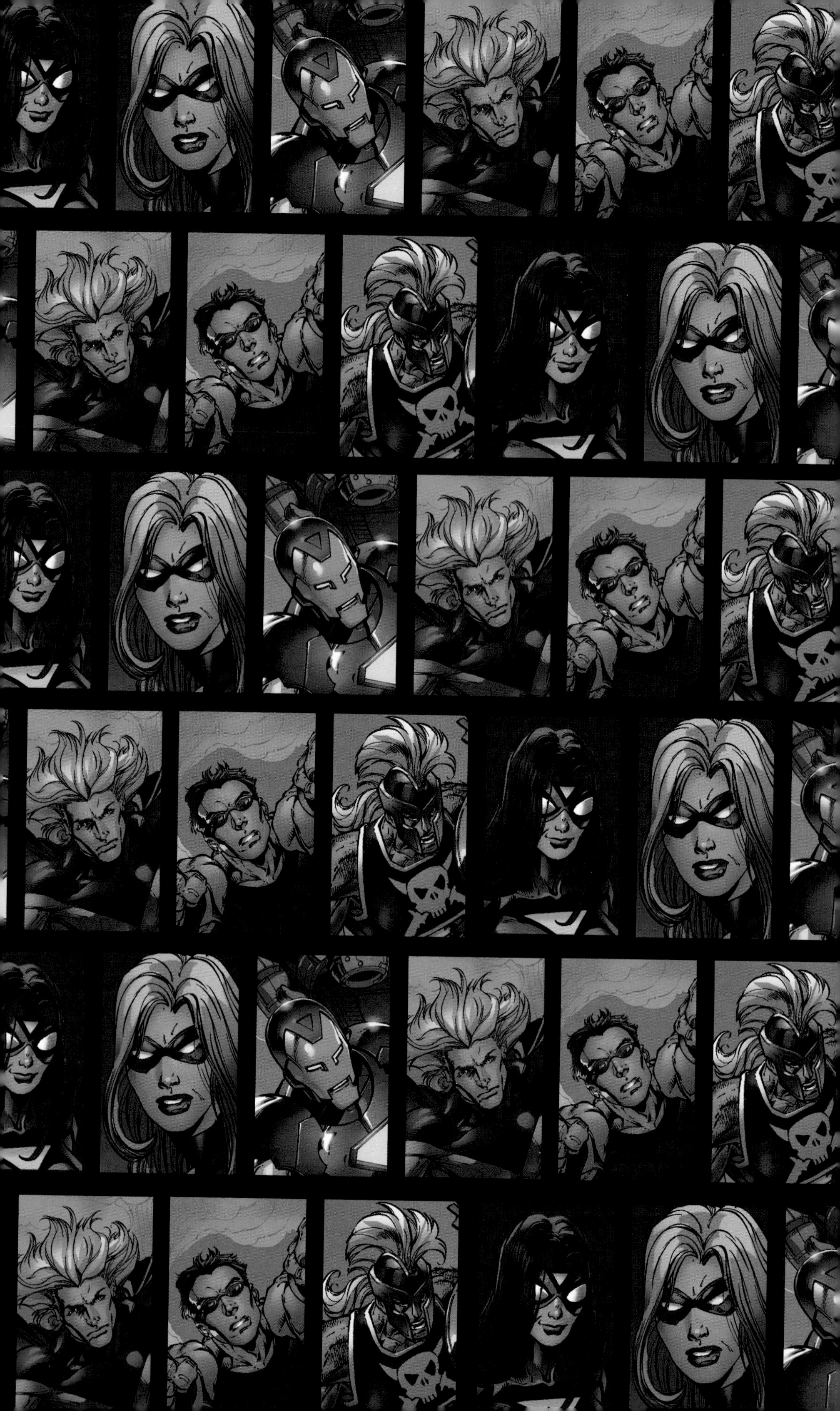

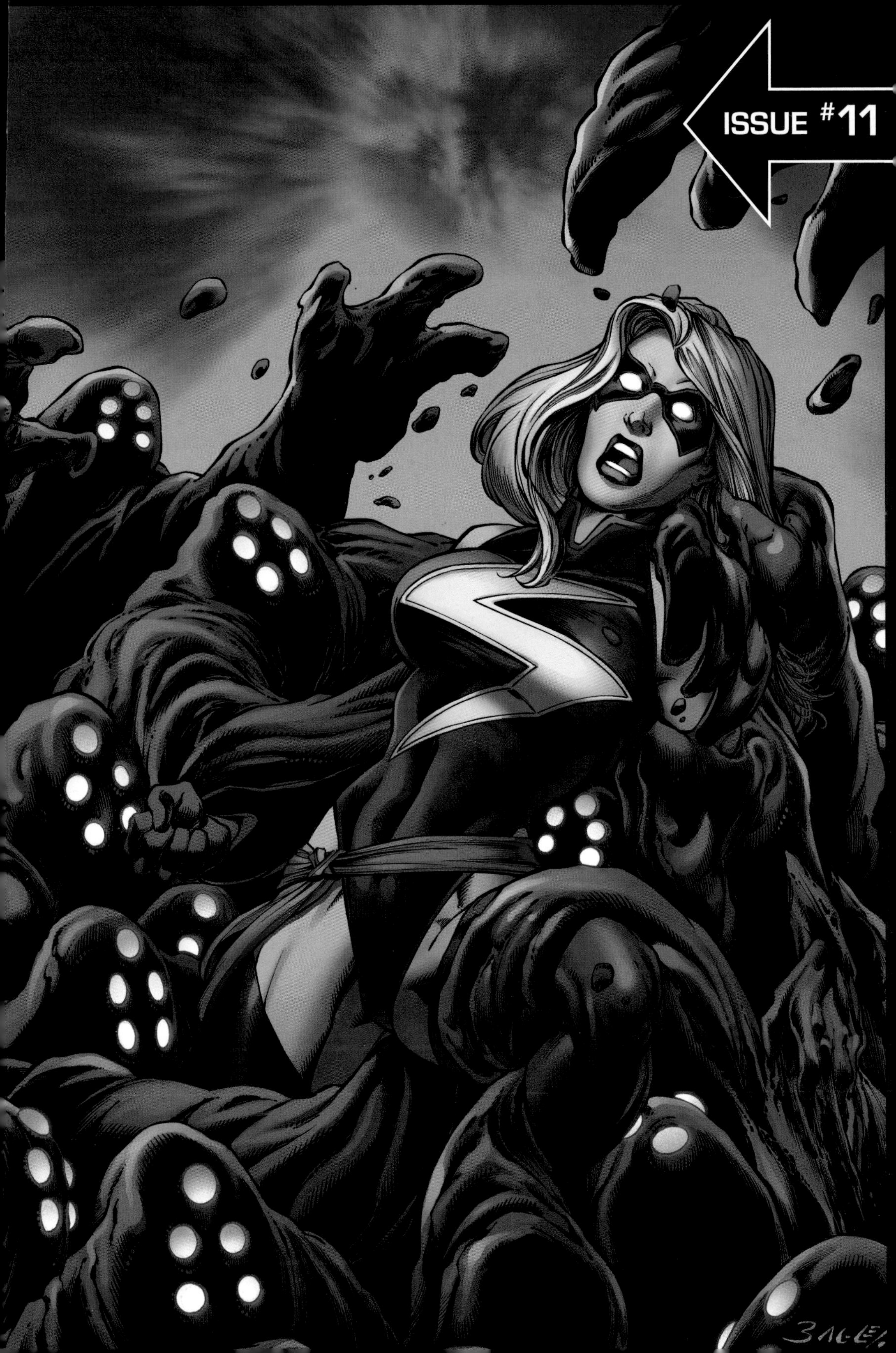
ISSUE #11

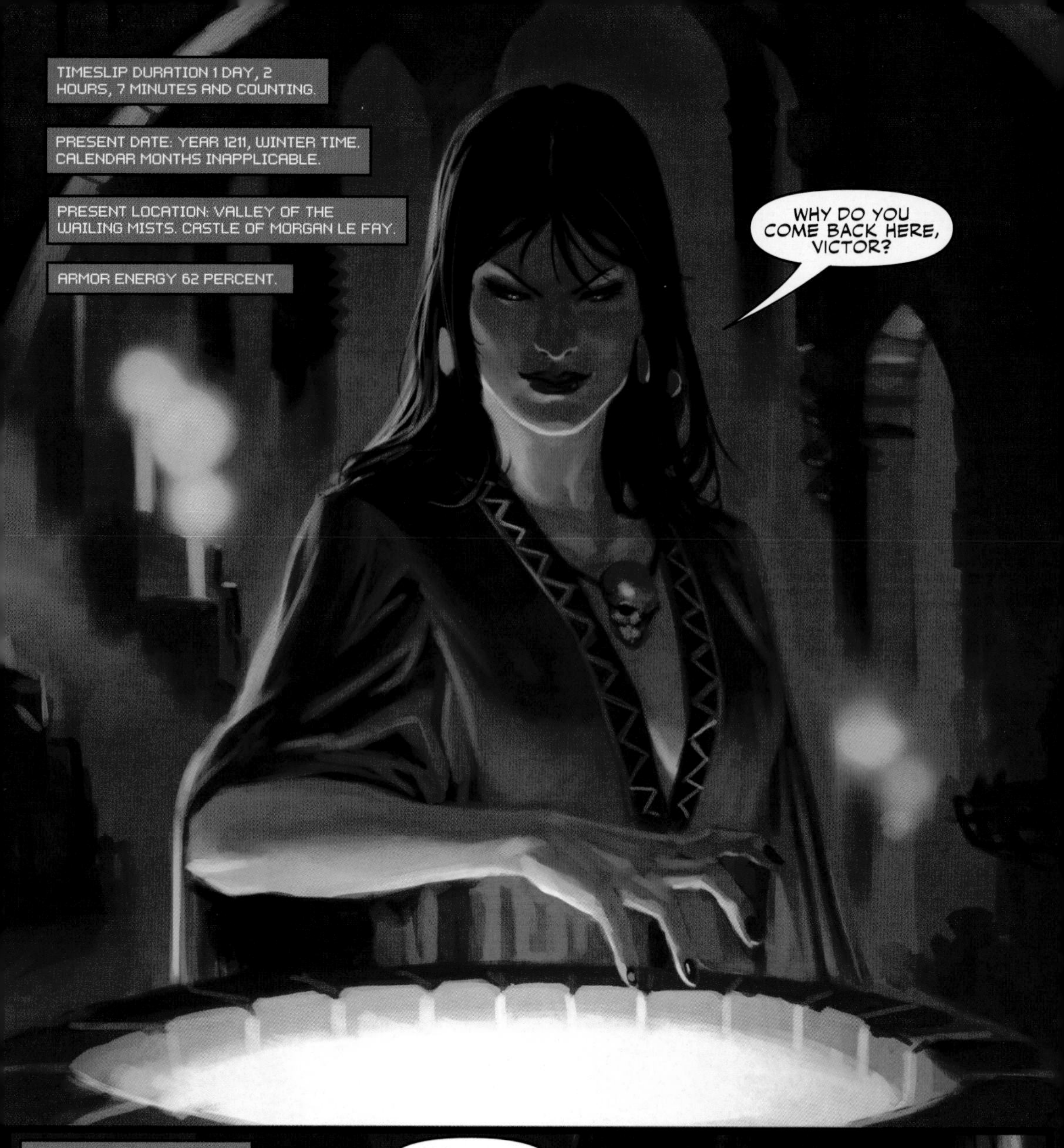
TIMESLIP DURATION 1 DAY, 2 HOURS, 7 MINUTES AND COUNTING.
PRESENT DATE: YEAR 1211, WINTER TIME. CALENDAR MONTHS INAPPLICABLE.
PRESENT LOCATION: VALLEY OF THE WAILING MISTS. CASTLE OF MORGAN LE FAY.
ARMOR ENERGY 62 PERCENT.
WHY DO YOU COME BACK HERE, VICTOR?

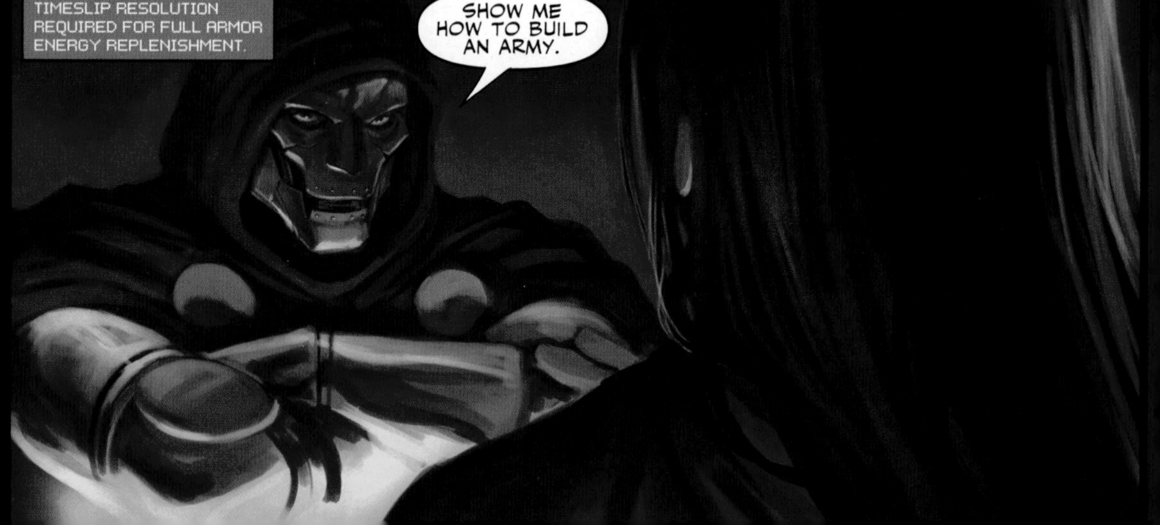
TIMESLIP RESOLUTION REQUIRED FOR FULL ARMOR ENERGY REPLENISHMENT.
SHOW ME HOW TO BUILD AN ARMY.

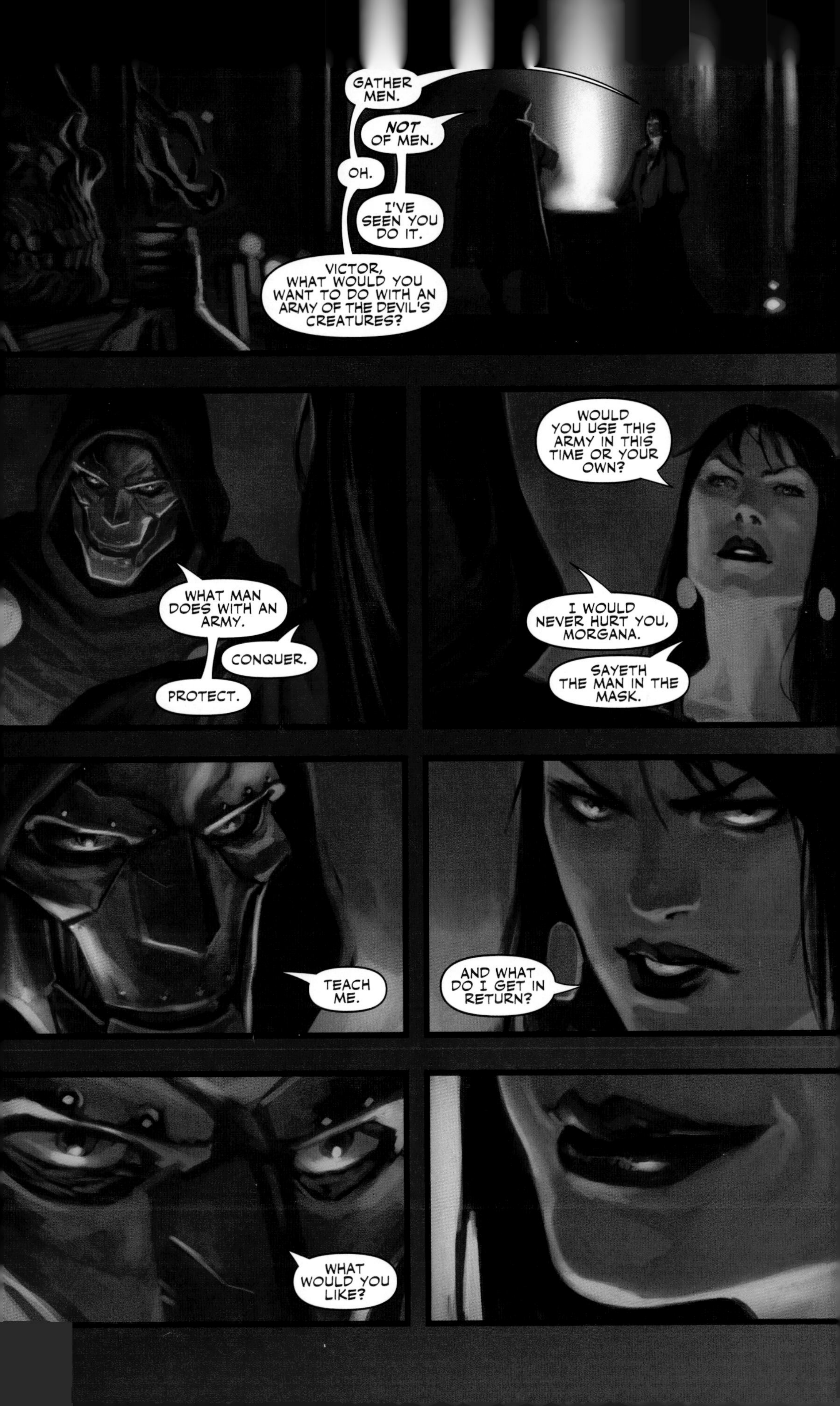
GATHER MEN.
NOT OF MEN.
OH.
I'VE SEEN YOU DO IT.
VICTOR, WHAT WOULD YOU WANT TO DO WITH AN ARMY OF THE DEVIL'S CREATURES?
WHAT MAN DOES WITH AN ARMY.
CONQUER.
PROTECT.
WOULD YOU USE THIS ARMY IN THIS TIME OR YOUR OWN?
I WOULD NEVER HURT YOU, MORGANA.
SAYETH THE MAN IN THE MASK.
TEACH ME.
AND WHAT DO I GET IN RETURN?
WHAT WOULD YOU LIKE?

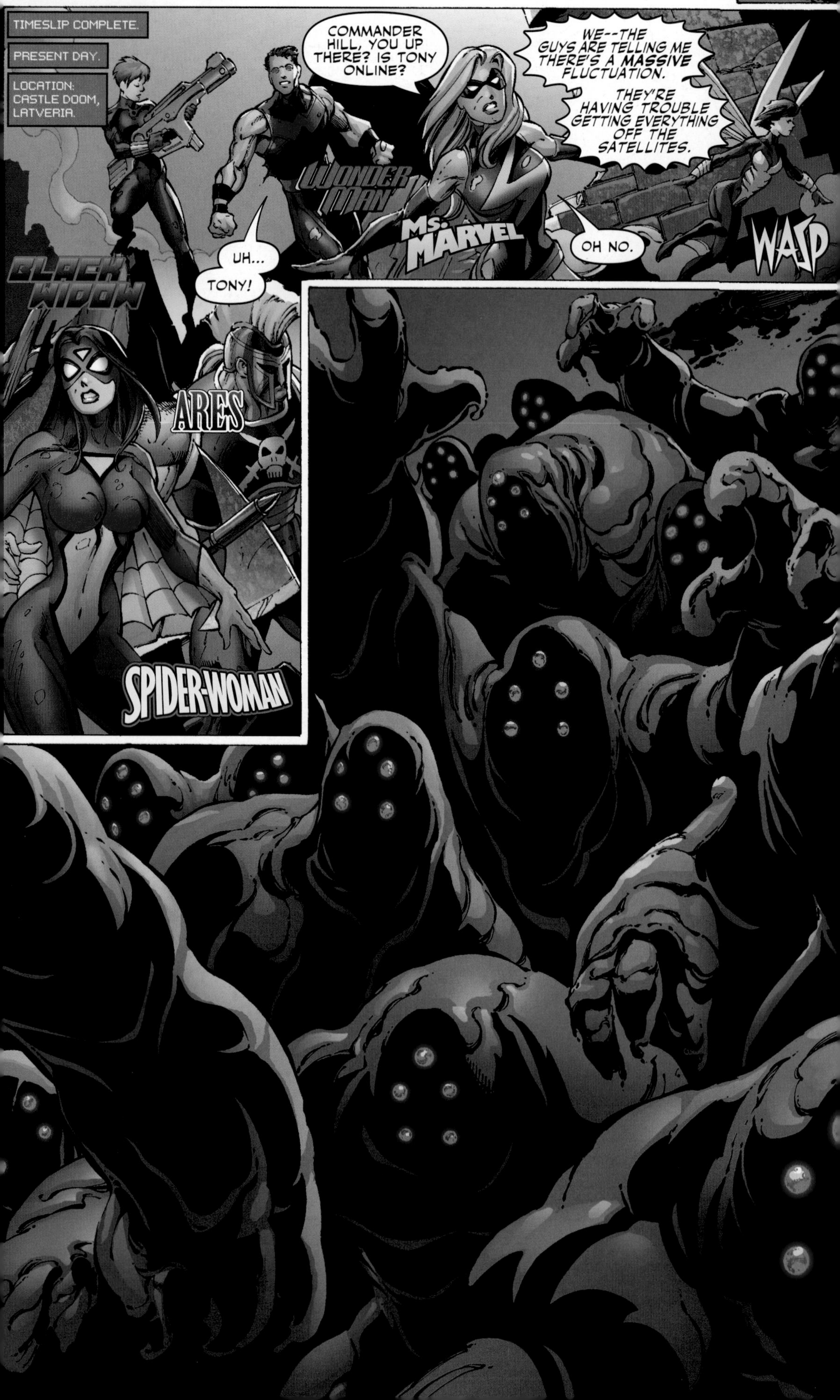

TIMESLIP COMPLETE.
PRESENT DAY.
LOCATION: CASTLE DOOM, LATVERIA.
COMMANDER HILL, YOU UP THERE? IS TONY ONLINE?
WE--THE GUYS ARE TELLING ME THERE'S A MASSIVE FLUCTUATION.
THEY'RE HAVING TROUBLE GETTING EVERYTHING OFF THE SATELLITES.
WONDER MAN
MS. MARVEL
WASP
BLACK WIDOW
UH... TONY!
OH NO.
ARES
SPIDER-WOMAN

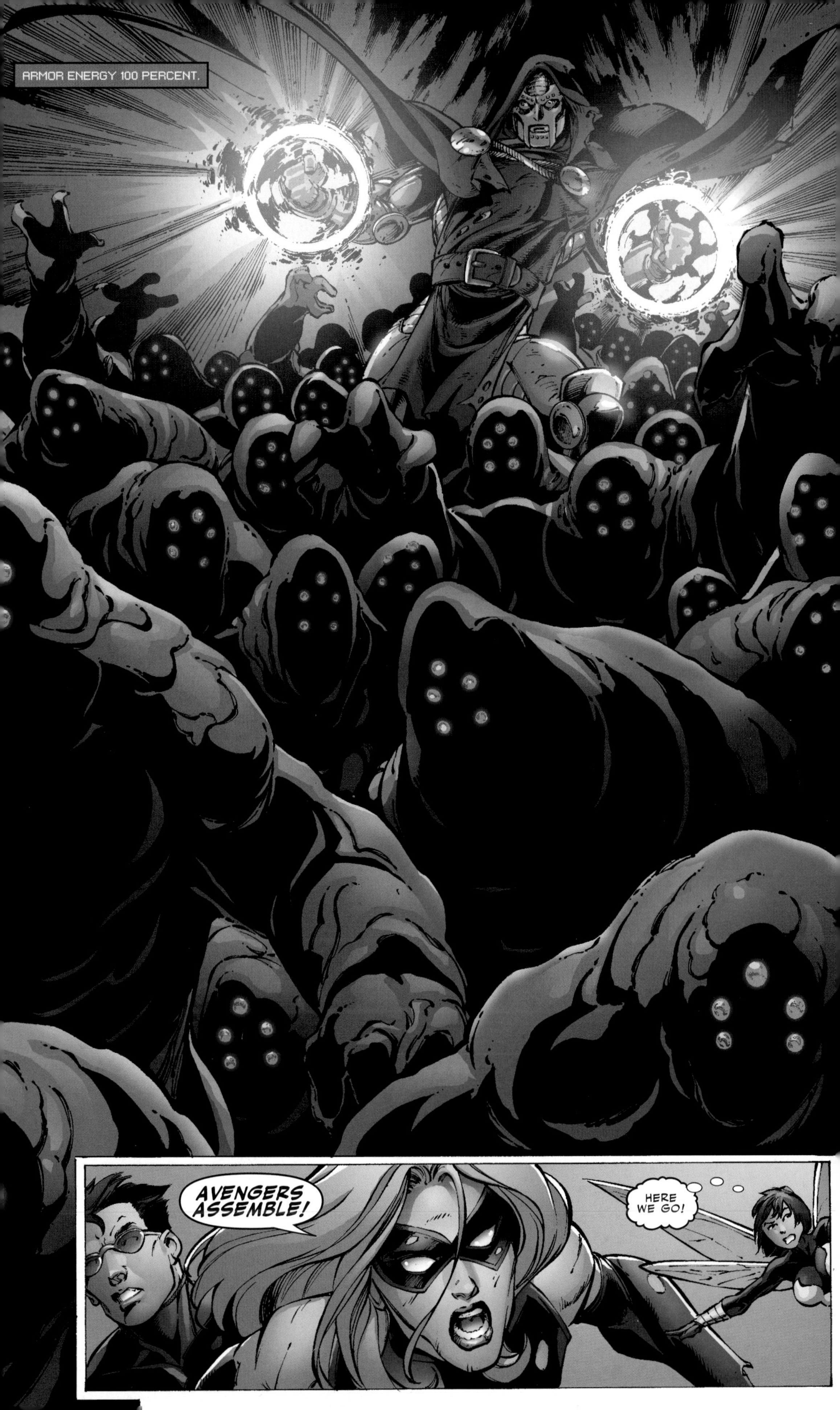
ARMOR ENERGY 100 PERCENT.
AVENGERS ASSEMBLE!
HERE WE GO!

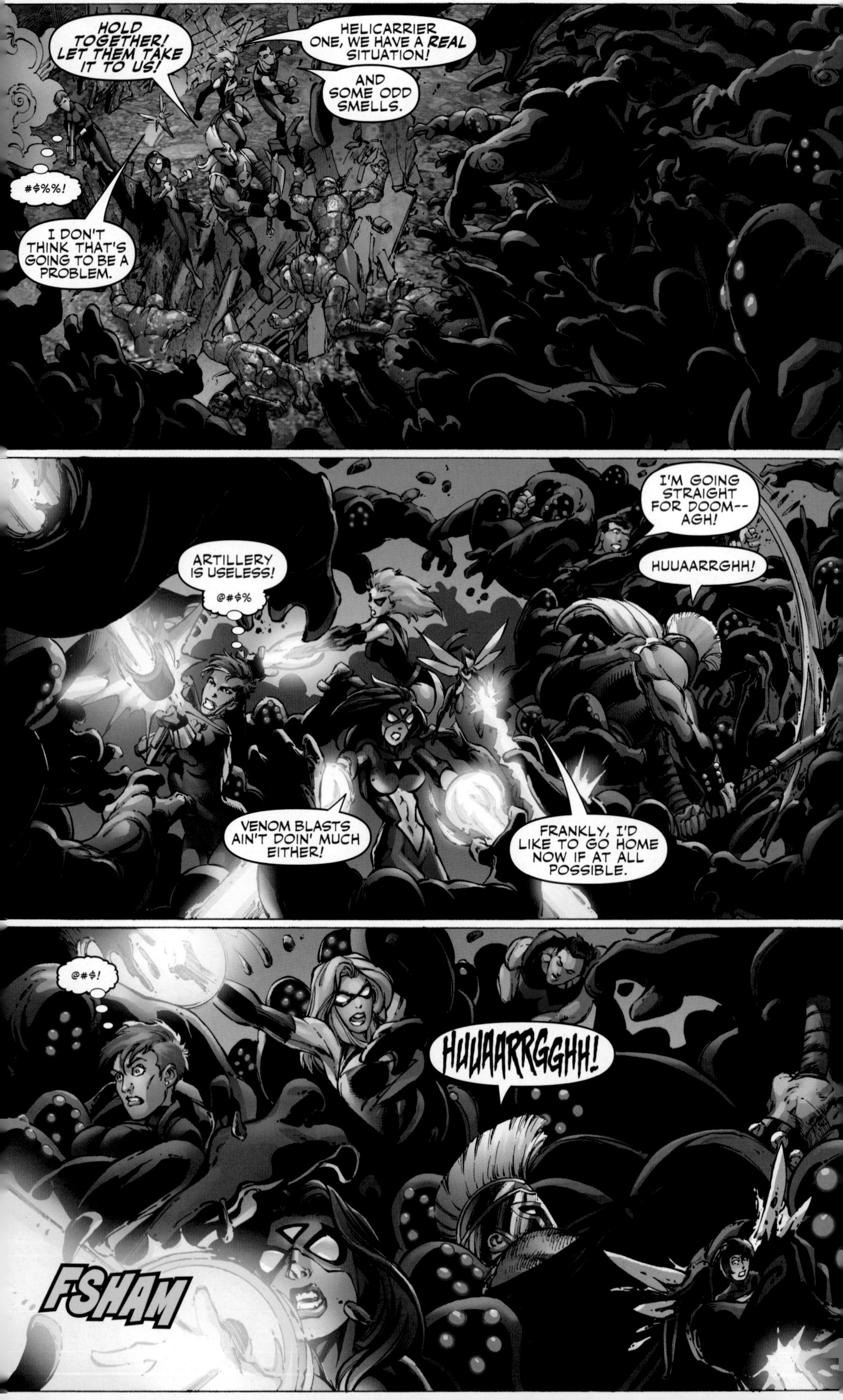

HOLD TOGETHER! LET THEM TAKE IT TO US!
HELICARRIER ONE, WE HAVE A REAL SITUATION!
AND SOME ODD SMELLS.
#$%%!
I DON'T THINK THAT'S GOING TO BE A PROBLEM.
I'M GOING STRAIGHT FOR DOOM--AGH!
ARTILLERY IS USELESS!
@#$%
HUUAARRGHH!
VENOM BLASTS AIN'T DOIN' MUCH EITHER!
FRANKLY, I'D LIKE TO GO HOME NOW IF AT ALL POSSIBLE.
@#$!
HUUAARRGGHH!
FSHAM

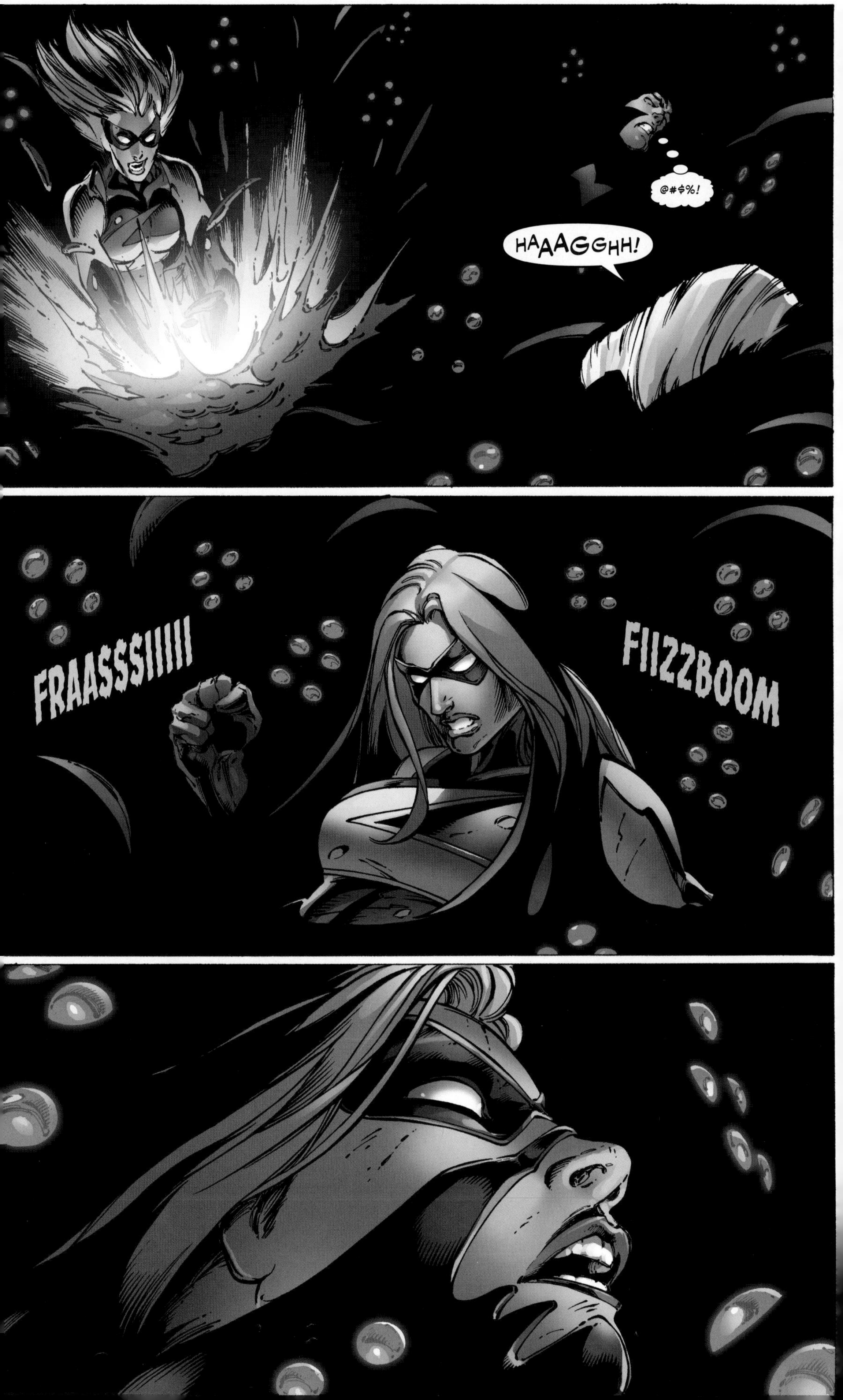
@#$%!
HAAAGGHH!
FRAASSSIIIIII
FIIZZBOOM

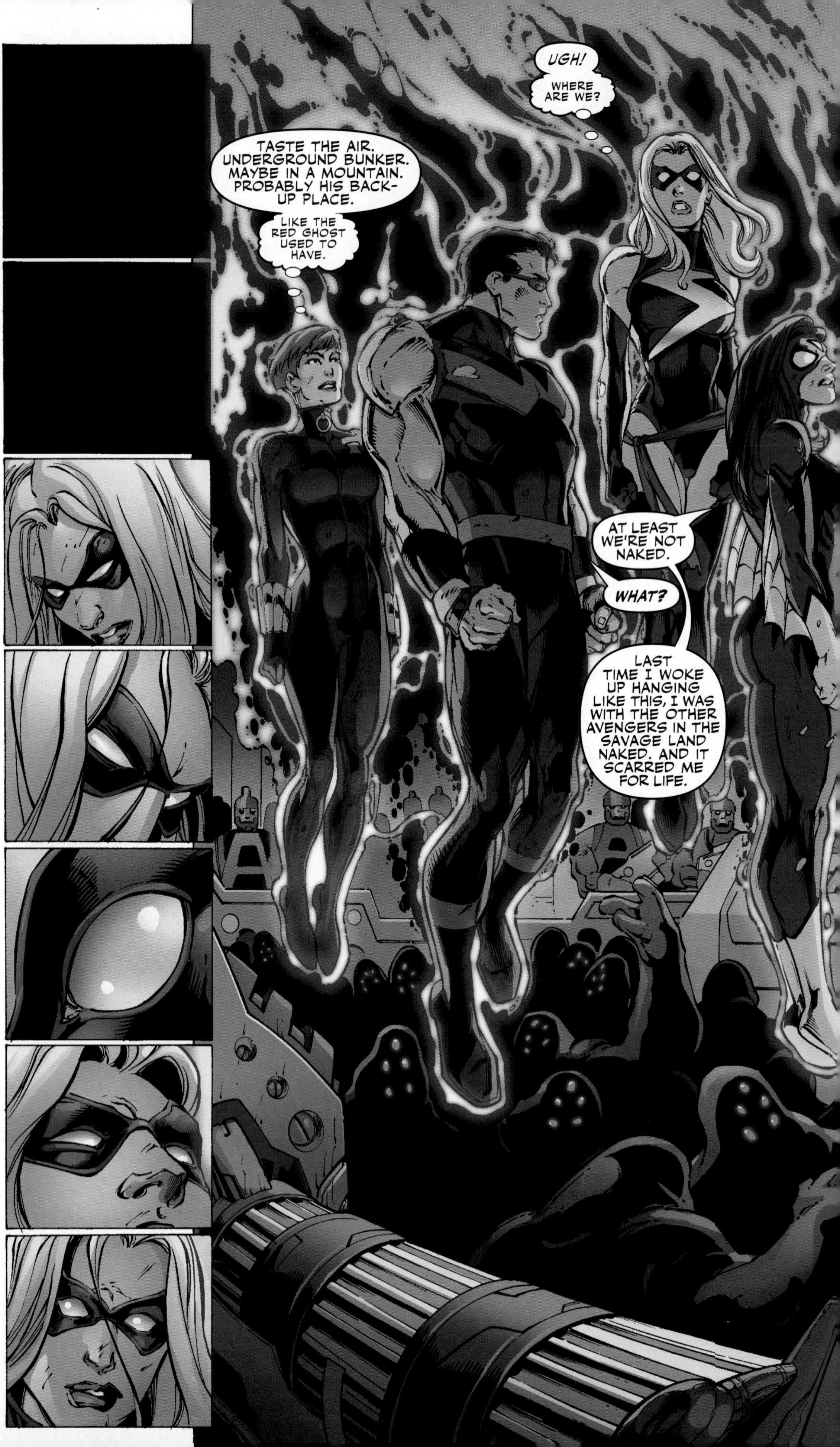
UGH!
WHERE ARE WE?
TASTE THE AIR. UNDERGROUND BUNKER. MAYBE IN A MOUNTAIN. PROBABLY HIS BACK-UP PLACE.
LIKE THE RED GHOST USED TO HAVE.
AT LEAST WE'RE NOT NAKED.
WHAT?
LAST TIME I WOKE UP HANGING LIKE THIS, I WAS WITH THE OTHER AVENGERS IN THE SAVAGE LAND NAKED. AND IT SCARRED ME FOR LIFE.

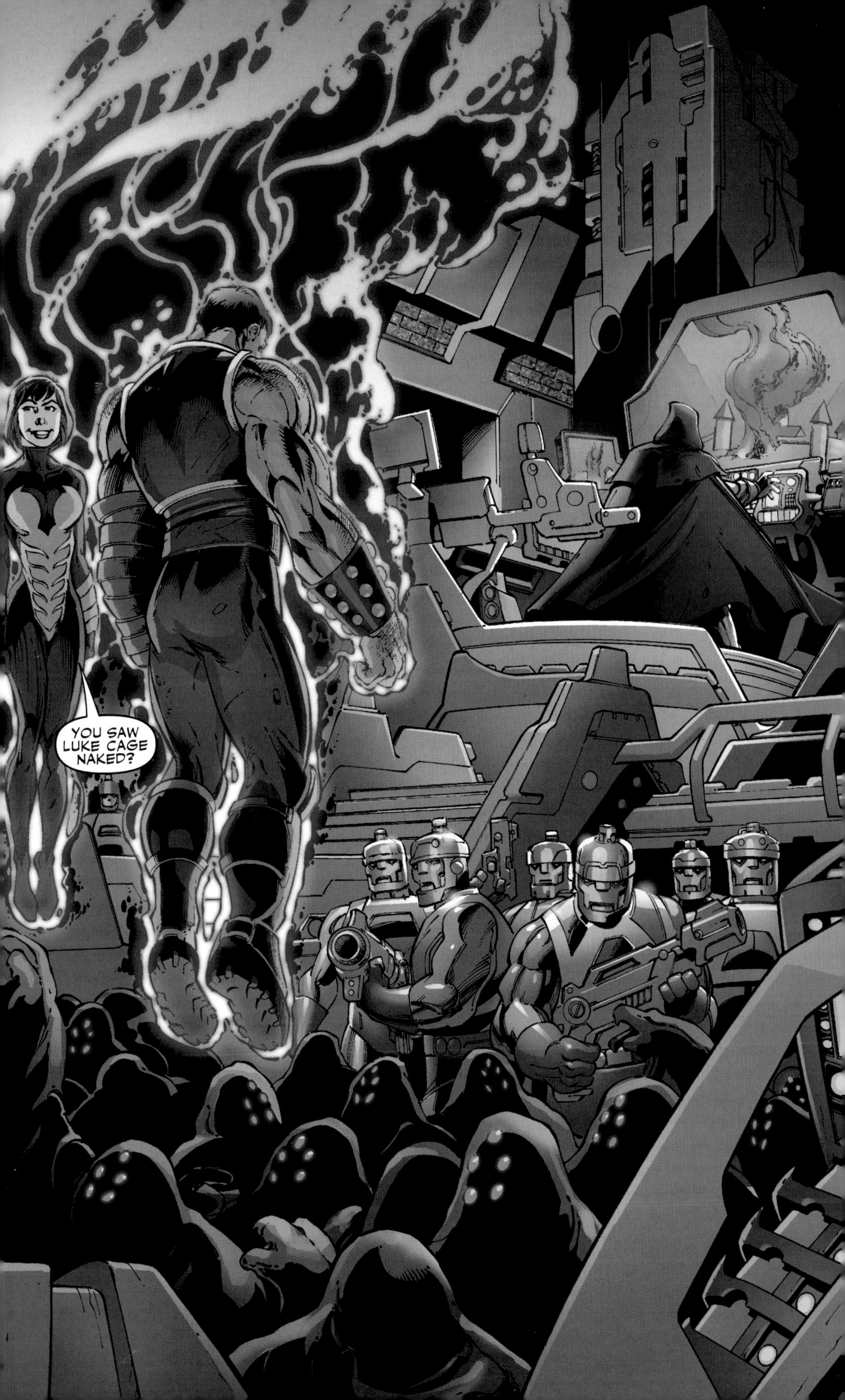
YOU SAW LUKE CAGE NAKED?

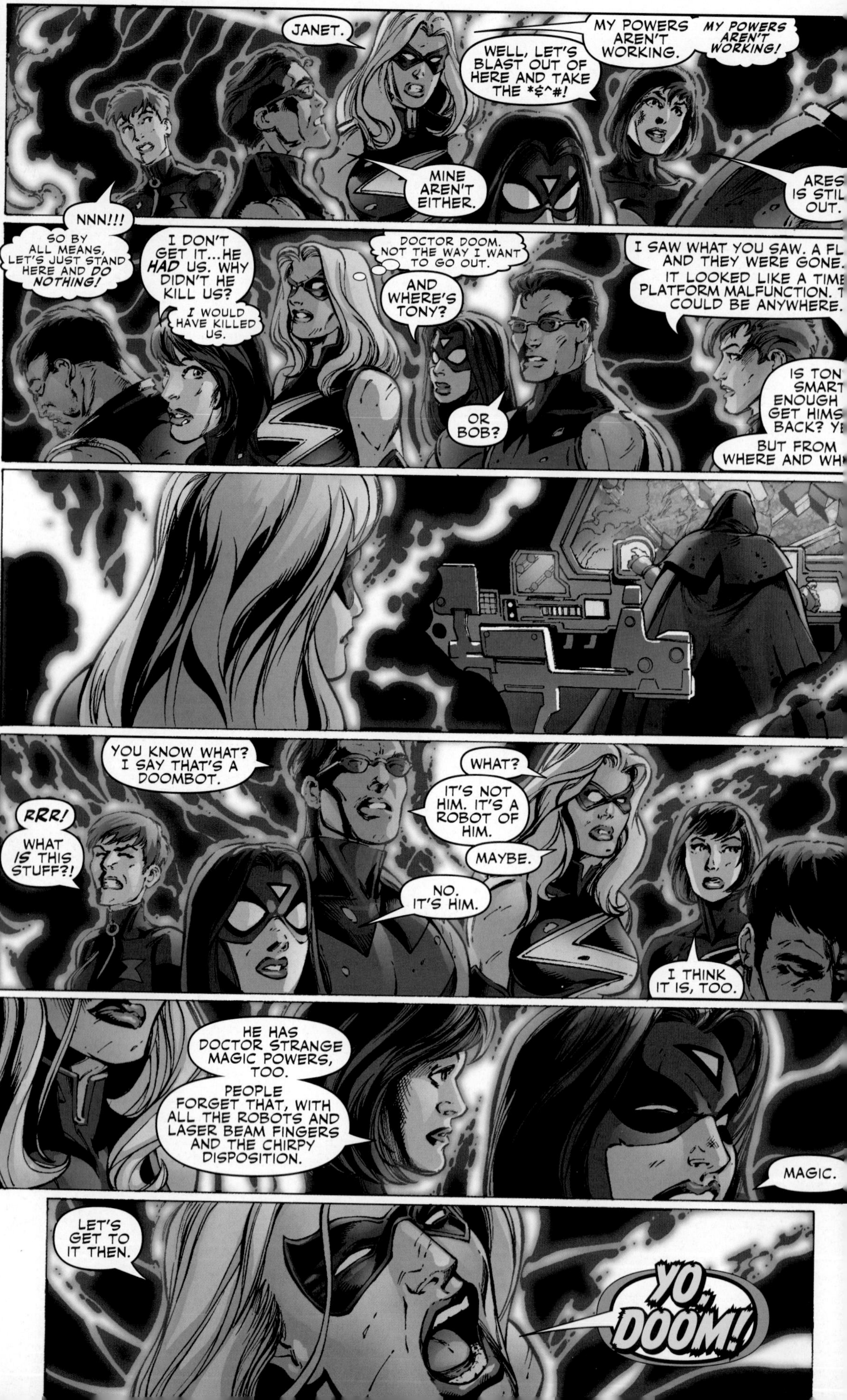

JANET.
WELL, LET'S BLAST OUT OF HERE AND TAKE THE *$^#!
MY POWERS AREN'T WORKING.
MY POWERS AREN'T WORKING!
MINE AREN'T EITHER.
ARES IS STIL OUT.
NNN!!!
SO BY ALL MEANS, LET'S JUST STAND HERE AND DO NOTHING!
I DON'T GET IT...HE HAD US. WHY DIDN'T HE KILL US?
I WOULD HAVE KILLED US.
DOCTOR DOOM. NOT THE WAY I WANT TO GO OUT.
AND WHERE'S TONY?
OR BOB?
I SAW WHAT YOU SAW. A FL AND THEY WERE GONE. IT LOOKED LIKE A TIME PLATFORM MALFUNCTION. T COULD BE ANYWHERE.
IS TON SMART ENOUGH GET HIMS BACK? YE
BUT FROM WHERE AND WH
YOU KNOW WHAT? I SAY THAT'S A DOOMBOT.
WHAT?
IT'S NOT HIM. IT'S A ROBOT OF HIM.
MAYBE.
RRR!
WHAT IS THIS STUFF?!
NO. IT'S HIM.
I THINK IT IS, TOO.
HE HAS DOCTOR STRANGE MAGIC POWERS, TOO.
PEOPLE FORGET THAT, WITH ALL THE ROBOTS AND LASER BEAM FINGERS AND THE CHIRPY DISPOSITION.
MAGIC.
LET'S GET TO IT THEN.
YO, DOOM!

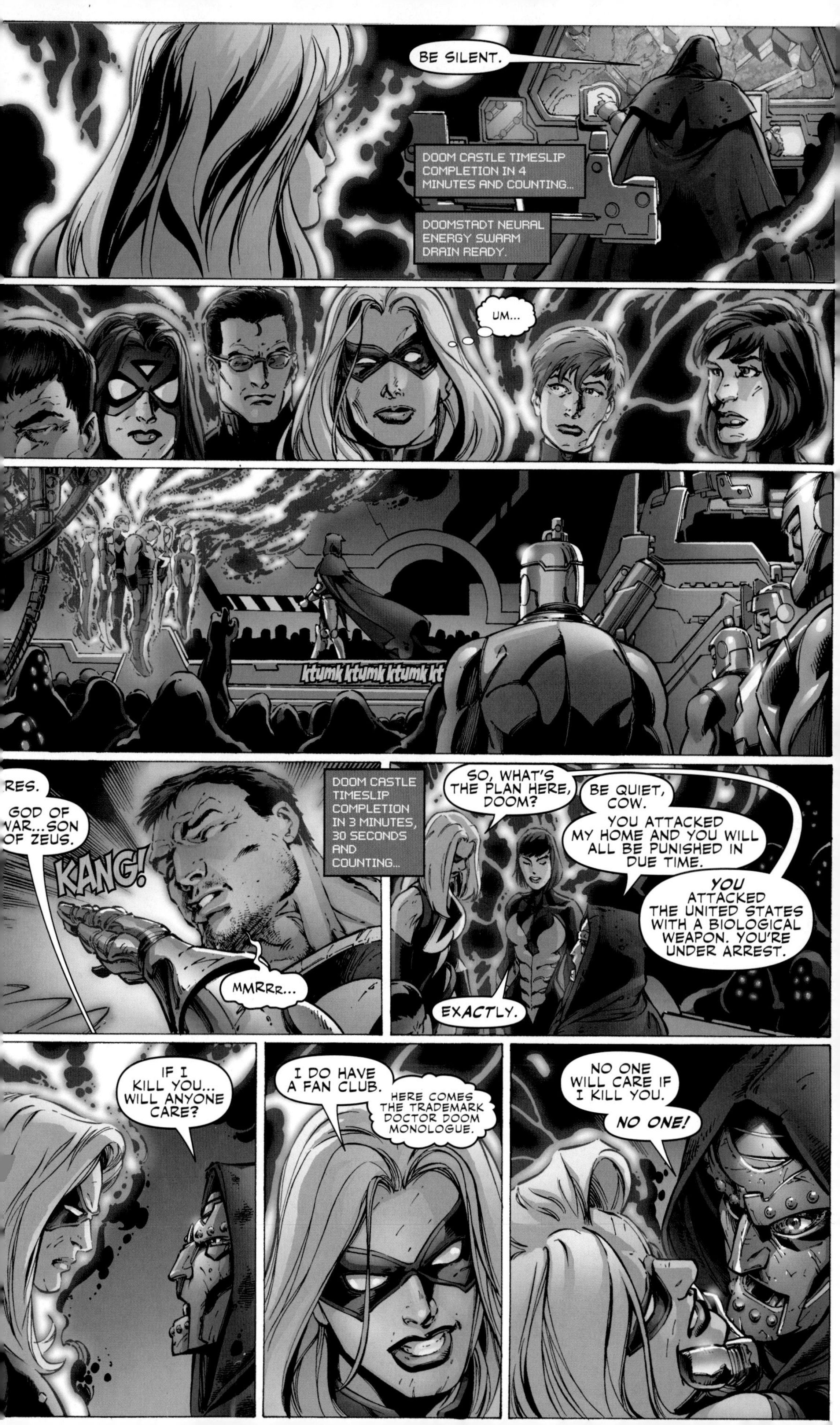
BE SILENT.
DOOM CASTLE TIMESLIP COMPLETION IN 4 MINUTES AND COUNTING...
DOOMSTADT NEURAL ENERGY SWARM DRAIN READY.
UM...
ktumk ktumk ktumk kt
RES.
GOD OF WAR...SON OF ZEUS.
KANG!
MMRRR...
DOOM CASTLE TIMESLIP COMPLETION IN 3 MINUTES, 30 SECONDS AND COUNTING...
SO, WHAT'S THE PLAN HERE, DOOM?
BE QUIET, COW.
YOU ATTACKED MY HOME AND YOU WILL ALL BE PUNISHED IN DUE TIME.
YOU ATTACKED THE UNITED STATES WITH A BIOLOGICAL WEAPON. YOU'RE UNDER ARREST.
EXACTLY.
IF I KILL YOU... WILL ANYONE CARE?
I DO HAVE A FAN CLUB.
HERE COMES THE TRADEMARK DOCTOR DOOM MONOLOGUE.
NO ONE WILL CARE IF I KILL YOU.
NO ONE!

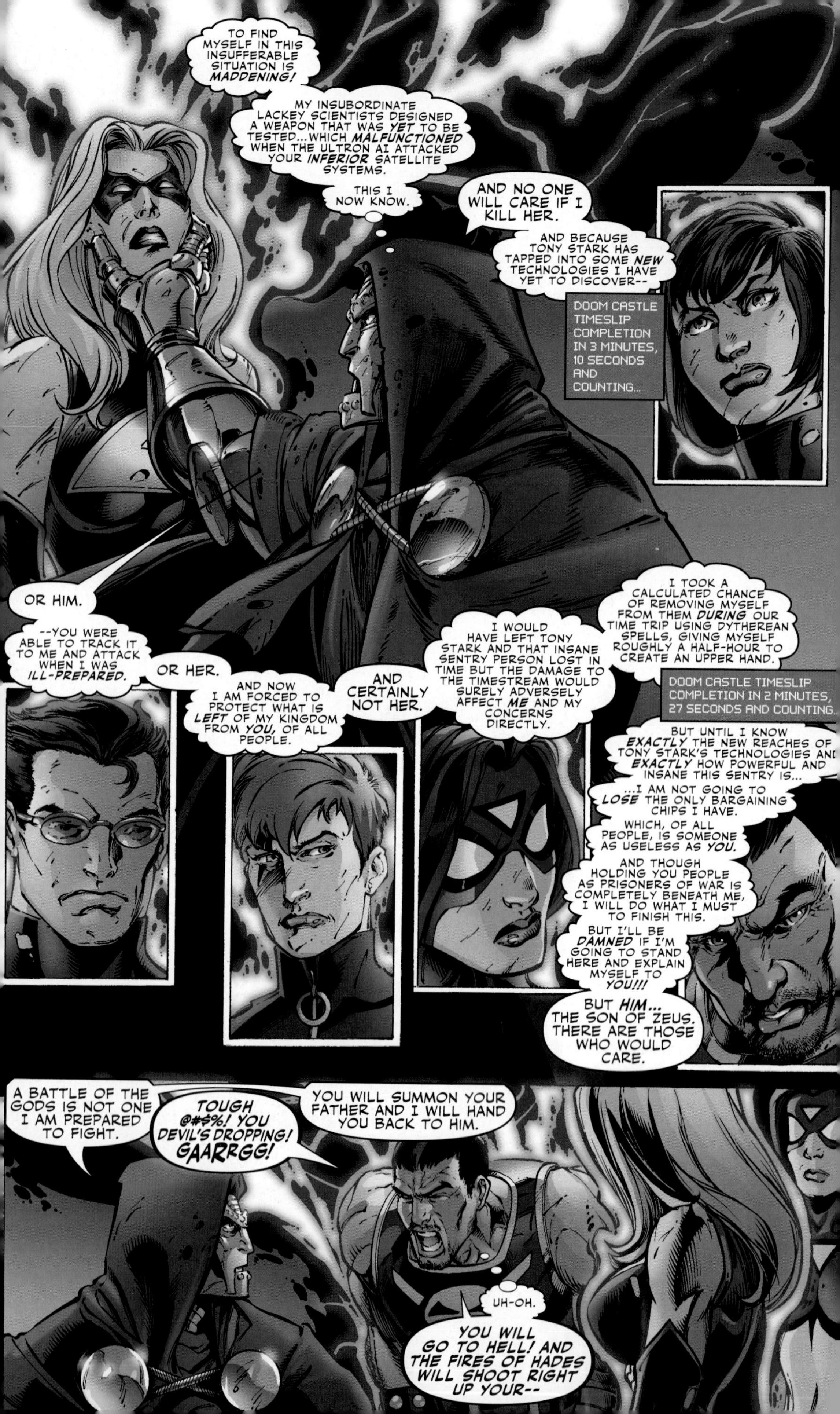

TO FIND MYSELF IN THIS INSUFFERABLE SITUATION IS *MADDENING!*
MY INSUBORDINATE LACKEY SCIENTISTS DESIGNED A WEAPON THAT WAS *YET* TO BE TESTED...WHICH *MALFUNCTIONED* WHEN THE ULTRON AI ATTACKED YOUR *INFERIOR* SATELLITE SYSTEMS.
THIS I NOW KNOW.
AND NO ONE WILL CARE IF I KILL HER.
AND BECAUSE TONY STARK HAS TAPPED INTO SOME *NEW* TECHNOLOGIES I HAVE YET TO DISCOVER--
DOOM CASTLE TIMESLIP COMPLETION IN 3 MINUTES, 10 SECONDS AND COUNTING...
OR HIM.
--YOU WERE ABLE TO TRACK IT TO ME AND ATTACK WHEN I WAS *ILL-PREPARED.*
OR HER.
AND NOW I AM FORCED TO PROTECT WHAT IS *LEFT* OF MY KINGDOM FROM *YOU,* OF ALL PEOPLE.
AND CERTAINLY NOT HER.
I WOULD HAVE LEFT TONY STARK AND THAT INSANE SENTRY PERSON LOST IN TIME BUT THE DAMAGE TO THE TIMESTREAM WOULD SURELY ADVERSELY AFFECT *ME* AND MY CONCERNS DIRECTLY.
I TOOK A CALCULATED CHANCE OF REMOVING MYSELF FROM THEM *DURING* OUR TIME TRIP USING DYTHEREAN SPELLS, GIVING MYSELF ROUGHLY A HALF-HOUR TO CREATE AN UPPER HAND.
DOOM CASTLE TIMESLIP COMPLETION IN 2 MINUTES, 27 SECONDS AND COUNTING.
BUT UNTIL I KNOW *EXACTLY* THE NEW REACHES OF TONY STARK'S TECHNOLOGIES AND *EXACTLY* HOW POWERFUL AND INSANE THIS SENTRY IS...
...I AM NOT GOING TO *LOSE* THE ONLY BARGAINING CHIPS I HAVE.
WHICH, OF ALL PEOPLE, IS SOMEONE AS USELESS AS *YOU.*
AND THOUGH HOLDING YOU PEOPLE AS PRISONERS OF WAR IS COMPLETELY BENEATH ME, I WILL DO WHAT I MUST TO FINISH THIS.
BUT I'LL BE *DAMNED* IF I'M GOING TO STAND HERE AND EXPLAIN MYSELF TO *YOU!!!*
BUT *HIM*... THE SON OF ZEUS. THERE ARE THOSE WHO WOULD CARE.
A BATTLE OF THE GODS IS NOT ONE I AM PREPARED TO FIGHT.
YOU WILL SUMMON YOUR FATHER AND I WILL HAND YOU BACK TO HIM.
TOUGH @#$%! YOU DEVIL'S DROPPING! GAARRGG!
UH-OH.
YOU WILL GO TO HELL! AND THE FIRES OF HADES WILL SHOOT RIGHT UP YOUR--

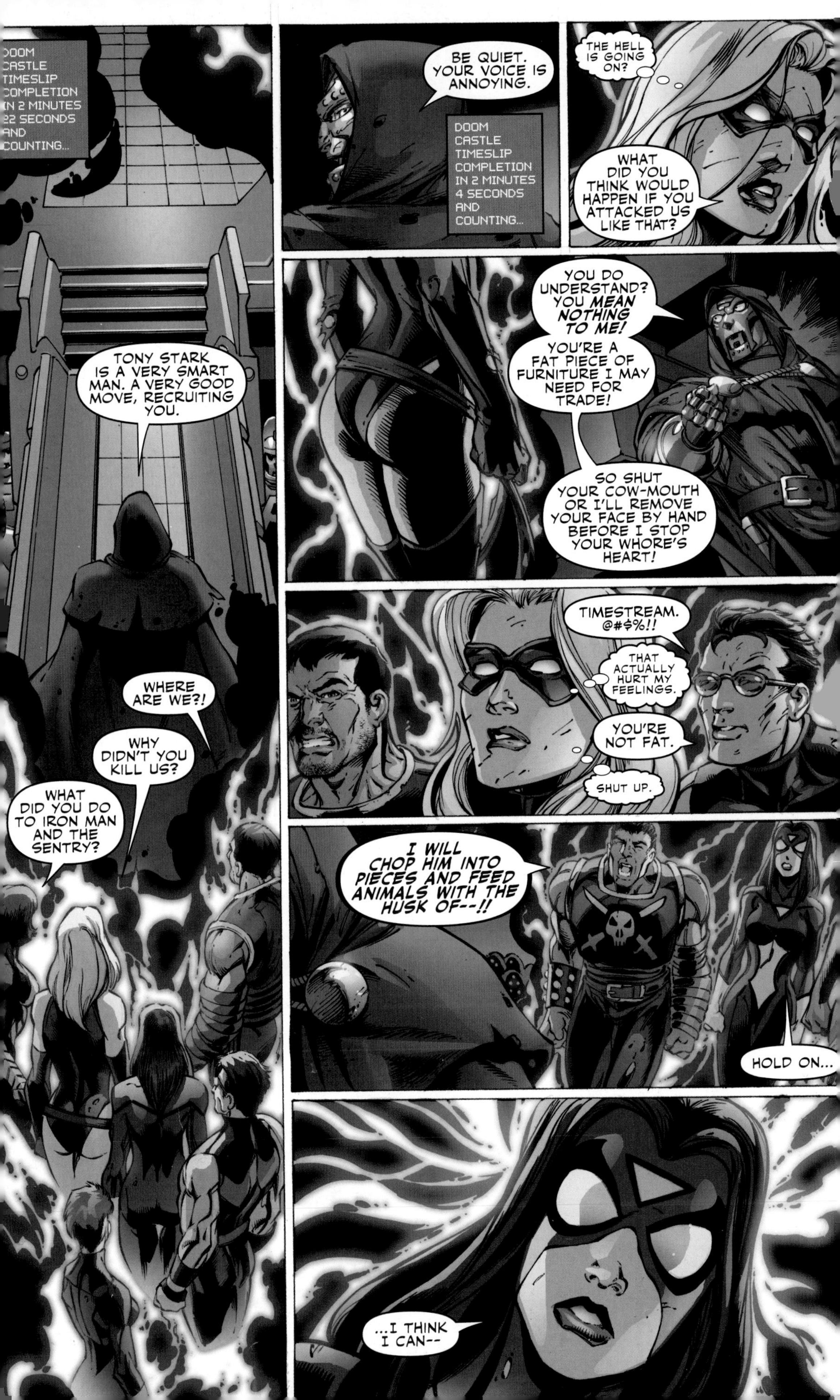

DOOM CASTLE TIMESLIP COMPLETION IN 2 MINUTES 22 SECONDS AND COUNTING...
TONY STARK IS A VERY SMART MAN. A VERY GOOD MOVE, RECRUITING YOU.
WHERE ARE WE?!
WHY DIDN'T YOU KILL US?
WHAT DID YOU DO TO IRON MAN AND THE SENTRY?
BE QUIET. YOUR VOICE IS ANNOYING.
DOOM CASTLE TIMESLIP COMPLETION IN 2 MINUTES 4 SECONDS AND COUNTING...
THE HELL IS GOING ON?
WHAT DID YOU THINK WOULD HAPPEN IF YOU ATTACKED US LIKE THAT?
YOU DO UNDERSTAND? YOU MEAN NOTHING TO ME!
YOU'RE A FAT PIECE OF FURNITURE I MAY NEED FOR TRADE!
SO SHUT YOUR COW-MOUTH OR I'LL REMOVE YOUR FACE BY HAND BEFORE I STOP YOUR WHORE'S HEART!
TIMESTREAM. @#$%!!
THAT ACTUALLY HURT MY FEELINGS.
YOU'RE NOT FAT.
SHUT UP.
I WILL CHOP HIM INTO PIECES AND FEED ANIMALS WITH THE HUSK OF--!!
HOLD ON...
...I THINK I CAN--

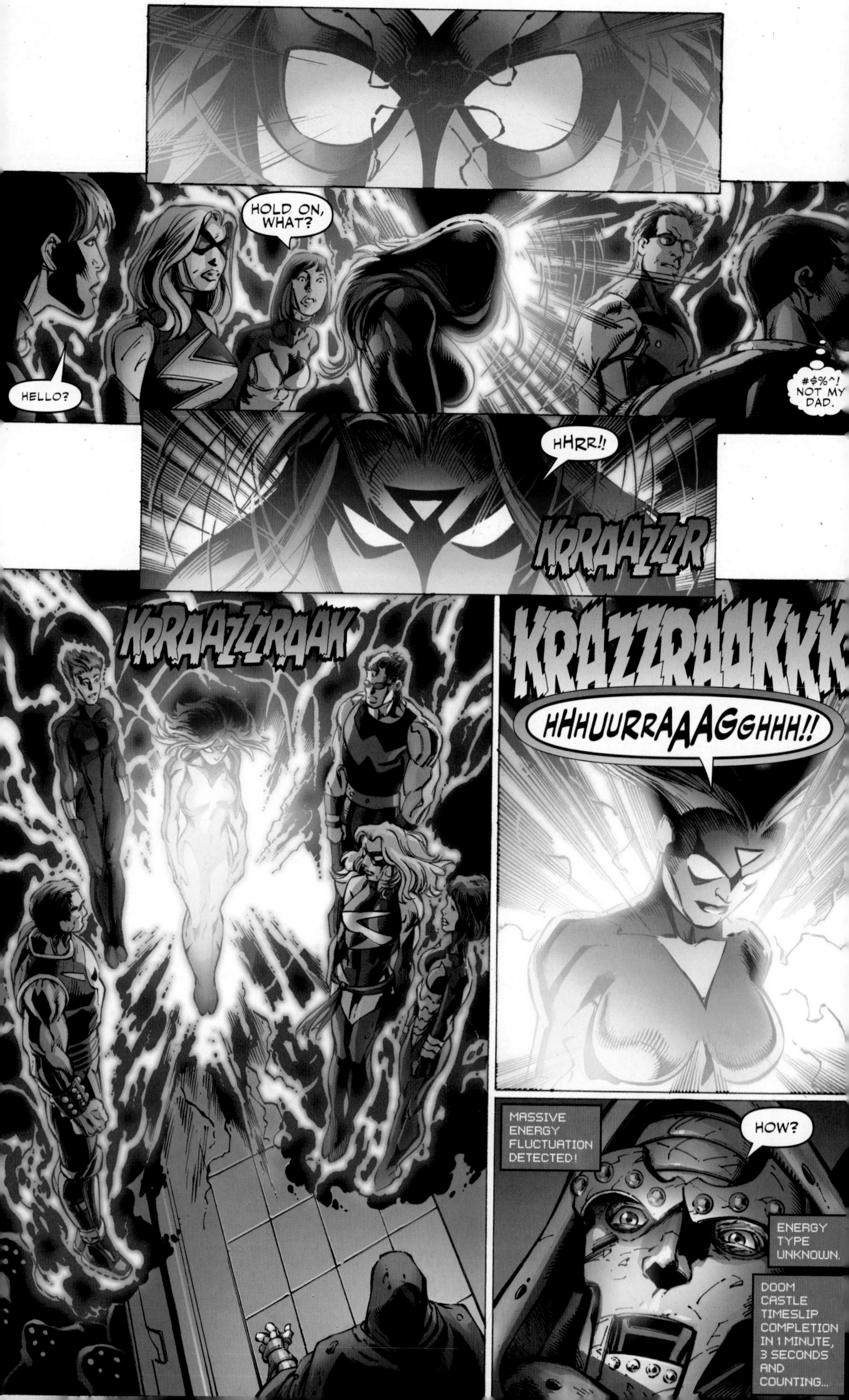
HOLD ON, WHAT?
HELLO?
#$%^! NOT MY DAD.
HHRR!!
KRRAAZZZR
KRRAAZZZRAAK
KRAZZRAAKKK
HHHUURRAAAGGHHH!!
MASSIVE ENERGY FLUCTUATION DETECTED!
HOW?
ENERGY TYPE UNKNOWN.
DOOM CASTLE TIMESLIP COMPLETION IN 1 MINUTE, 3 SECONDS AND COUNTING...

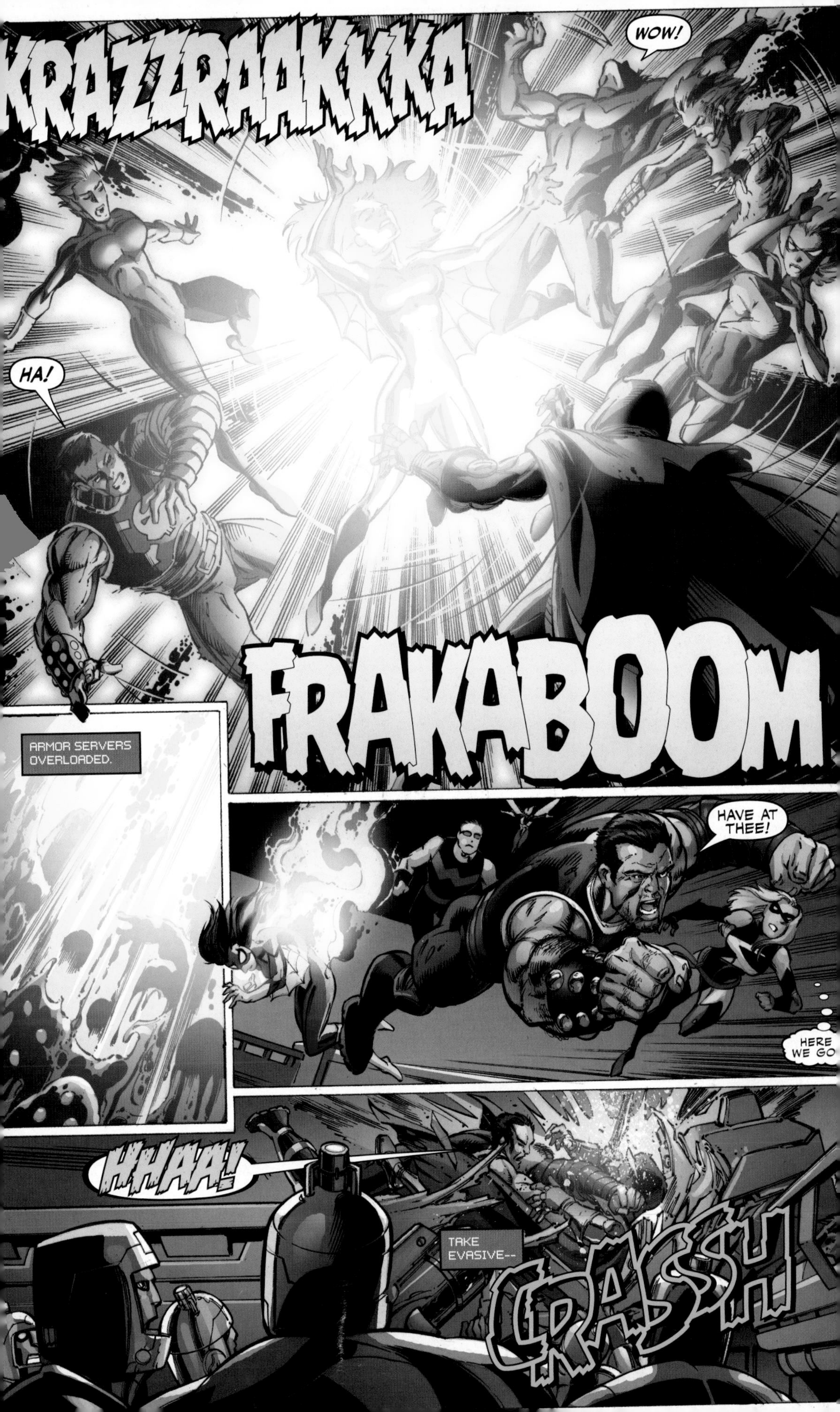
KRAZZRAAKKKA
WOW!
HA!
FRAKABOOM
ARMOR SERVERS OVERLOADED.
HAVE AT THEE!
HERE WE GO
HHAA!
TAKE EVASIVE--
CRASSH

DOOM CASTLE TIMESLIP COMPLETION IN 22 SECONDS AND COUNTING...

SIMON, POUND DOOM!

WIDOW, GET THE HELICARRIER ONLINE AND FIND OUT WHERE WE ARE!

I'M GOING TO GO FIND TONY AND BOB!

THERE'S A COUNTDOWN CLOCK!

I SEE IT.

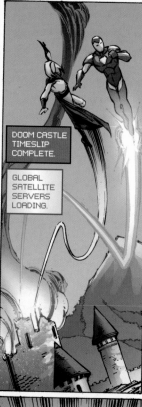

DOOM CASTLE TIMESLIP COMPLETE.

GLOBAL SATELLITE SERVERS LOADING.

SERVERS LOADING. STAND BY.

WHAT IS THAT?

BOB. HEAD IT OFF!

GET OUT OF THERE!

DOOMSTADT NEURAL ENERGY SWARM DRAIN INTERFACE ACTIVATED. LAUNCH.

DOOMSTADT NEURAL ENERGY SWARM DRAIN ACTIVATED.

OH NO!

CAROL?

GET OUT OF THERE!

SERVER CONNECTION SUCCESSFUL

SATELLITE CONNECTION ONLINE.

UNIDENTIFIED ENERGY SOURCE DETECTED.

UNIDENTIFIED ENERGY FLUX.

EVASIVE ACTION REQUIRED.

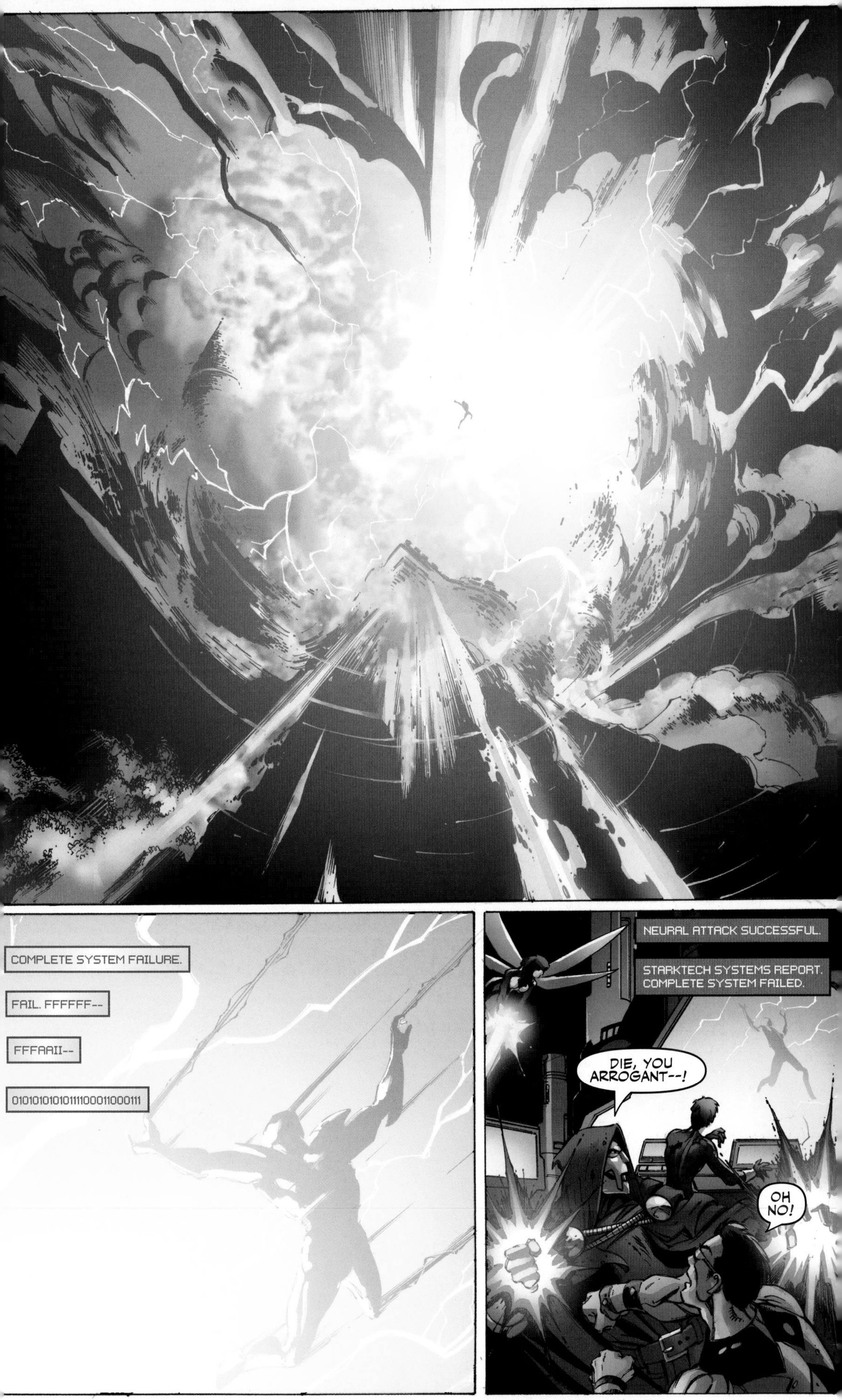
COMPLETE SYSTEM FAILURE.
FAIL. FFFFFF--
FFFAAII--
0101010101011110001100011
NEURAL ATTACK SUCCESSFUL.
STARKTECH SYSTEMS REPORT. COMPLETE SYSTEM FAILED.
DIE, YOU ARROGANT--!
OH NO!

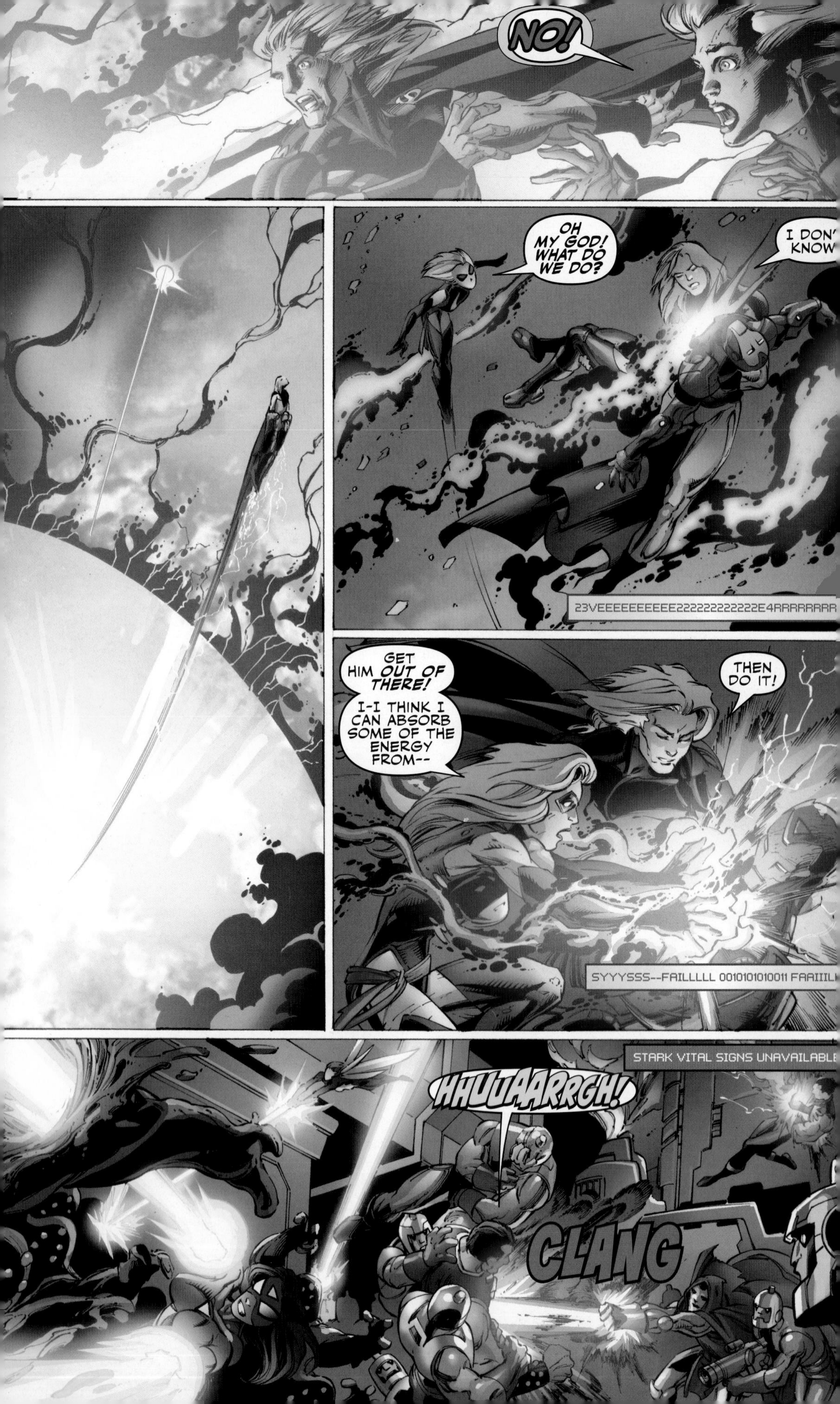
NO!
OH MY GOD! WHAT DO WE DO?
I DON' KNOW
23VEEEEEEEEEE22222222222E4RRRRRRRR
GET HIM OUT OF THERE!
I-I THINK I CAN ABSORB SOME OF THE ENERGY FROM--
THEN DO IT!
SYYYSSS--FAILLLLL 0010101010011 FAAIIIL
STARK VITAL SIGNS UNAVAILABL
HHUUAARRGH!
CLANG

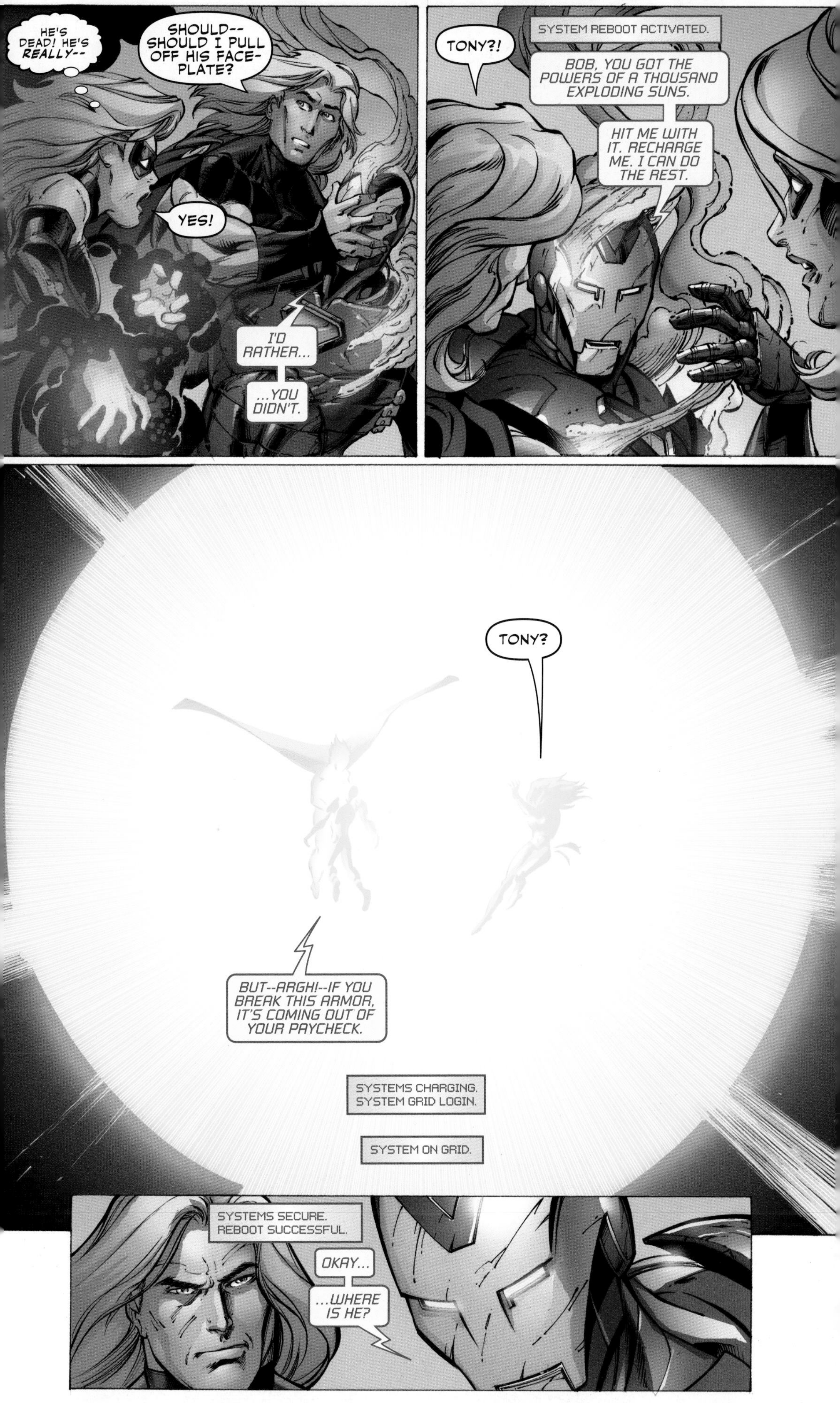
HE'S DEAD! HE'S REALLY--
SHOULD--SHOULD I PULL OFF HIS FACE-PLATE?
YES!
I'D RATHER...
...YOU DIDN'T.
TONY?!
SYSTEM REBOOT ACTIVATED.
BOB, YOU GOT THE POWERS OF A THOUSAND EXPLODING SUNS.
HIT ME WITH IT. RECHARGE ME. I CAN DO THE REST.
TONY?
BUT--ARGH!--IF YOU BREAK THIS ARMOR, IT'S COMING OUT OF YOUR PAYCHECK.
SYSTEMS CHARGING. SYSTEM GRID LOGIN.
SYSTEM ON GRID.
SYSTEMS SECURE. REBOOT SUCCESSFUL.
OKAY...
...WHERE IS HE?

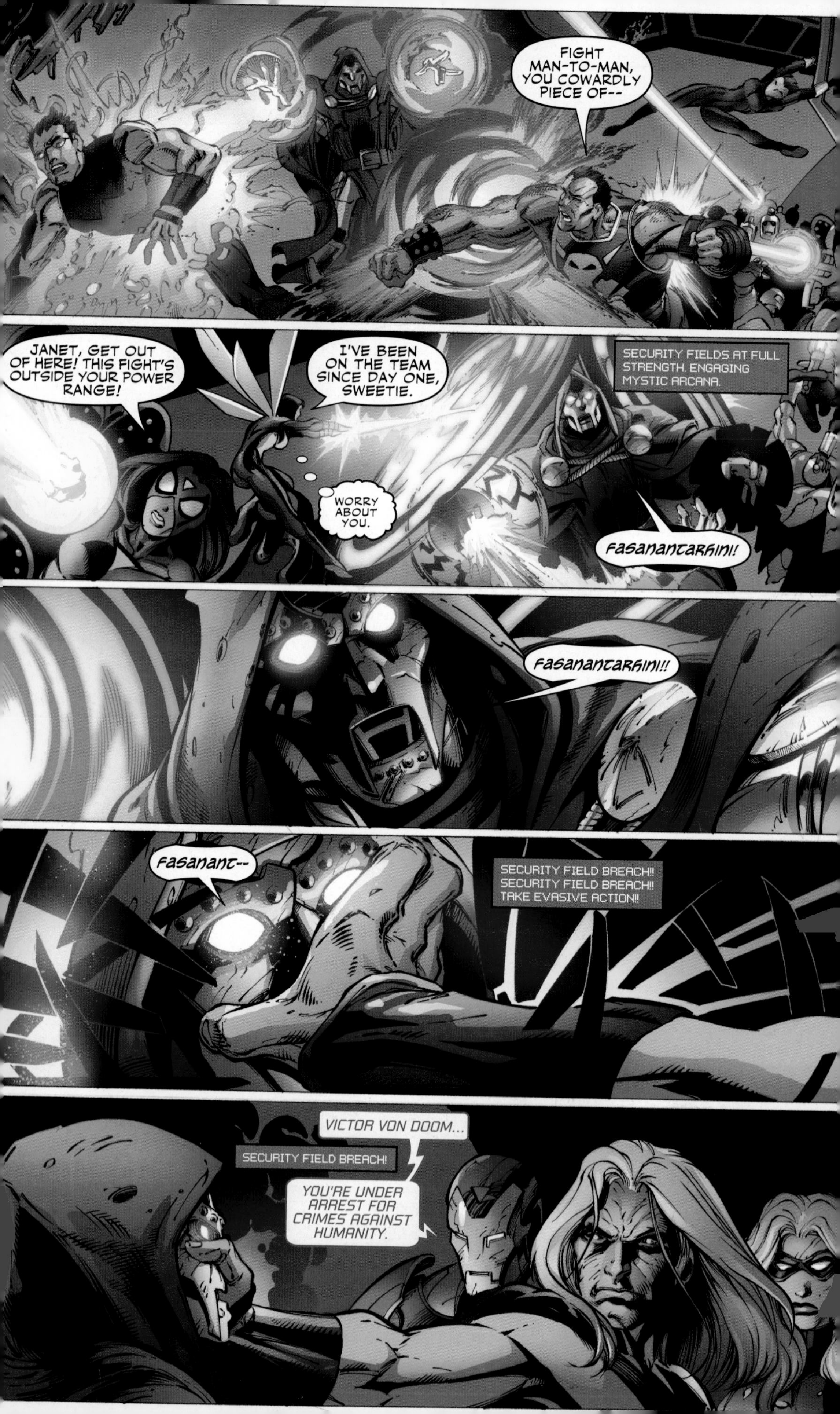

FIGHT MAN-TO-MAN, YOU COWARDLY PIECE OF--
JANET, GET OUT OF HERE! THIS FIGHT'S OUTSIDE YOUR POWER RANGE!
I'VE BEEN ON THE TEAM SINCE DAY ONE, SWEETIE.
WORRY ABOUT YOU.
SECURITY FIELDS AT FULL STRENGTH. ENGAGING MYSTIC ARCANA.
FASANANTARHINI!
FASANANTARHINI!!
FASANANT--
SECURITY FIELD BREACH!! SECURITY FIELD BREACH!! TAKE EVASIVE ACTION!!
VICTOR VON DOOM...
SECURITY FIELD BREACH!
YOU'RE UNDER ARREST FOR CRIMES AGAINST HUMANITY.

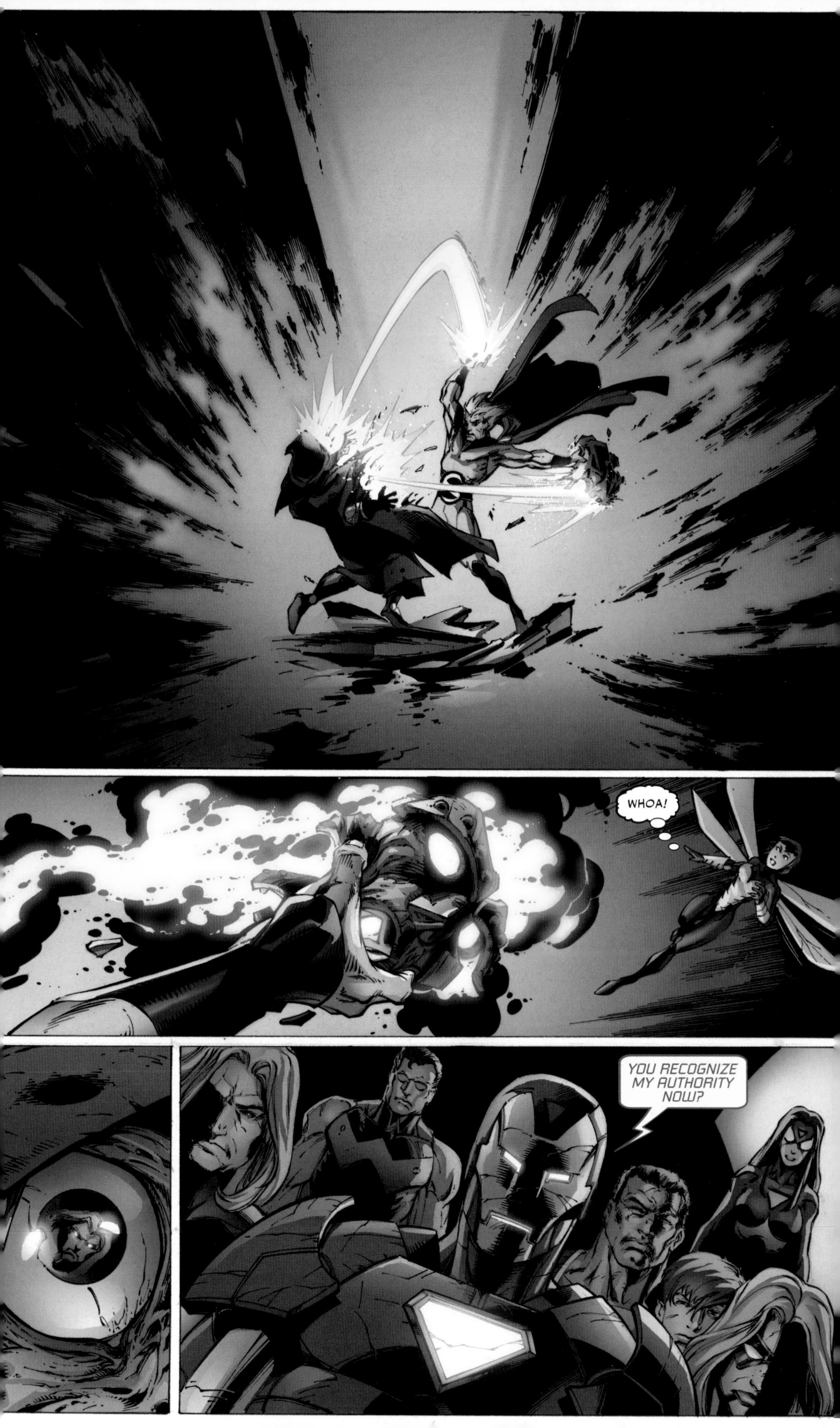
WHOA!
YOU RECOGNIZE MY AUTHORITY NOW?

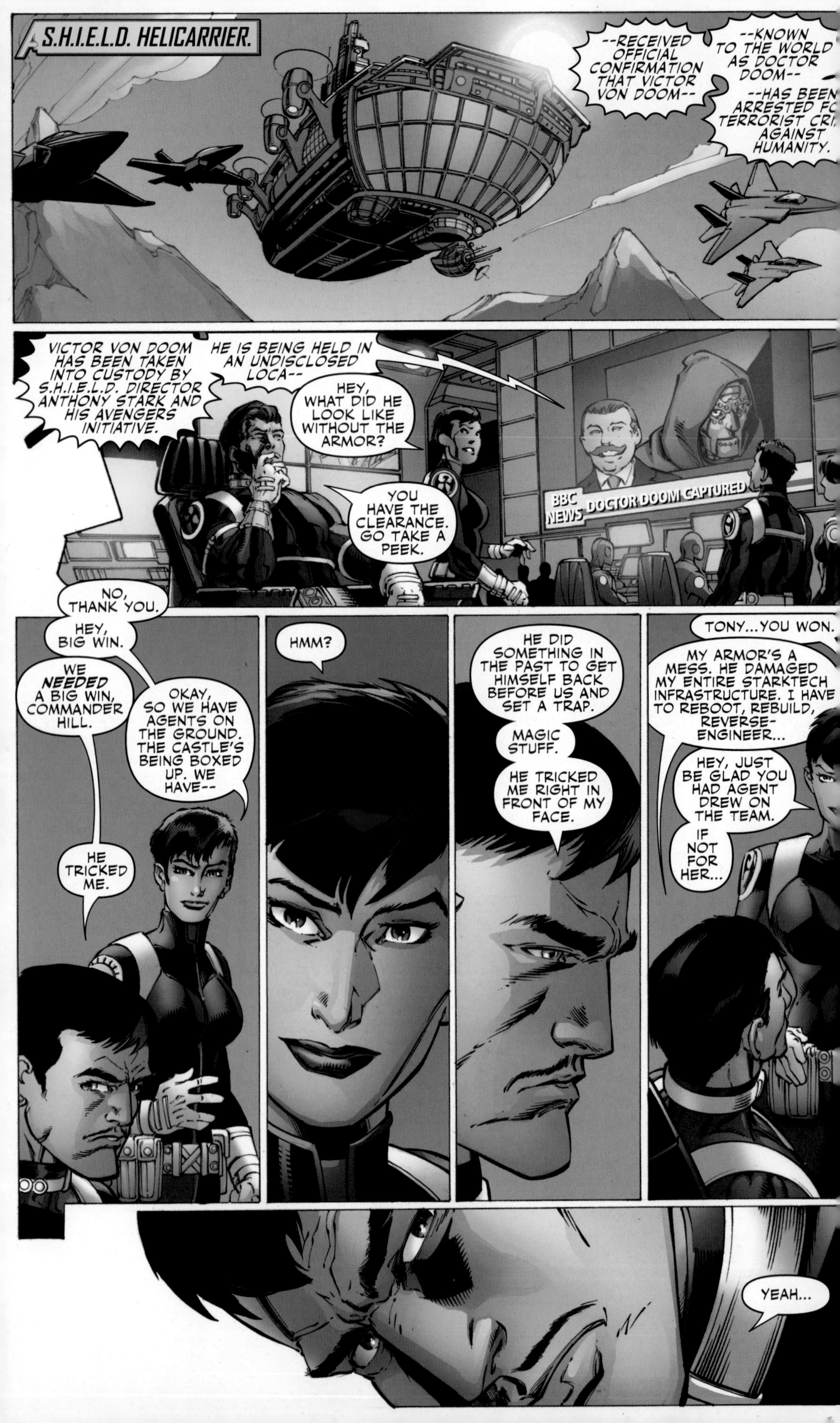
S.H.I.E.L.D. HELICARRIER.
--RECEIVED OFFICIAL CONFIRMATION THAT VICTOR VON DOOM--
--KNOWN TO THE WORLD AS DOCTOR DOOM--
--HAS BEEN ARRESTED FO TERRORIST CRI AGAINST HUMANITY.
VICTOR VON DOOM HAS BEEN TAKEN INTO CUSTODY BY S.H.I.E.L.D. DIRECTOR ANTHONY STARK AND HIS AVENGERS INITIATIVE.
HE IS BEING HELD IN AN UNDISCLOSED LOCA--
HEY, WHAT DID HE LOOK LIKE WITHOUT THE ARMOR?
BBC NEWS
DOCTOR DOOM CAPTURED
YOU HAVE THE CLEARANCE. GO TAKE A PEEK.
NO, THANK YOU.
HEY, BIG WIN.
WE NEEDED A BIG WIN, COMMANDER HILL.
OKAY, SO WE HAVE AGENTS ON THE GROUND. THE CASTLE'S BEING BOXED UP. WE HAVE--
HE TRICKED ME.
HMM?
HE DID SOMETHING IN THE PAST TO GET HIMSELF BACK BEFORE US AND SET A TRAP.
MAGIC STUFF.
HE TRICKED ME RIGHT IN FRONT OF MY FACE.
TONY...YOU WON.
MY ARMOR'S A MESS. HE DAMAGED MY ENTIRE STARKTECH INFRASTRUCTURE. I HAVE TO REBOOT, REBUILD, REVERSE-ENGINEER...
HEY, JUST BE GLAD YOU HAD AGENT DREW ON THE TEAM.
IF NOT FOR HER...
YEAH...

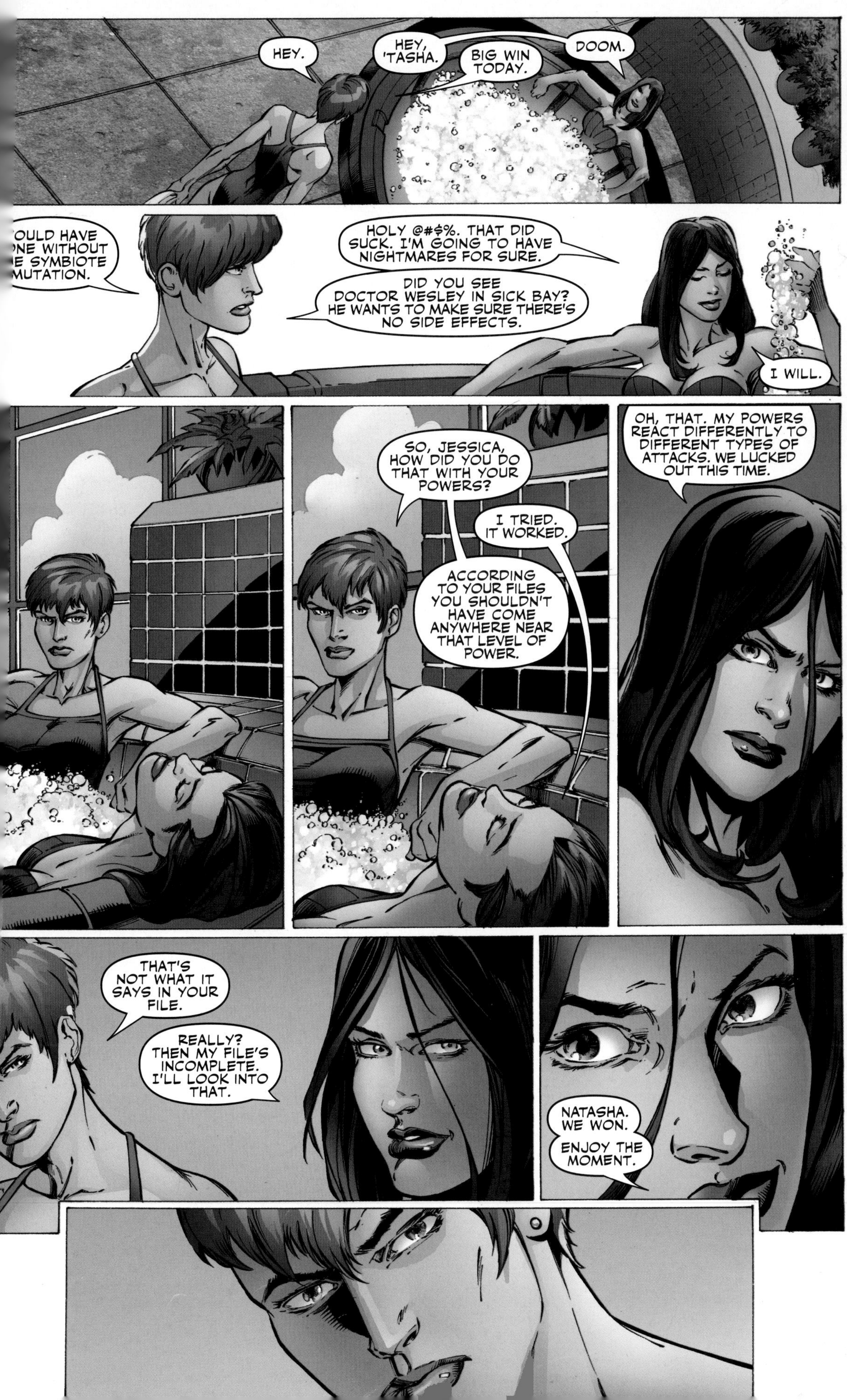
HEY.
HEY, 'TASHA.
BIG WIN TODAY.
DOOM.
OULD HAVE NE WITHOUT E SYMBIOTE MUTATION.
HOLY @#$%. THAT DID SUCK. I'M GOING TO HAVE NIGHTMARES FOR SURE.
DID YOU SEE DOCTOR WESLEY IN SICK BAY? HE WANTS TO MAKE SURE THERE'S NO SIDE EFFECTS.
I WILL.
SO, JESSICA, HOW DID YOU DO THAT WITH YOUR POWERS?
I TRIED. IT WORKED.
ACCORDING TO YOUR FILES YOU SHOULDN'T HAVE COME ANYWHERE NEAR THAT LEVEL OF POWER.
OH, THAT. MY POWERS REACT DIFFERENTLY TO DIFFERENT TYPES OF ATTACKS. WE LUCKED OUT THIS TIME.
THAT'S NOT WHAT IT SAYS IN YOUR FILE.
REALLY? THEN MY FILE'S INCOMPLETE. I'LL LOOK INTO THAT.
NATASHA. WE WON.
ENJOY THE MOMENT.

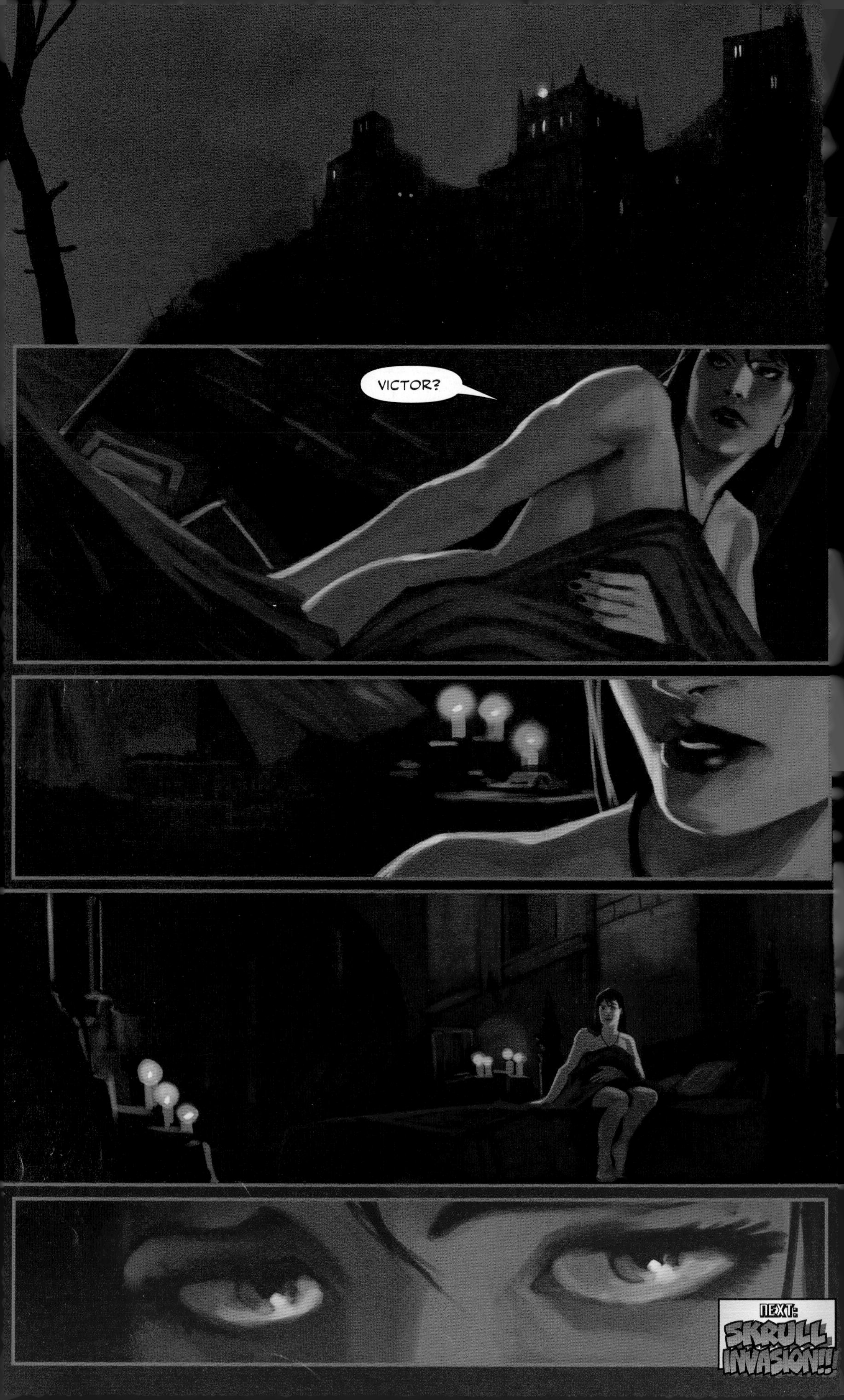
VICTOR?
NEXT:
SKRULL INVASION!!

ISSUE #7 COVER INKS
by Fank Cho

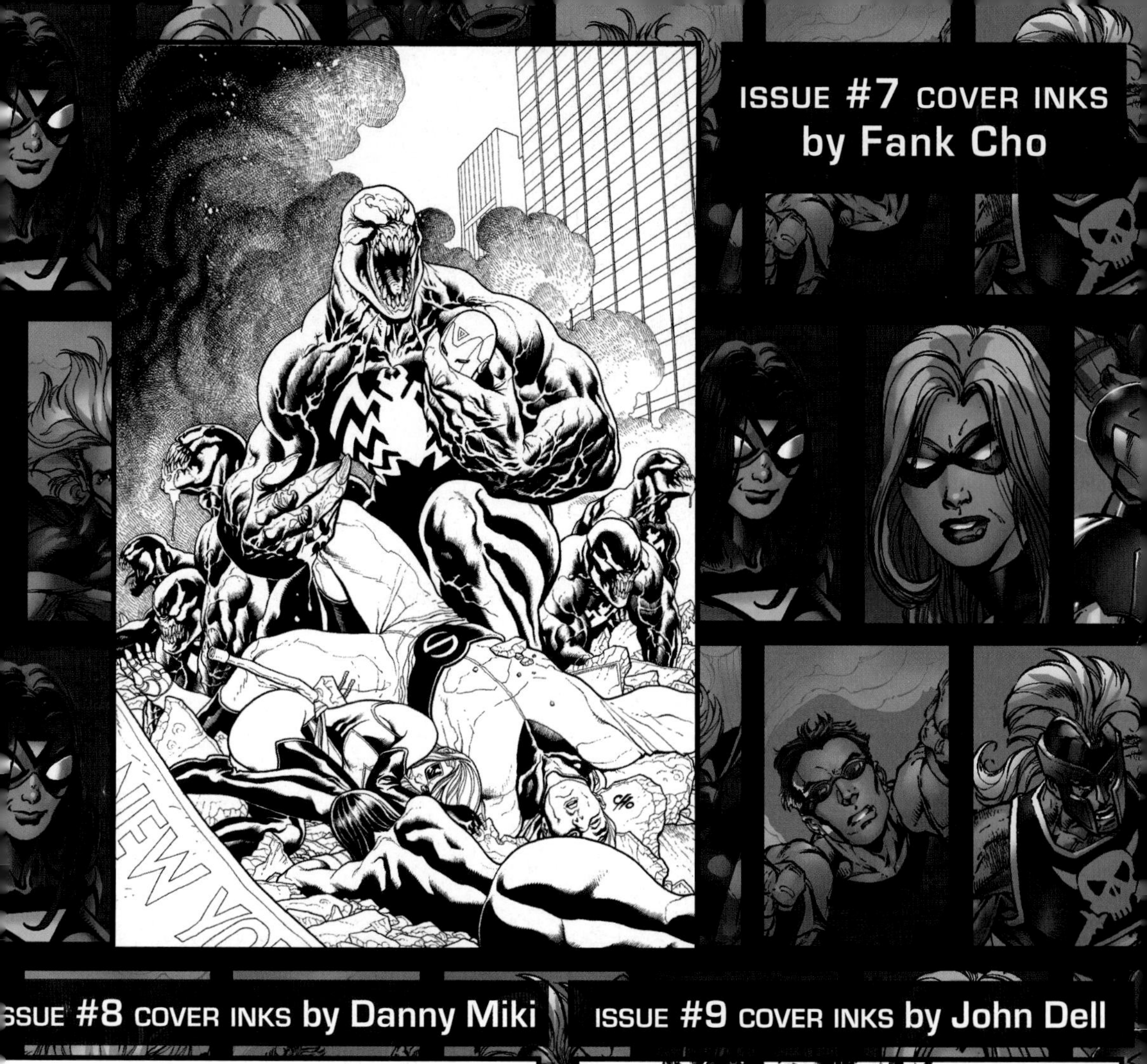

SSUE #8 COVER INKS by Danny Miki

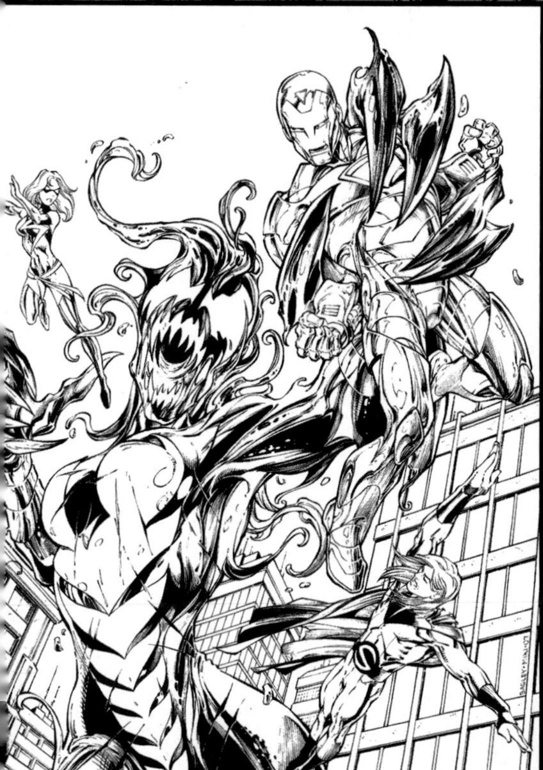

ISSUE #9 COVER INKS by John Dell

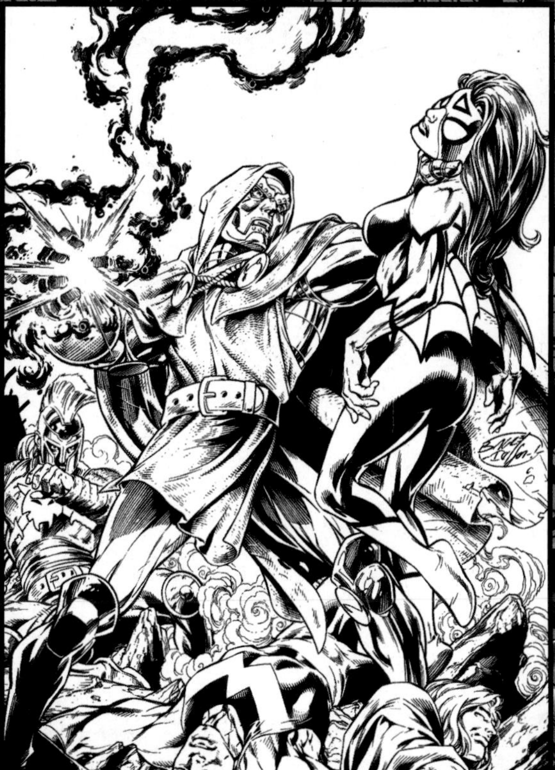

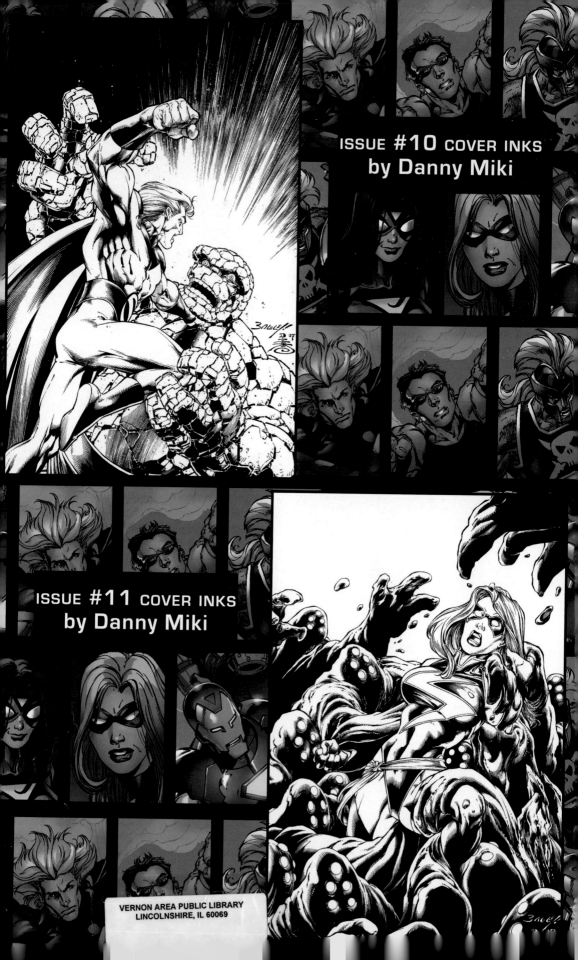

ISSUE #10 COVER INKS
by Danny Miki

ISSUE #11 COVER INKS
by Danny Miki